Columbia Northwest Classics

Chris Friday, Editor

Columbia Northwest Classics

Columbia Northwest Classics are reprints of important studies about the peoples and places that make up the Pacific Northwest. The series focuses especially on that vast area drained by the Columbia River and its tributaries. Like the plants, animals, and people that have crossed over the watersheds to the east, west, south, and north, Columbia Classics embrace a Pacific Northwest that includes not only Oregon, Washington, and Idaho but also British Columbia, the Yukon, Alaska, and portions of Montana, California, Nevada, and Utah.

Mountain Fever:
Historic Conquests of Rainier
by Aubrey Haines

To Fish in Common:
The Ethnohistory of Lummi Indian Salmon Fishing
by Daniel L. Boxberger

Mexican Labor and World War II:
Braceros in the Pacific Northwest, 1942–1947
by Erasmo Gamboa

Gyppo Logger
by Margaret Elley Felt

The Boys of Boise:
Furor, Vice, and Folly in an American City
by John Gerassi

THE BOYS OF BOISE

Furor, Vice & Folly in an American City

JOHN GERASSI

With a Foreword by Peter Boag
and a New Preface by the author

UNIVERSITY OF WASHINGTON PRESS
Seattle and London

Library of Congress Cataloging-in-Publication Data
Gerassi, John.
The boys of Boise : furor, vice and folly in an American city / John Gerassi ;
with a foreword by Peter Boag and a new preface by the author.
p. cm. — (Columbia Northwest classics)
Originally published: New York : Macmillan, 1966.
Includes index.
ISBN 0–295-98167-9 (alk. paper)
1. Homosexuality—Idaho—Boise.
I. Boag, Peter. II. Title. III. Series.
HQ76.U52B654 2001 306.76'6'0979628—dc21 2001044282

CONTENTS

FOREWORD TO THE
2001 PAPERBACK EDITION

In modern times, few social issues in America have consistently attracted as much attention, controversy, and backlash as has homosexuality. Beginning in the 1950s, but more vigorously since about 1970, lesbians and gays in the United States have undertaken a campaign to secure basic human rights, acceptance or at least tolerance from broader society, and the ability to live freely without fear of persecution or worse.[1] Since the late 1980s, this campaign has realized important successes, but no sea change has occurred: gays and lesbians still confront anger, outrage, and harassment emanating from the local to the national levels. On a regular basis they face, among other things, fundamentalist religious attacks, anti-gay initiatives, "Don't Ask Don't Tell," the Defense of Marriage Act, blame for the "ruin" of the American family, loss of jobs, and in some places the continued criminalization of their private and consensual sexual activities. They also endure injury and even death at the hands of detractors who often go unpunished.

Generally speaking, lesbians and gays have experienced different levels of persecution depending upon where they have lived. Although this conclusion is far from absolute, especially for the Pacific Northwest, larger cities have traditionally provided relative havens for gays and lesbians and the communities that they have forged. On the other hand, what we often refer to as "middle America," that is, small towns and rural areas, has been less inviting. Written in 1965 about a same-sex sexual scandal that occurred in 1955 in Boise, Idaho, John Gerassi's classic study depicts both middle America's traditional response to homosexuality as well as an era in the country's history before the modern gay rights movement really got underway. In the story and the way it is told, *The*

---

1. See, for example, John D'Emilio, *Sexual Politics, Sexual Communities: The Making of a Homosexual Minority in the United States, 1940–1970* (Chicago: University of Chicago Press, 1983).

Boys of Boise is a period document important for what it reveals about past social understandings and responses to homosexuality, reflecting a mentality that has changed in some ways since the 1950s and 1960s. But because much of what Gerassi wrote about and the perspective he offered when writing it persist in today's struggles over gay and lesbian issues, his book has much to tell us about how contemporary society reacts to, and misunderstands, homosexuality.

The Boys of Boise originated as a piece of investigative journalism, not as an academic tome. As a result, it is powerful in ways that often fail more scholarly studies. Gerassi provides fascinating personal insight into how a community attempts to protect its less than glorious past and he shows us some of the difficulties that anyone who wishes to investigate a controversial subject might encounter. For example, even the Idaho governor attempted to block Gerassi's research. Perhaps most important, because of how it is written and what it reports, this book offers readers much to respond to intellectually and viscerally.

As far as the modern history of gay and lesbian literature goes, *The Boys of Boise* is among the first widely read popular offerings that called for a more compassionate view of gays. Among other things, Gerassi advocated the decriminalization of homosexuality. Great Britain had recently accomplished this, but society in mid-1960s America had little interest in the possibility. With Gerassi's overall positive approach in mind, however, it should be noted that understandings of homosexuality have changed. Because of this shift, at least four troublesome points about homosexuality emerge in Gerassi's work that are in need of a more modern perspective in order for readers to consider how ideas about the subject have altered since the time *The Boys of Boise* first appeared. In this way we can appropriately place the book in its historical context, appreciate Gerassi's efforts, and note the volume's substantial significance as an historical document.

First, two of Gerassi's central foci are the psychology and psychological treatment of homosexuality. He summarizes, for example, some of the popular psychological theories for the "causes" of homosexuality to which many in the 1960s subscribed. He also repeatedly laments the failure of Idaho officials to live up to their promises to provide therapy for the adult men convicted of consensual sex acts with each other, and sometimes argues that this therapy was needed. Such sentiments were common at the time, but seven years after this volume appeared, the American Psychiatric Association removed homosexuality from its list of recognized mental illnesses. Since that re-evaluation, the mainstream psychological and psychiatric professions have increasingly discredited various psychological explanations for homosexuality, such as that which Sigmund Freud had proposed, and which Gerassi offers as possible etiologies. Current scientific research into the "causes" of sexuality concentrate almost solely on biological factors.[2]

Second, Gerassi refers to the men arrested for sex with teenage males in 1950s Boise as "child molesters." Throughout the twentieth century, social fears over possible contact between homosexuals and children were consistently manifested as such charges and were made fact by the legal system. These popular and legal conceptions undoubtedly influenced Gerassi in the 1960s.[3] But a variety of sociological and historical studies support Gerassi's other suggestion that Boise's "boys" (ranging from older high school aged youths to twenty-one-year-old men) were either prostitutes or chose on their own accord to enter into same-sex sexual relations. Indeed, the literature reveals that teenage male sex workers have had a ubiquitous presence in America's urban and rural settings at least since the late nineteenth century.[4]

2. Stephen C. Halpert, "'If it ain't broke, don't fix it': Ethical Considerations Regarding Conversion Therapies," *International Journal of Sexuality and Gender Studies* 5, no. 1 (January 2000), 19–35; J. Michael Bailey, "Homosexuality and Mental Illness," *Archives of General Psychiatry* 56, no. 10 (October 1999), 883–84; Stephen F. Morin and Esther D. Rothblum, "Removing the Stigma: Fifteen Years of Progress," *American Psychologist* 46, no. 9 (September 1991), 947–49. An example of the dominance of Freudian explanations for homosexuality in the 1960s is revealed in one of the reviews of *The Boys of Boise:* see Jack Leavitt, "The Ordinariness of Sodomy," *The Nation*, January 9, 1967, 54–57.

3. Social theorist Michel Foucault noted that as heterosexual expressions between adults became the established sexual standard in the western world only in the late nineteenth century, broader society then began to view all other sexualities as outside the norm and therefore deviant. Among these "deviancies" are counted both children's sexuality and homosexuality. In the social mind's eye, the "dangers" of the two became not only linked but conflated. See Michel Foucault, *The History of Sexuality: An Introduction*, trans. Robert Hurley (New York: Pantheon Books, 1978), 38–39.

4. On teenage male sex work and the willingness of boys to engage in sex with men, see Lilburn Merrill, "A Summary of Findings in a Study of Sexualism Among a Group of One Hundred Delinquent Boys," *Journal of Delinquency* 3, no. 6 (November 1918), 255–69; William Marlin Butts, "Boy Prostitutes of the Metropolis,"

Third, gay and lesbian readers in particular, but also their supporters, might react strongly against the tone of midcentury American stereotypes unwittingly perpetrated in many journalistic accounts. The repeated use of the phrase "the homosexuals" not only denied individuality, but also provided only a one-dimensional view of those involved. Such terminology pejoratively painted the men implicated in the affair as the "other" and allowed for an eerie feeling that collectively they really may have posed a furtive threat to society.

Finally, the related issue of exactly how we define someone as a homosexual or a heterosexual merits attention. Gerassi's work demonstrates the 1950s and 1960s struggle that mainstream society and even sometimes sympathetic onlookers had over this very concern. Is one a homosexual because he or she engages in sexual activities with someone of the same sex? Or is there something more to sexuality than simply what one deduces from its physical expressions? *The Boys of Boise* sometimes implies that acts prove decisive and that a homosexual, therefore, is defined by what he or she does in bed. Modern sexual-rights advocates, historians, sociologists, and various other scholars have been less convinced and have amply demonstrated that people's sexual expressions are culturally and temporally specific. They have also decisively demonstrated that people enter into sexual relations with members of their own sex, or the opposite sex, for any number of reasons not related to homo-

Journal of Clinical Psychopathology 8, no. 4 (April 1947), 673–81; H. Ross Lawrence, "The 'Hustler' in Chicago," *A Journal of Student Research* 1, no. 1 (fall 1959), 13–19; Albert J. Ross, Jr., "The Social Integration of Queers and Peers," *Social Problems* 9, no. 2 (fall 1961), 102–20; Steven Maynard, "'Horrible Temptations': Sex, Men, and Working-Class Male Youths in Urban Ontario, 1890–1917," *Canadian Historical Review* 78, no. 2 (June 1997), 191–235. Merrill, "A Summary of Findings," is also instructive on the notion of different past sexualities and sexual activities between males of different ages which had little to do with homosexuality as we understand it today. On this point, see also Josiah Flynt, "Homosexuality among Tramps," Appendix A in *Studies in the Psychology of Sex*, vol. 4, *Sexual Inversion*, by Havelock Ellis, 2d ed. (Philadelphia: F. A. Davis, 1904), 219–24; Nels Anderson, "The Juvenile and the Tramp," *Journal of the American Institute of Criminal Law and Criminology* 14 (August 1923), 290–312; and George Chauncey, *Gay New York: Gender, Urban Culture, and the Making of the Gay Male World, 1890–1940* (New York: Basic Books, 1994), 65–97. Another useful volume to consider in light of these ideas is Paul H. Gebhard, John H. Gagnon, Wardell B. Pomeroy, and Cornelia Christenson, *Sex Offenders: An Analysis of Types* (New York: Harper & Row and Paul B. Hoeber, 1965).

sexuality or heterosexuality.[5] Readers need to keep in mind such recent scholarly findings before taking at face value arguments presented in the 1950s and 1960s.

One notable aspect of Gerassi's work that has withstood the test of time concerns the fact that Boise's homosexual panic in the 1950s directly related to the anti-communist hysteria which enveloped America during the early Cold War. In recent years, scholars of homosexuality have shown that severe social disruptions resulting from the Great Depression and World War II left the American family in a relatively unsettled condition by the late 1940s. At precisely this moment, frightening political developments in Eastern Europe and Asia and the Soviet Union's detonation of an atomic bomb made it appear as though communism was unstoppable. More disconcerting was that even the United States seemed vulnerable, as the case of Alger Hiss suggested. The tenuousness of the family and the perceived defenselessness of the government led to an explosive situation. Quickly, opportunistic politicians took advantage. They linked communism and homosexuality together and posed them as the primary threats to the American social and political fabric. The result of such irresponsible actions led to a frightening national witch-hunt that destroyed many innocent people.[6]

Before reaching Boise, this Cold War anti-homosexual panic had already enveloped other Pacific Northwest communities. From about 1952 to the early 1960s, the subject of sexual deviancy generally, and homosexuality specifically, fixated the residents of Portland. And already as early as the summer of 1950, hysteria "rocked" even the small, heavily Mormon eastern Idaho community of Rexburg. In the same local newspaper that used banner headlines to describe frightening communist actions in Korea, local officials reported "widespread homosexual practices . . . concentrated in Madison county" and fretted about it "extend[ing] into other counties

5. See Kathy Peiss, Christina Simmons, with Robert A. Padgug, eds., *Passion and Power: Sexuality in History* (Philadelphia: Temple University Press, 1989) for an introduction.

6. John D'Emilio, "The Homosexual Menace: The Politics of Sexuality in Cold War America," in Peiss et al., *Passion and Power,* 226–40; George Chauncey, Jr., "The Postwar Sex Crime Panic," in *True Stories from the American Past,* ed. William Graebner (New York: McGraw Hill, 1993), 160–78; David K. Johnson, "The Lavender Scare: Gays and Lesbians in the Federal Civil Service, 1945–1975" (Ph.D. diss., Northwestern University, 2000).

of the Upper Snake river valley." By September, area authorities had undertaken extensive investigations and two local men had lost their jobs after admitting to sodomy.[7] Although Gerassi did not pursue in great detail these connections between national or regional events and what happened in Boise, he did accurately gauge Idahoans' anti-communist sentiment in the 1950s and drew parallels between how Boiseans readily participated in McCarthyism and how they reacted against homosexual men in 1955–56. Moreover, the undercover detective brought in to investigate the city's homosexual scene had recently worked to expel gays from the U.S. State Department.[8]

It is clear in the examples of these few cases that national developments can play a primary role in how local sex panics begin and work themselves out. The anti-homosexual craze that afflicted the Pacific Northwest in the 1950s was not the first time in which same-sex vice scandals in the region, or even in Boise for that matter, had connections to larger, country-wide uncertainties. Immediately following World War I, the United States endured a period of heightened xenophobia and anti-communism not unlike that which would occur three decades later in the aftermath of World War II. In 1920, in the midst of this atmosphere, Boise authorities discovered a small number of men having sexual relations with each other in the lavatories of a downtown business building. A lengthy and highly publicized trial of two of the suspects ensued. One of those charged, E. E. Gillespie, a man of good education, owner of several ranches in the state, Republican party official, and retired War Department civil servant, realized that the local commotion over suspect sexual activities could be linked to the frightening national mood. He de-

7. See, for example, the following articles in the *Portland, Oregon Journal*: "Prison Terms Change Talked in Sex Crimes," February 25, 1952, 1; "Pervert Curb On Plan List," February 29, 1952, 1 and sec. 2, p. 12; "Today's Guest Editorial: Facts About Deviates," March 27, 1952, 20; "Today's Guest Editorial: Sex Deviate Laws," February 18, 1953, 22; "Sex Deviate—Cure of Problem Lagging in Oregon," December 1, 1954, 1; and in the *Portland, Oregonian:* "Police Juvenile Division Says Deviate Ring Broken," January 20, 1956, sec. 3, p. 10; "Police Say Arrest of Two Portlanders Exposed Statewide Homosexual Ring Activities," October 25, 1963, 25; and in the *Pocatello, Idaho State Journal:* "Rexburg Investigates Moral Practices," September 14, 1950, 1.

8. Jim Hopkins, "The Boy Most Likely," *Boise, Idaho Statesman*, October 15, 1995, 9A.

cried, for instance, the "after war period of distrust, jealousy and revenge" which had played a role in his conviction. But wisely, Gillespie also noted that local conditions might influence a campaign against someone suspected of socially unacceptable activities. He believed that many Boiseans had "misunderstood and misinterpreted" him for years. Gillespie even implicated a local newspaper, which had publicly impugned him in 1918 as "the man of mystery." "My enemies, both personal and political," he charged on the day of his conviction, "will now undoubtedly . . . rejoice."[9]

While sex scandals such as those that occurred in Boise, Rexburg, and Portland did have intimate connections to national developments, they were also rooted in local events, as E. E. Gillespie so well understood in 1920. Importantly, Gerassi connects Boise's 1955 anti-homosexual hysteria to local politics and society. He points out that the scandal partly originated from the desire of the Boise elite—a group of businessmen who controlled the economy and polity of the city and much of the state—to "get" one of their own members who they understood flagrantly participated in homosexual activities. Gerassi also blames much of what happened to the homosexual men of Boise on the provincialism and ignorance of the Idaho populace. Gerassi's rather harsh assessment of the state's people might make some uncomfortable. Even in the 1950s there were progressive thinkers in the state. And Idaho has made significant advancements on social issues in the last half century. In 1994, for example, Idahoans, albeit by the slimmest of margins, held off an anti-gay initiative. The following year, the sponsors of that measure—who also had direct connections with the anti-gay movement in Oregon and Washington State—failed to get enough signatures to place a second initiative on the Idaho ballot. Also in 1995, forty years after the events that Gerassi described, Boise's *Idaho Statesman* revisited the affair. In 1965, Gerassi had singled out that newspaper for particular criticism, especially blaming it for whipping up anti-homosexual fears in 1955 and 1956. But four decades later, editorial policy was decidedly more favorable to gays. In its critical review of

---

9. *Boise Evening Capital News*, "Minimum Sentence in Gillespie Case," November 20, 1920, 8; Peter Boag, "'Peeping Toms' and Tearooms in 1920s Boise: A Case Study of the Emergence and Suppression of Gay Male Community," *Northwest Gay and Lesbian Historian* 1, no. 3 (summer 1996), 4–5.

the scandal, the *Statesman* even drew parallels between the unfortunate events of 1955 and the less than desirable developments occurring in the state in the mid-1990s.[10]

Despite these auspicious advances in Idaho, the provincialism that Gerassi decried in 1965 remains strong and gives *The Boys of Boise* great currency even after nearly forty years. For its 1995 article on the Boise scandal, for example, the *Statesman* interviewed Gene Thomas, who had been a deputy prosecutor in Boise in 1955. "That chapter in Boise's history," Thomas proclaimed in the 1990s, "is a proud chapter no matter what the homosexual community has to say."[11] Thomas's comments mirror the sentiments of many Idahoans and their officials, as I have discovered on both the personal and professional levels since moving to the state in 1989. In 1996–97 I made application to a grant competition which, at the time, the Idaho Board of Education sponsored in order to facilitate and promote the scholarship of the state's university professors who work in the humanities and social sciences. I requested funds to pursue research on a book-length project devoted to the study of the history of homosexuality in the Pacific Northwest. After a lengthy external peer review process, my project received scores that qualified it for funding. The Idaho Board of Education, however, chose to deny my grant, despite the fact that it funded all other proposals that earned the same marks. The executive director of the board, Rayburn Barton, announced that the "project was out of sync with the [values of] Idaho state taxpayers." Board member Harold Davis revealed that he had commiserated with an eastern Idaho farmer over my scholarly pursuits and finally concluded, in light of the fact that potato prices were down, that "this is not the way we want to spend money." As the story over my grant rejection took on a more public dimension, a number of Idahoans weighed in on the matter. One resident resorted to the old tradition of linking homosexuality to the endangerment of the family, suggesting my historical study would deliver yet another blow to that which he valued most. "My-

10. Jim Hopkins, "Initiative revives 'Boys' rhetoric," *Boise, Idaho Statesman*, October 15, 1995, 9A; Hopkins, "The Boy Most Likely," 1A, 8A–9A. These articles describe many of the tragic personal consequences of the Boise scandal which Gerassi did not report. They also reveal the identities of some of the individuals for whom Gerassi used pseudonyms.

11. Hopkins, "The Boy Most Likely," 8A.

self and others," he wrote in congratulating the board for its decision, "stand for the only institution of marriage, husband and wife, male and female, man and woman. . . . As I have five children ages ranging from 15 years old to 4 months, I pray that you will stand firm on your decision . . . thank you for choosing to know the difference between night and day." Some Idahoans addressed their vitriol directly to me in personal letters. One wrote, "If all you have to do is study the gays perhaps you should be released from your job so you can get out in the real world and do something productive. Like for example, spray knapweed or pull weeds, or dig ditches." Because of the controversy surrounding my project and the fact that I chose to fight the board's decision, the state legislature solved the problem once and for all. In the spring of 1998 it discontinued the decade-long grant program. A major source of funding for the humanities and social sciences in Idaho dried up.[12]

During my struggles with the Idaho Board of Education, I did of course receive encouragement from more enlightened individuals, mostly faculty and students at the state's various public universities and colleges. Support from these quarters was not universal and some faculty members and organizations remained inactive, fearing a withdrawal of their own funding or perhaps simply unwilling to support any scholarly investigations of homosexuality. For example, the faculty senate at Boise State did not condemn the board's actions (of the state's universities and four-year state colleges it was the only one not to do so), but rather expressed the hope that funding would not be threatened for all. Even in my own department at Idaho State University, the situation made some people uncomfortable. When my colleagues circulated a letter of protest to the board, the department chair chose not to sign it.[13]

12. Kim Strosnider, "Idaho Board, Fearful of Offending Taxpayers, Blocks Funds for Study on Gay History," *The Chronicle of Higher Education,* May 2, 1997, A37; Dan Popkey, "State Board of Education kills grant for gay study," *Boise, Idaho Statesman,* May 4, 1997, B1; Harold Davis, Tape Recorded Minutes, Idaho Board of Education Meeting, Boise, April 17, 1997; Michael R. Wickline, "Credibility or politics?," *Lewiston (Idaho) Morning Tribune,* May 10, 1997, 7A; Sy Thompson to author, August 2, 1997.

13. Boise State University Faculty Senate Minutes, May 13, 1997; Nick Casner to author, May 14, 1997; Members of the Idaho State University History Department to Idaho State Board of Education, April 29, 1997. Casner, a faculty member of BSU, reported to me an eyewitness account of the BSU faculty senate meeting.

I have not been alone in bearing the brunt of such actions. After my debacle, Idaho Public Television (IPTV) became embroiled in controversy because it insisted on airing national documentaries, such as *It's Elementary* and *After Stonewall,* which deal with gay and lesbian issues and history in an evenhanded manner. The planned broadcast of these programs, in 1998 and 1999 respectively, brought forth incredible outrage from certain sectors of Idaho's public who wanted them canceled. As a compromise, IPTV delayed their broadcast until the late hours of the night. It also prefaced the showing of *It's Elementary* with a taped statement from a member of the Board of Education who offered a strongly worded caution to the audience. Nonetheless, IPTV's attempt to modify these programs and their airing did not go far enough for some. Immediately after the *It's Elementary* ruckus the state's legislature began threatening privatization of IPTV. In the summer of 2000, in hopes of warding off such action, IPTV began periodically running a rather convoluted disclaimer which stated that the station occasionally aired documentaries dealing with actions that, if committed within the borders of the state, would constitute crimes. Such a warning, of course, inaccurately suggests that homosexuality is against the laws of the state, when in fact sodomy is. The state's sodomy law originated in the territorial days of the 1860s and still carries the possibility of life imprisonment.

If legislative actions, Board of Education behaviors, minutes of meetings, letters to the editor, personal notes to me, sentiment expressed on airwaves, and complacency of those who know better is any accurate gauge of how the general public in Idaho feels, then it is clear that many in the state still retain a deep fear of homosexuality even a half century after the boys of Boise scandal. This alone gives reason to pursue steadfastly historical inquiry into the subject. For Idaho and the Pacific Northwest such inquiry is only in its infancy, but a few studies have appeared in recent years and others are due out soon.[14] The republication of John Gerassi's *The Boys of Boise* is therefore timely. The book reacquaints us with an older literature on the region's gay and lesbian history at a time when we are just setting out in new scholarly directions. Moreover, the book's

14. Among the few historical works on gay, lesbian, and transgender history of the Pacific Northwest are Terry L. Chapman, "'An Oscar Wilde Type': 'The Abominable Crime of Buggery' in Western Canada, 1890-1920," *Criminal Justice History*

insights, methods, and conclusions shed light on the contentious debates of our time and invite yet more interest in the disturbing events of our shared past.

PETER BOAG
April 2001
Pocatello, Idaho

---

4 (1993), 97–119; Nancy Krieger, "Queen of the Bolsheviks: The Hidden History of Dr. Marie Equi," *Radical America* 17, no. 5 (1983), 55–73; Don Paulson, with Roger Simpson, *An Evening at the Garden of Allah: A Gay Cabaret in Seattle* (New York: Columbia University Press, 1996); Peter Boag, "Sex and Politics in Progressive-Era Portland and Eugene: The 1912 Same-Sex Vice Scandal," *Oregon Historical Quarterly* 100, no. 2 (summer 1999), 158–81. My book, tentatively entitled *Same-Sex Affairs: Society and Male Homosexuality in Portland and the Northwest, 1890–1930,* is under contract with the University of California Press. Portland's Gay and Lesbian Archives of the Pacific Northwest occasionally publishes historical articles in *The Northwest Gay and Lesbian Newsletter.* Other works that touch on the Pacific Northwest include D. Michael Quinn, *Same-Sex Dynamics among Nineteenth-Century Americans: A Mormon Example* (Urbana: University of Illinois Press, 1997), which includes some information on Idaho; and Jonathan Ned Katz, *Gay/Lesbian Almanac: A New Documentary* (New York: Harper & Row, 1983); and Jonathan Ned Katz, *Gay American History,* rev. ed. (New York: Meridian, 1992).

PREFACE TO THE
2001 PAPERBACK EDITION

When *The Boys of Boise* was first published in 1966, it elicited en-
thusiastic reviews. No one chastised me for my tone, which was a
bit too superior. No one criticized me for sharing the common as-
sumptions of the day about homosexuality: that some kinds of lusts
are improper, perhaps even sick. Sociologists, social workers, jour-
nalists, and most other readers praised the book without reserva-
tion. Except in Boise. There, folks scoffed at it, but for the wrong
reasons. Boise's *Idaho Daily Statesman* panned it—understandably,
of course, since the town's only daily newspaper was most responsible for creating the hysteria the book described. And mainstream
politicians were equally reluctant to say a nice word; those who knew
the book was dead on target avoided embarrassment by claiming
they had not read it. The local bookstore refused to display *The
Boys of Boise,* while continuing to order more copies from the publisher, hide them under the counter, and profit from the huge demand, especially after CBS ran a special on homosexuality in
America and focused a segment on Boise and my book.

The 1955 witch-hunt of homosexuals in Boise was never really
aimed at gay men but rather at the more progressive politicians
who wanted to modernize the city. The hunters were members of
the established elite, those Idaho aristocrats who met at the exclusive Arid Club and plotted against all innovations which might
threaten their sinecures and power. That in the process they ruined
the lives of many people bothered none of them. The Boise witch-
hunt was aimed at the good guys, at a City Hall then run by decent
reformers, at a hapless councilman, at a "queen" who hoped to create new jobs through a program of urban renewal. (In my original
manuscript, I named that "queen," but my publisher's lawyers refused to reveal his identity for fear of lawsuits, especially since he
was too powerful even for Arid Clubbers and survived unscathed.)
Of course most of the victims were poor—a shoeshiner, a clerk, a
railroad worker.

But not all. One was a young man named Frank Anton Jones, whom I called Jim Morton in the book. His father, Harold T. "Buck" Jones (Henry Morton in the book), was a New Jersey–born councilman who had moved to Idaho in 1924 to buy wool from the area's Basque sheepherders and had married into one of that community's better-known families. Shortly after their son Frank and a sister were born, the Joneses moved to Boise, where Buck ran a clothing store and got involved in local politics. He was elected to the City Council in 1951 and was so active in city activities that his name soon appeared on the walls of City Hall, public swimming pools, and other town buildings.

In 1955, when the homosexual scandal broke out, Buck was one of the loudest proponents of "crushing the monster," to quote the *Statesman* front-page editorial. That year, son Frank trudged through the grueling application for West Point, got the required congressional nomination, and was admitted—the beginning of a would-be brilliant career. On January 7, 1956, C. L. "Doc" House, the rather distasteful Ada County sheriff, traveled to San Francisco and brought back a former Boise gay named Melvin W. Dir, who waived extradition and confessed to having had homosexual relations with various Boise men, including Frank Jones three years earlier when Frank would have been fourteen. Doc House then journeyed to West Point, got Frank dismissed from the military academy, and brought him back to Boise.

"Disgusting," cried Buck. "They could have told me about it, and I would have had him brought home on an emergency leave and then we could have gone into the whole thing. Instead they send this Sheriff Doc House and he gets a confession from my kid and they boot him out of West Point then and there. It was dirty. In their investigation there were other names"—in all, a private investigator hired by the cops grilled 1,472 men. With the collusion of the police, the investigator then dodged subpoenas to avoid testifying on his methods—"big shots involved, one very big name. But nothing happened to him." Well, yes, Buck, but that's what you get for trusting your political system and playing power politics.

Frank was a minor and was never charged. But his life was ruined. He tried to adapt, moved to Portland, then Philadelphia, married, adopted two children, considered divorce, returned to Boise, separated from his wife, and on Monday, February 15, 1982, at about

9 p.m., committed suicide. He was forty-four. Buck died of a heart attack shortly thereafter. His wife followed three years later.

Eventually the Boise City Council admitted that there had never been a homosexual underground as the *Statesman* and *Time* magazine had squawked, just a normal share of gay men doing their thing. In the meantime, a "lesbian" plot was also "uncovered" among Boise policewomen, but that too eventually faded from the front page.

Nothing much has changed since then in Boise, Idaho. True, witch-hunts are harder to unleash now, and so are smear campaigns. But some still work: the radical right did go after Senator Frank Church, mostly because he was pro-choice, and beat him. Some of the main characters from *The Boys of Boise* are dead; others have left the state. Today, whatever principals survive don't want to talk about the past. The *Statesman* tried to weasel itself back into a moderate position, without ever apologizing or sharing with its readers the lesson it should have learned. In 1995, Jim Hoskins, a young reporter for the *Statesman*, tried to update the story, but few people would talk to him. The main prosecutor, Blaine Evans, whose political ambitions were crushed by the scandal when it turned sour, was still practicing law then, but he refused to give Hoskins an interview.

A week after *The Boys of Boise* was published, the Sunday *Los Angeles Times/Washington Post Book Week* came out with a rave review. I was ecstatic. I bubblingly called my editor, Peter Ritner, who was then managing editor of the Macmillan Company. "Stop jumping up and down," he yelled at me over the phone. "The review just killed your book. It will now be taken seriously and used in law schools. That means it won't sell very much."

And the victims? Most were freed long before my book came out. One had not been, but the book seemed to have rectified the situation. He wrote me a fantastic letter (which he asked me not to reveal) thanking me for in effect getting him out of jail.

So I didn't get rich. But that letter sure made the whole book very worthwhile.

JOHN GERASSI
April 2001

INTRODUCTION TO THE
ORIGINAL EDITION

Glancing through *Time* magazine one day in December 1955, I was suddenly struck by a story headed "Idaho Underworld." Immediately I wondered what kind of underworld could possibly exist in such a sparsely populated, basically poor state, where no city was big enough for an organized crime syndicate to operate either extensively or profitably. But the first paragraph set me straight. It explained that there is a kind of underworld I had not imagined, or rather it referred to an underworld that I, born and bred in a big city, would never have characterized as an underworld at all:

> Boise, Idaho (pop. 50,000), the state capital, is usually thought of as a boisterous, rollicking he-man's town, and home of the rugged Westerner. In the downtown saloons of the city a faint echo of Boise's ripsnorting frontier days can still be heard, but its quiet residential areas and 70 churches give the city an appearance of immaculate respectability. Recently, Boiseans were shocked to learn that their city had sheltered a widespread homosexual underworld that involved some of Boise's most prominent men and had preyed on hundreds of teen-age boys for the past decade.

My first impulse was not to believe it—unless, of course, the local police and law-enforcement agencies were part of that underworld, and had been all along. For how else, I asked myself, could such an underworld flourish for so long? In a city of 50,000 people, surely the cops must be aware of everything that goes on. And unless the ringleaders were so highly placed in the state's political machinery that they were untouchable, someone certainly would have exposed their operations long before.

Even if the cops, the politicians, the judges, the newsmen and the big businessmen were part of this underworld—a very unlikely possibility—would not a group of outraged parents have banded together to clean up the mess? After all, kids are kids, and no matter how pleasant or profitable their extracurricular activities may be, they are bound to talk, to brag, or at least to betray themselves accidentally. What's more, not all of these "hundreds of teen-age boys" could possibly have grown up to be confirmed homosexuals. Surely some, reaching adulthood during "the past decade" and having kids of their own, would have made an attempt to put a stop to it.

The article went on to say:

> In the course of their investigation, police talked with 125 youths who had been involved. All were between the ages of 13 and 20. Usually, the motive—and the lure—was money. Many of the boys wanted money for maintenance of their automobiles (Idaho grants daylight driving permits to children of 14, regular licenses to 15-year-olds). The usual fees given to the boys were $5 to $10 per assignation.

Clearly, therefore, not all the "125 youths" were homosexual. Many simply catered to the adult homosexuals for money. But would not their parents have been suspicious of their children's sudden independent wealth? Obviously, there was more to the story than *Time* reported.

Perhaps, I thought, Boise had become as liberal as New York, where homosexuals are rarely arrested (except in shakedowns), where young men and even teen-age boys freely drag the streets in makeup and wigs. After all, I reasoned innocently, Idaho had produced one of the most radical senators of the union—Glen Taylor, who had been on the Progressive Party ticket with Henry Wallace in 1948. But no, Boise was a small town, and no such American town could ever become so liberal as to allow homosexuals to wander about freely picking up thirteen-year-olds—for a whole decade!

Sure enough, the last paragraph of that *Time* story read:

> This week the shocked community and the state began a rehabilitation program for the boys. Social workers began to investigate each case, to work out family problems. A citizens' committee representing

virtually every organization in Boise began a campaign to get after-school jobs for the boys, and a special team of psychiatrists will arrive this week from Denver, at the expense of the State Board of Health, to treat the young victims.

But now my suspicions were aroused from a different angle. Where could Boise get the finances to carry out such a program of rehabilitation? If the community was really shocked, why had nothing been done for ten years? And where would Idaho find so many qualified social workers to handle the job?

Three weeks later, *Time* printed a short follow-up story on the Boise underworld. In two quick paragraphs, it reported that more homosexuals had been arrested—and sentenced. But it also said:

Dr. John L. Butler, chief of Idaho's Department of Mental Health, had publicly opposed sentencing the homosexual adults to prison terms: "We have to build up community supports for them," he said. "One alternative might be to let them form their own society and be left alone."

This statement raised all sorts of new questions. For one thing, how did Idaho ever get such a progressive-minded mental-health chief, one who dared to propose measures even New York would consider outrageous? Secondly, what happened to the kids? Did not Dr. Butler's suggestion that the homosexuals should simply live together imply that they were all consenting adults?

Nor did the sentences make much sense. The range seemed to be from six months to life—in prison. What kind of a judge would send a homosexual to prison for life—prison being a notorious breeding ground for homosexuality anyway? There were other unanswered questions: How were the youths rehabilitated? If hundreds were involved, what happened to the schools? And what, in fact, did the community do about it, besides creating a few after-school jobs?

Two years later, I became an editor at *Time* magazine, and one of my first acts was to look up the Boise file in the morgue. But there was nothing more on the matter. No one had seemed interested in following it up. I decided that someday I would.

My preoccupation with international politics kept me pretty busy for the next few years, however, and instead of going to Boise, I went all over South America and wrote a book on the revolutionary upheavals gripping that continent. But I never forgot the Boise story, and in 1965, ten full years after the scandal broke, I finally took the time to check it out. I went to Boise.

Before doing so, I read everything I could find on homosexuality and on child molesters. I interviewed many psychiatrists and psychologists who specialized in the subject, including some who had worked on the Kinsey reports. I also did as much research on Idaho, its history, customs, politics and resources, as was possible from the outside.

Once in Boise, I rapidly discovered that it was going to be harder to find the answers than I had thought. First of all, some of the court records had disappeared, while others had to be traced down to individual law offices. Also, very few people were willing to cooperate. The memory of the scandal was still fresh, and often sore. Many city and state officials wanted the scandal kept buried, not only because it reflected adversely on their city and their state, but also for personal reasons: Their own behavior during the scandal had been far from irreproachable. Finally, many of the principals no longer lived in Boise.

Nevertheless, as I persisted, I did get some breaks. I met a group of young lawyers and newsmen who began to help me. Although my investigation was bound to hurt the Republican Party, which was in power in 1955 and still ruled Boise in 1965, these people came from both sides of the political fence. Indeed, I obtained some very useful information from members of the Radical Right, despite the fact that they were (and, I presume, still are) stanchly opposed to all mental-health laws.

Some of these young men had been teen-agers during the scandal, and a few remembered particular details that gradually helped me fit together the over-all puzzle: why the scandal broke, how it was exploited and by whom, and what happened to the town as a result. Eventually I was able to track down many of the principals who had left Boise and were now living in Seattle,

San Francisco, Florida and elsewhere. Dr. Butler, for example, did turn out to be the progressive-minded psychiatrist that the *Time* article had implied, but he had understandably fared poorly in Boise and was no longer there. I found him, as dedicated as ever, in Portland, Oregon.

With each new piece of evidence, my questions became more precise. But with each such question, I apparently became more of a threat. I began to receive anonymous phone calls warning me to drop my investigation. One day I got another anonymous phone call, but this time it was a friendly one. "Your motel is going to get ransacked," the voice said. "You'd better hide whatever material you've accumulated." I immediately put all my documentation into a suitcase, drove out to the airport, and sent it to New York. When I returned to my motel, sure enough, someone had gotten in and turned every drawer inside out.

Finally I heard that the governor himself, Robert E. Smylie, had written a letter to *Newsweek*'s man in charge of the northwestern territory. I had made it perfectly clear that though I was (then) a *Newsweek* editor I was in Boise on my own time for a story or a book that did not involve *Newsweek*, and so I had violated no rules of conduct. But the very fact that he had written such a letter, or that it was so reported to me, made me apprehensive. I asked a friendly lawyer to make sure that he heard from me or contacted me at least once a day.

I stuck it out until I had documented the whole affair. When I did, I realized that the *Time* article had been misleading in many ways. I also concluded that the whole scandal was one of the most shocking examples of legalized prejudice, involving politics and personal vendettas, that I had ever come across. Homes were shattered, families were broken and individual careers were ruined, sometimes with incredible viciousness. And the fabric of a whole town was laid bare, revealing to what extent it rested on pettiness, intolerance and the personal ambition of a few.

I also understood, perhaps for the first time, what life in a small town is really like, and since America is ultimately made up of such small towns, I understood what America is really like. Because Boise is one of those typical American communities that has a single daily newspaper, I realized that the freedom of the press we cherish so much can be just as much of a farce in America as it is in countries where the press is controlled by the government. For what is the difference between a newspaper that prints only what the government tells it to and a newspaper that prints only what an all-powerful editor, catering to the establishment of the community, decides is news or fact?

Many of the men convicted for "infamous crimes against nature" in Boise in 1955 and 1956 should have been separated in some way from society: They were indeed child molesters. But the way the cases were handled not only illustrates the moral corruption of a small city wrought by its own stifling conformity and fears, it also exposes the quicksand on which so much of our American society is erected.

Acknowledgments

A great many people made this book possible. But unfortunately most of them cannot be named, since they live and work in Boise, Idaho, and would undoubtedly suffer social and economic reprisals from those who will take offense at what is reported herein—instead of realizing that this book was written in the hope that there may never be reason to write another like it about any town in America. Nevertheless, I would like to single out the staff of the struggling weekly *Idaho Observer* and especially its daring, crusading editor, Sam Day. Though Sam is not responsible for the contents of this book, his spirited honesty inspired me to carry out my investigations even after it became dangerous to do so. I would also like to thank my assistant, Susan, and all those Idahoans who, in the name of eradication of prejudice, intolerance, hate, and the mental illnesses derived therefrom, gave me so much of their valuable time.

CHRONOLOGY

1955 October 31	First arrests on morals charges in what was to become the great scandal of 1955–56: a shoe repairman (Cooper), a clothing-store clerk (Cassel), and a freight-line worker (Brokaw, sometimes incorrectly spelled Brocaw). Ada County (Boise) probation officer Emery Bess claims "about 100 boys" are involved in a homosexual ring.
November 3	*The Idaho Daily Statesman* panics community with highly emotional editorial.
November 10	Cooper, pleading guilty, sentenced to life in prison.
November 14	Joe Moore, vice president of the Idaho First National Bank, arrested.
November 16	Defining the homosexual as a "criminal," the *Statesman* demands the removal of "this sordid mess."
November 20	With Boiseans becoming nearly hysterical, the *Statesman* reverses itself, says that the homosexual is not a criminal and calls for calm.
November 24	Dr. John Butler, a psychiatrist with special training in sexual deviations, arrives in Boise to visit family, becomes consultant to the Board of Health.
November–December	A dozen men, some very prominent, and including Gordon Larsen, are arrested on homosexual charges on December 11, 1955.
December 2	Charles Herbert Gordon, a decorator, pleading guilty to lewd and lascivious conduct, is sentenced to fifteen years.
December 9	Brokaw also pleads guilty but is recommended for leniency by Prosecuting Attorney Blaine Evans

because of his "cooperation." Psychiatric evidence is introduced in Brokaw's defense. Reginald Shaffer, Gordon's half-brother by adoption, is sentenced to fifteen years.

have been interviewed concerning the homosexual cases.

April 10   Probation officer Emery Bess is asked to resign.

April 13   Dir pleads not guilty.

May   Former Democratic Senator Glen Taylor and Frank Church, rivals for the nomination to oppose the incumbent, Republican Senator Herman Welker, in the November elections, launch vitriolic campaigns. (Church won the nomination by 200 votes in September.)

June 7   William Baker goes on trial for the murder of his father.

June 8   Baker is found guilty of manslaughter.

June 11   Baker is sentenced to ten years.

June 13   Prosecutor Blaine Evans announces he will run for the state senate.

August 24   Dir changes his plea to guilty.

September 21   Dir is granted a withheld five-year sentence but goes to Ada County jail.

November 6   General elections: Eisenhower defeats Stevenson in Idaho 166,979 to 105,868, but Church beats Welker 149,096 to 102,781, with Taylor, running as an independent, getting 13,415.

November 19   Larsen goes on trial.

November 20   Larsen guilty.

December 4   Moore loses appeal, told to report to the sheriff for confinement in the penitentiary on December 27.

December 7   Larsen's attorney files motions for new trial and withheld sentence (see appendices).

December 12   Wilson loses appeal. Senator-elect Church appoints John Carver, Jr., Moore's defense attorney, as his special assistant.

December 14   Idaho's director of the Board of Health, who had testified in defense of various of the convicted homosexuals, is reported fed up and will resign.

December 21	Larsen's motions are denied.
1957	Larsen is sentenced to five years. His attorney ap-
January 11	peals to the Idaho Supreme Court (eventually loses).
January 16	Dir is charged with violating the terms of his probation.
January 21	Dir is sentenced to seven years in the penitentiary. The scandal comes to an end, although its consequences are still being felt today.

1

CRUSH THE MONSTER

ON THE MORNING of Wednesday, November 2, 1955, the people of Boise were stunned by a front-page headline in their local newspaper, *The Idaho Daily Statesman:* THREE BOISE MEN ADMIT SEX CHARGES.

Beneath it, the article claimed that an investigation "into immoral acts involving teen-age boys was being launched," thereby adding to the first hint of a sex scandal the unsettling information that minors were involved. The article also stated that such an investigation had been announced on Tuesday by Emery Bess, Ada (Boise) County probation officer, "after three Boise men were arrested late Monday night."

Why it was a probation officer and not the police or prosecuting attorney who made the announcement was not explained. Nor were any reasons offered as to why the story had not been reported in the Tuesday issue of the *Statesman*.

The article continued:

Charged with lewd and lascivious conduct with minor children under the age of 16 are Charles Brokaw, 29, a freight line dock worker, and Ralph Cooper, 33, a local shoe store employee. The third is Vernon H. (Benny) Cassel, 51, local clothing store clerk, charged with infamous crimes against nature.

Once again, explanations were missing. What, in point of fact, did these three men actually do, or what were they accused of doing? What is the difference between "lewd and lascivious conduct" and "infamous crimes against nature"? To the uninformed people of Boise, the second charge sounded much more vicious than the first—whatever the phrases meant legally. In either case, the reader's curiosity was whetted by the article. But his curiosity remained mostly unsatisfied.

According to the article, Bess insisted that the authorities had barely "scratched the surface," though there was partial evidence against "several" other adults and "about 100 boys." With that, of course, the reader really became alarmed—though still ignorant. Bess went on to say that the arrests were the results of the investigation of Howard Dice, a private detective, carried out "at the request of a client."

In the elevators and hallways of their office buildings that morning, the people of Boise were full of questions, doubts, anger—and gossip. Was there a particular complaint by a particular father against these three arrested men for having committed an immoral act against his son? Who was the client, anyway? Why were not the police involved? If the client was not a father of one of the boys, what was his concern? Or, if he felt he should make it his business out of civic duty, why did he not reveal himself, and why did he not go to the police instead of hiring a private detective?

The article answered none of these questions. It did say that Blaine Evans, Ada County's prosecuting attorney, had obtained tape-recorded confessions from each of the three men, but this only confused matters even more, for it implied that though the police were not involved in the investigation, the prosecuting attorney was. The article further said that the three men had been taken into custody by two deputy sheriffs *after* the three had made their statement, and that they had been locked up in jail because they did not, or could not, post bail. There were no references to defense attorneys.

At lunch that day, conversation in Boise was unusually lively. All along the main street, along the rows of small shops, at the Boise Hotel (a rambling, brownstoned, old-fashioned edifice one block away from the State Capitol), at the Idanha (an ugly, fading hotel a few blocks west) and at the many eating places

frequented by the city's white-collar workers—state employees, sec-
retaries, lawyers, influence peddlers, accountants—the buzzing
sounds revolved around the same theme: sex in Boise. Although
the three arrested "deviates" were rather harmless, atypical residents of the basically middle-class town, everyone seemed already
convinced that scores if not hundreds of "respected" citizens were
somehow connected in a vast secret organization of perverts and
that every kid in high school had been poisoned by that organization. It was incredible what the imagination of those calm,
churchgoing, law-abiding people came up with—on the barest
and, as yet, most confusing bits of evidence.

Boise's mothers, of course, were the most imaginative of all.
They frantically called the authorities at the Boise High School
(the only one at the time), at police headquarters, at the *Statesman*. And, naturally, from their comfortable, white-shingled, two-
story houses, which cram the straight, tree-lined residential streets,
these mothers were calling each other, embellishing the story,
adding names to the list of "known perverts" and emphatically
stressing the acute seriousness of the whole matter.

On the next day, November 3, the *Statesman* itself stressed
that seriousness equally fervently, perhaps even irresponsibly, in
its editorial:

CRUSH THE MONSTER

Disclosure that the evils of moral perversion prevail in Boise on an
extensive scale must come as a distinct and intensely disagreeable
shock to most Boiseans. It seems almost incredible that any such can-
cerous growth could have taken roots and developed in our midst.

It's bad enough when three Boise men, overhauled and accused as
criminal deviates, are reported to have confessed to violations involving 10 teen-age boys; but when the responsible office of the probate
court announces that these arrests mark only the start of an investigation that has only "scratched the surface," the situation is one that
causes general alarm and calls for immediate and systematic cauteriza-
tion.

The situation might be dismissed with an expression of regret and
a sigh of relief if only one could be quite sure that none other than

these three men and these 10 boys have been infected by the monstrous evil here. But the responsible court officer says that only the surface has been scratched and that "partial evidence has been gathered showing that several other adults and about 100 boys are involved."

So long as such possibility exists, there can be no rest.

Involved in it are the roots of a manifestation of juvenile delinquency quite beyond the ken of most welfare advancement agencies or interests.

It's a challenge of greater danger than most of us could have thought possible here.

It must, by all means, be met promptly and effectively.

The operation as projected involves a task and a responsibility that's entirely too big and too sinister to be left alone to a private detective and an officer of the probate court.

Until the whole sordid situation is completely cleared up, and the premises thoroughly cleaned and disinfected, the job is one in which the full strength of county and city agencies should and must be enlisted.

That's what we demand: and that's what we expect.

Such an editorial was bound to generate panic, and it did. For one thing, Boiseans, who were used to the *Statesman*'s habit of covering local crime news in inside pages, were now convinced that the newspaper was really alarmed—proof that all decent Boiseans should be even more alarmed, because the staid, conservative daily had a reputation of underplaying every crisis. Secondly, the editorial, which seemed to believe every word that Emery Bess had spouted, called upon every city and state agency to pursue and "crush the monster" as if the life of the community were at stake.

How could the *Statesman* arrive at such conclusions from the mere facts that three men had been arrested and that a probation officer had made a couple of sweeping generalizations? Unless, of course, the paper had additional information, which it had not printed. That would explain how it knew that "10 boys" had been involved when the article had mentioned only "minor children." It would also explain why the editorial carefully twice repeated Emery Bess's remark that the surface had only been scratched.

But why did the *Statesman* pointedly avoid reference to the mysterious client? Did it know who he was? Was the newspaper somehow linked to the investigation? If so, it would then know for sure that there were other men involved, and perhaps even who they were. And if these men turned out to be important members of the community, then its headlines and strong editorial made sense.

One thing is certain: On November 3, 1955, when the *Statesman* exploded with its inflammatory editorial calling on all agencies to crush the monster, there was no such thing. Three rather unimportant, unassuming, unpolitical individuals had been arrested for doing something either infamous or lewd with some minors, and a probate-court officer, who gave no proof that he knew what he was talking about, claimed that about a hundred kids were perhaps doing the same thing with several other adults. On that kind of evidence, most newspapers would only demand more information.

And, for a while, it appeared as if there were no more information to be had. On Friday, November 4, as reported in the *Statesman* the next day, Cooper pleaded guilty in the Third District Court with no lawyer representing him. Cassel appeared with attorney J. Charles Blanton but did not enter a plea. And Brokaw requested a preliminary hearing, which was set for November 10.

The only interesting item in that day's report was the name J. Charles Blanton, for he had worked in the prosecuting attorney's office just before the scandal broke. I will come back to Blanton later, but it might be useful to quote part of an interview that I had with him in 1965. He said, as recorded verbatim by my assistant: "Like every city, Boise had its homosexuals. But we didn't have any evidence, and we didn't make any effort to seek it out. We had prosecuted homosexuals. I don't know how many. But we handled them normally, without any sensation. The individual was treated. I had left the office in September of 1955."

Yes, like every city, Boise had always had its homosexuals. And, said a former assistant prosecuting attorney, evidence against homosexuals was not sought out deliberately. When such men were caught violating the law, they were prosecuted—routinely. Yet Blanton left in September and less than two months later, a whole "monster" corrupting "about 100 boys" was denounced. Somebody must have worked incredibly fast to discover such a monster so quickly.

A week later, on Friday, November 11, the *Statesman* had something new to report about that monster, which now took the form of one pitiful character—Ralph Cooper. On page 14, as if it had to be shamefully buried, the news was topped by this two-column head: "Cooper Draws Life Term in Idaho Penitentiary."

2

THE REPAIRMAN AND
THE BANKER

RALPH COOPER was no innocent victim. At thirty-three, he had a long police and FBI record and, as the *Statesman* said, "a record of crime dating back to the time he was 13 years old." But perhaps for that very reason, a closer scrutiny of his background should have been undertaken. In the court records, his history is described thus:

> Ralph Cooper, the defendant, has admitted the charge stated in the Information in its entirety ["Lewd conduct with a minor child," made by Lee Gibson for a crime committed on July 1, 1954]. In addition to this instance, he also admits a relationship with another minor named * * *. The latter affair occurred in December of 1953. The defendant further admits that when he was fifteen years of age he was committed to the State Industrial School at St. Anthony, Idaho, on a charge of burglary and there served a 13-months term. Shortly after his release from St. Anthony, he was returned to serve an additional 18 months as a parole violator. In 1943 he was convicted of burglary in the State of Idaho and was sentenced to the Idaho State Penitentiary where he served until 1945. In 1948 he was convicted of forgery, again in Idaho, and served a term at the Idaho State Penitentiary until 1950. In 1951 the defendant was convicted in the Probate Court of Ada County for contributing to the delinquency of minors. This offense had to do with liquor; however, Judge Jackson, as a condition of his release, required that the defendant stay away from young boys.

With reference to out-of-state charges and convictions, the defendant relates that he was convicted of a felony in the State of California
in 1941 and served a penitentiary sentence at San Quentin.

The Prosecuting Attorney's office has also been informed that this
defendant had sexual relations with other minor boys, aside from
those he has admitted. One young man has informed us that while
working at the shoe repair shop where Cooper was employed, the
defendant had homosexual relations with him; that he bought and
provided liquor for himself and three other young boys and that on
one occasion the defendant took the said boys on a trip to Kuna
Caves, during which trip they drank the liquor he had provided and
during which trip he committed homosexual acts on their persons
involving the use of his mouth. The statement with reference to the
Kuna Caves incident is corroborated by statements given to our office
by other young men who supposedly also made the trip. In addition,
the Prosecuting Attorney's office has signed written statements from
other young men describing the homosexual activities of the defendant with respect to them.

The defendant has stated that he desires psychiatric treatment and
would like to discontinue homosexual activities. Although he denies
certain of the charges made against him in the above-referred-to statements, with reference to the two incidents first mentioned, he has
been open and cooperative in providing this office with information.

This synopsis, filed by the prosecuting attorney's office on November 4, 1955, was in the records available in the Court House,
District Court of the Third Judiciary District of the State of
Idaho, in and for the County of Ada. What I found extremely
curious was that in Cooper's file, none of the other statements
mentioned was included. Nor were there any other depositions,
by or against the defendant.

The *Statesman* article gave a few more details. It said that
District Judge Merlin S. Young, who sentenced Cooper to life
imprisonment, "asked him if any statements were to be made in
his behalf. There were none." It then quoted Young as saying
that "it appears that all of your actions have been with teen-age
youths." It pointed out that Cooper's previous convictions were

for shoplifting, car theft, grand theft, first-degree burglary and forgery. And it included this paragraph:

Warden L. E. Clapp [1] told a reporter that Cooper must serve ten years of the sentence before he can be considered for parole "and that doesn't mean he will be considered," Clapp said. He stressed that the State Board of Pardons has the power to establish the conditions and that in Cooper's case, even if he would in some future time be paroled, it could only be to a state hospital and not to society.

In reviewing his case, that statement haunted me. If even the state penitentiary's warden, who had and has no meaningful training in psychology, was aware at the very moment of Cooper's sentencing that he should be in a state hospital—that is, that Cooper obviously needed psychiatric help—why did the court never consider it? Surely, Cooper's criminal record indicated that there might have been a general breakdown in his moral fabric. And why was he not represented by a lawyer?

These questions must remain without definite answers. But guesses are possible, and the probability is high that we can guess accurately. Suppose, for example, that Cooper had been promised psychiatric help if he did plead guilty. Would he not do so, assuming he was guilty as charged?

Cooper served nine years in the state penitentiary, which is just outside Boise's city limits. When he was paroled, he was not sent to a state hospital, despite Warden Clapp's assurances (but the reason for that, as we shall see, may well be that Idaho's two mental hospitals are not equipped to handle sexual "deviates"). In any case, Cooper was freed, and as far as the police or anyone else knew, he had been well behaved for more than a year when I interviewed him.

He was, as he had been in the 1955 mug shots, tall and pockmarked, perhaps a little thinner. He was neither mad nor bitter, although he admitted that he had been both for a few years. He

---

[1] Clapp resigned as warden after twenty-one years in March 1966 to become Idaho's Secretary of State.

considered himself a tiny pawn in the whole sordid mess, the first
to be sentenced, to feel the full impact of the *Statesman*'s screech-
ing editorial. He talked freely and calmly, about everything from
his arrest to life in the pen. Here's how it all began according to
him:

"First thing I know about the whole story was when this deputy
sheriff comes up to the house and asks me to go to the station, says
they want to talk to me. I go. When I get there they book me for
homosexual activity with minors. They got statements, two signed by
kids I never heard of, and by this kid Lee Gibson, and that was true
all right. They toss me in jail and then Blaine Evans [the county
prosecuting attorney] comes around and the chief of police and the
sheriff and they keep asking me where I was on such a date and such
a date and so on. They try to pin all sorts of murder raps on me, but
either I got alibis or else, when I don't and they keep pressing, I ask
that they give me a lie-detector test. That finally got them off my tail.
They ask me to sign a confession, well, I figure they got me with that
Gibson statement, and then they tell me that I'll get about five years
or seven at the most, and Evans tells me that I could get off, released
to a psychiatrist, so I sign the statement. Then I was brought up in
front of Judge Young and he asked me what I plead and I said guilty.
I never had a lawyer nor did anyobdy suggest I could get a state-
appointed one, but I wouldn't want one anyway. I know from experience that whenever you get a court lawyer, all he wants is money
and tells you to fall on the mercy of the court. So I plead guilty and
that's it. They took me back to the county jail and on the way the
sheriff tells me, 'Don't worry, most you'll get is seven years.' Then
two days later, eleven days after I got picked up, I went up before
Judge Young and he says, 'By the power vested in me, I sentence you
to the penitentiary for the rest of your natural life.' I'll never forget
that. It took me two weeks to get out of my daze. . . . I heard from
my sister that the cops had gone through my house and taken every
photograph they could find, old photos of my parents and friends.
They had nothing to do with the case, there were no photographs of
Gibson or anybody else involved, but I never again saw the albums.
There was no search warrants issued either. . . ."

A poor, maladjusted fellow—that was my impression of Ralph
Cooper. Under Idaho state law, lewd and lascivious conduct is

a felony, and as an oft-convicted felon, Cooper got life in prison, but he never really understood why. If he had killed somebody, yes. If he had robbed another time, yes again. But to play around with little boys—somehow that never seemed to him a crime. A perversion, perhaps. Thus he hoped for a cure. In his mind, so it appeared to me, he realized that homosexuality was something sick, not evil, though robbery and forgery were evil. "The law must convict you if you get caught—that's the chance you take —but not if you're sick." It never really occurred to Cooper that the law rarely makes such a separation, nor indeed that he might be sick in *all* his habits. That is why I believed him when he insisted that somebody had told him that he would get psychiatric care if he cooperated. I later found more reasons to believe it.

Yet no one so suggested in court, and Cooper was sentenced to life in prison. The "monster" was put away. But there was still no proof that the monster was quite as bad as the *Statesman* had claimed. Nor was there any new information on how the case had been solved, or, for that matter, on how and why the investigation had begun. The *Statesman* article reporting Cooper's sentence once again repeated that the arrests had come about as a result of "an investigation conducted by Howard Dice, owner of the Gem State Investigation Service, at the request of a client." But there were no details on the mysterious client. Nor was there any explanation of why a crime committed on July 1, 1954, had suddenly been investigated after September 1955.

And then, suddenly, a big fat clue hit the front page of the *Statesman*, proving that Cooper had indeed been only a tiny pawn in the sordid drama that was just beginning to unfold, a drama whose main stars had been unknown when Cooper was arrested—except, of course, to those who had written the script. With Cooper out of the way, with Lee Gibson's statement duly recorded and Cooper's guilty plea firmly supporting that statement, the real star was ready to be exposed. And he was—in a catchy box on page 1 of the November 15, 1955, issue of the *Statesman*.

The article said that late the night before, a Monday, Joe Moore, 54, vice president of the Idaho First National Bank, had been arrested on felony charges of committing an infamous crime against nature. The complaint was signed by Prosecuting Attorney Blaine Evans and Sheriff C. L. "Doc" House, based on a statement by a seventeen-year-old youth with a corroborating statement by a fifteen-year-old. House had taken Moore into custody after he had been called to the courthouse, where the prosecuting attorney's office was, for interrogation. Said Evans: "Our office will continue these investigations, and will use every facility at our disposal to eliminate this despicable condition in the community."

So, it *was* the prosecuting attorney who was carrying out the investigation after all. The article certainly implied that. Yet when I checked out the files, I found that the two boys' statements against Moore had been witnessed by Howard Dice, Emery Bess and, in the case of the seventeen-year-old, by James C. Hunt, Criminal Investigator (CID), U.S. Army, Fort Carson, Colorado. But the people of Boise were not told this. What they were told, in the words of the *Statesman* editorial on November 16, was:

THIS MESS MUST BE REMOVED

The decent foundations of the Boise community were jolted beyond description recently with the arrest of three local men on morals charges involving young boys. It did not seem possible that this community ever harbored homosexuals to ravage our youth. Yet it was true as confessions of both men and young boys made disgustingly clear.

Understanding of the difficulty law enforcement officers face in exposing these enemies of society, there has not been public demand that our law enforcement officials act immediately. Rumors that investigations were being made may have held demands in check.

Monday night Ada County's Prosecuting Attorney Blaine Evans revealed another arrest of the same sordid nature. There is no comfort in knowing that another of these arrests could be made but there is great satisfaction in the realization that the prosecutor has made such an arrest. And there is additional comfort in his statement that he will use every facility at his command to continue these investigations and rid the community of this scourge. Those were the words the community wanted to hear. Those were the words the community required.

The prosecutor faces no easy task. Tracking down this kind of *criminal*,[2] obtaining the necessary evidence and getting it to court is perhaps the most difficult of all law enforcement. But progress has been made. We are completely confident there will be more.

It might not be a bad idea for Boise parents to keep an eye on the whereabouts of their offsprings. To date a number of boys have been victimized by these perverts. The greatest tragedy of all is the fact that young boys so involved grow into manhood with the same inclinations of those who are called homosexuals.

No matter what is required, this sordid mess must be removed from this community.

Aside from the fact that medically and psychiatrically the editorial is wrong, it could certainly claim good cause to be alarmed. After all, a banker—and a big one—had been arrested. No one bothered to mention that one of the two boys testifying against the banker Moore was the same "boy"—Lee Gibson—who had signed the convicting statement against Cooper.

What difference did that make? Suppose, for a moment, that Cooper did not know Moore—as it turned out. Isn't it then strange that the young, innocent Lee Gibson should have been "victimized" by two so different homosexuals? Of course, said the accusers, the Gibson boy was only fifteen and therefore could not know what was going on. Or could he? Could it not have been Lee Gibson who had made the advances? Shocking? Revolting? A boy of fifteen? We'll see!

Meanwhile, the noose tightened. The prosecuting attorney became a hero and the investigation was identified as his. The town was more alarmed than ever, but it was convinced that something was being done. Oh yes, people went on the rampage denouncing men who stopped to talk to young boys, men who paused to look at football practice, men who were not good, kind, obedient hus-

[2] My italics. See page 16.

bands. In fact, within the next few days, more anonymous phone calls poured into the prosecuting attorney's office, the police station, the sheriff's office and the *Statesman* switchboard than ever before. But the town was on the move.

Many harmless homosexuals who had never touched or approached minors also panicked. One young fellow, a local teacher, obviously had the habit of reading the *Statesman* during breakfast. On the morning that Moore's arrest was reported and that Blaine Evans' promise to "eliminate" all homosexuals appeared in print, this young teacher had just begun to eat his eggs. He never finished them. He jumped up from his seat, pulled out his suitcases, packed as fast as he could, got into his car, and drove straight to San Francisco, never even bothering to call up the school to let it be known that he would be absent. The cold eggs, coffee and toast remained on his table for two days before someone from his school came by to see what had happened.

"Okay, so I'm gay," he told me in 1965, "but I've never hurt anyone, or let it affect my responsibilities. And then this thing breaks. Even before Moore got arrested, friends of mine warned me that a witch hunt was going on. I didn't believe it. But when they went after Moore, Christ, I saw the handwriting on the wall. And that editorial, too! First they say, 'Save the kids.' Then they say, 'Crush the homosexuals.' Enemies of society—that's what we were called. I remember very well. So I asked myself, where will this stop? I've never had any kind of relations except with consenting adults. But is Boise going to be calm enough to draw the difference? Will they *look* for the difference? No, I knew they'd go after anybody who wears a ring on their pinky. I wasn't going to take the chance and get swallowed up in a blind, raging witch hunt. I got the hell out."

As it turned out later, when this fellow's name appeared on the investigator's list, his evaluation of the panic was accurate. But, incredibly, the *Statesman* was also beginning to think things out. It had started the panic. It had called homosexuals criminals. It had demanded that every means possible be used to crush the monster. But now, perhaps too late, it sat back and listened to

its own voice—and to its effect. As the anonymous calls kept pour-
ing in, as outraged mothers continued to demand blood, as suspicion spread out on neighbors and friends, the *Statesman* suddenly realized that it had erred. And so it tried to rectify matters.
Thus on November 20, after Moore and Brokaw had been released on $2,500 bail but while Cassel was still in jail, it ran the
following editorial:

OBJECTIVE APPROACH AND INTELLIGENT PLAN ARE NEEDED FOR
        SOLUTION OF A SERIOUS SOCIAL PROBLEM IN BOISE

The Boise community, face to face with a homosexual situation exposed to public realization, comes now to the time when shock and
disgust must be replaced with calm and calculated analysis and consideration. Some homosexuals have been exposed, others are rumored
due for exposure; one has gone to prison for a life term, others await
court sentence or trial. Yet none of these steps is in the right direction, none of them accomplishes the necessary correction. Most important, the victims—the young boys who have been involved—are
left by the wayside for a future of considerable question.

The community's wrath leaped into vigorous demands with the first
arrests of homosexuals. Law enforcement was criticized, both at city
and county levels. Private detective assignment had caused the first
arrests and may cause more. To say that the city police administration, the sheriff and the prosecutor are in an embarrassing and difficult situation is to put the matter mildly. Each of these agencies is
functioning now in the direction of homosexuals as are the courts.
Public reaction generally is that something is being done. Yet nothing in the way of a remedy is even started.

Homosexuals are not singular to this community nor are they of recent vintage. We imagine they exist in every community in the country. They have been around as long as the weaknesses of the human
mind have been evident. Confessions by homosexuals invariably bring
out the stark fact that these victims of a puzzling physical or mental
quirk were themselves infected as young boys. There the die was
cast. They grew into manhood to infect other boys who, in turn,
unless effective intervention follows, will travel the same path and
carry the identical threat to the next generation of youth. Tragically,

the scourge multiplies since one adult homosexual usually infects several boys.

Those who are shocked at this kind of comment right about this distance in the analysis need only lift their head out of the sand and come face to face with one of society's greatest problems—the homosexual. There has to be the realization that he exists right here in Boise. And the most important admission has to be that *the homosexual is not a criminal*,[3] and that the proper correction is not an indefinite sentence to the state penitentiary where the homosexual may do society more damage.

Boise saw this fact well illustrated just two or three days ago. Two men were arrested who recently were paroled from the state penitentiary after serving time for homosexual offenses. Within a few months after they were turned loose they were back in the business of ravishing Boise boys. No one knows how quickly they were back in this sordid business. Everyone knows they were soon caught at the same activity for which they had been jailed.

There has to be a better system of correction than this one.

In the current issue of *Coronet* magazine, an article entitled "The Third Sex—Guilt or Sickness," may well have been prepared for special Boise consideration at the time.

"Homosexuality has been denounced as an outrageous crime, and dismissed as a trivial eccentricity. But it has rarely been examined objectively in the light of our present laws and existing medical knowledge," the *Coronet* article points out.

The challenge in this community is to examine this problem objectively and to organize into one effective group every available informed and interested individual and agency to work toward an intelligent and effective battle against this evil. To us there is greater importance in immediate aid for young victims than the adult homosexual. Fortunately for Boise there are now constructive steps being taken to organize for this part of this vital work.

Who will start the coordinated effort to bring this problem to a fair and sensible level of control? We suggest a public meeting of our courts, our law enforcement officers, members of the legal profession,

[3] My italics. See page 13.

the medical society, the agencies serving youth, the Parent-Teacher associations, the state pardon board and any and all other interested and connected groups.

The program appears to be simple:

Homosexuals must be sought out before they do more damage to youth, either by investigation of their past records or by appeal to their unbalanced minds. Psychiatric treatment should start wherever it will be accepted in order to work against further acts by homosexuals.

Immediate plans must be made for the proper assistance to boys who have been victimized in order that they do not grow into manhood to become homosexuals.

Otherwise the community must admit that there is no problem with homosexuals, and that there is no concern over the enormous damage from their activities.

No challenge ever has been as great as this one.

At this time it is proper to point out that the inclination of many people to regard this matter as a joke, and a source for various kinds of banter, is wrong. The exposé of homosexuals is cruel torture to the families of persons involved and to business associates. Common decency requires understanding in all these instances.

It is also in order to recall that no city or county law enforcement agency has either the funds or the personnel for a homosexual squad, and that well-known, uniformed police officers cannot cope with this problem. Until there is public reaction to a degree that provides law enforcement with the facilities for policing homosexuals all complaint is unfair and unjustified.

There are many who can say "something must be done." Certainly we agree. We are not defending any homosexual, or his acts. Instead, we hope for an objective approach to a serious social matter, and an intelligent plan arranged and carried out which will minimize, if not completely eliminate, one of the most unfortunate instances in the long and honorable history of one of the most respectable small communities in the nation—the good city of Boise.

In that same issue, one of the "constructive steps," referred to in the editorial was announced on page 12. It was that two weeks before, an organization had been formed to fight juvenile delinquency in Ada County. The organization, called Youth Advisory Committee and composed of leading businessmen, voted to secure medical help and treatment for the one hundred boys involved in the homosexual ring (of the existence of the ring there was as yet, of course, no proof), and appointed various people to various tasks, such as studying the possibility of employment for the boys, since, as Sheriff Doc House said, lack of money was one of the main causes of delinquency.

Dick Eardley was then working for the *Statesman,* where these committee meetings took place. In 1965, he was on the news staff for station KBOI-TV in Boise, and he told me what these constructive steps had amounted to. "I had just arrived a couple of weeks before, when the scandal broke. I was working for the *Statesman* and I hosted for the paper a series of conferences between the sheriff, the prosecuting attorney, some business leaders and ministers. They called themselves a committee, and the chairman was Martin Heuman, president of the Intermountain Food Equipment Company. They were all very shocked about the scandal and wanted to do something about the kids. The psychiatrists in town, Dale Cornell and John Butler [who arrived later, on Thanksgiving Day], offered their services. There were about five or six meetings during that first month of November-December, all held at the *Statesman,* with the purpose of seeing what they could do. They talked about different recreation facilities for the kids, better supervision, and so on. But nothing concrete was ever accomplished. Then the meetings trailed off, and that was the end of that."

And that too was the end of the *Statesman*'s sobering suggestions. The panic continued, and so did the arrests. In fact, the scandal had only barely begun. But with the arrest of a bank vice president, neither second thoughts by the *Statesman* nor genuine fear by many leading businessmen that the scandal was getting out of hand could put an end to it. But then, of course, those who did not want it curtailed, those who had launched it in the first place, were much too powerful.

3

THE CLIENT

SENATOR GLEN H. TAYLOR once referred to the powerful men of Boise as the "Boise gang"—a "small group of willful, well-heeled corporation politicians" who run the state. Although he coined that description during a political speech in 1956 when he was trying to win the Democratic nomination for the Senate, Taylor was not exaggerating. Idaho has long been ruled by a handful of rich Boise lawyers and businessmen, whose goal is not political power, but economic power.

That is not to say that their candidates have always been elected, nor that old-style, self-made politicos in Lewiston or Twin Falls or other Idaho cities have not wielded political power. Nor is it even to say that the governor has always been a pawn of the "Boise gang." In fact, when I was in Boise in 1965, Governor Robert Smylie was not at all popular with these bosses. But they certainly did run the state from behind the scenes. They influenced the legislature and the courts, benefited from the banking and utilities regulations and indirectly affected the daily lives of most Idahoans, as we shall see later.

These men have usually been Republicans, and extremely conservative ones. In 1964, for example, they helped Barry Goldwater carry Ada County 25,404 to 19,639, and although President Johnson won the state as a whole, the conservative strength was such that no other northern state gave him so small a plurality—5,363 out of almost 300,000 votes cast. But like most elites, the Boise bosses have always sat on both sides of the fence. What has con-

cerned them is not winning a Republican slot here or a Democratic post there. Rather it is to control the economy of the state.
Thus their preoccupation would be, say, to stop a federal power
project or an urban renewal program rather than to assure the
election of a John Birch extremist to Congress. Like the power
elites elsewhere in the United States, the "Boise gang" has always
been willing to sacrifice political ideology for economic gain.

Idaho's power elite has not been worried about foreign policy—
unless, of course, it affected business, such as when the huge Boise
construction firm of Morrison-Knudson was contracted by the
U.S. Government to build bases in South Vietnam. Normally,
it has focused its attention on such interstate problems as taxes,
licensing regulation, restrictions on out-of-state competitors, and
so on. On these issues, most of the members of the power elite,
whether Republicans or Democrats, have generally agreed, and
their power has been such that they have usually had their way.

There have been, of course, some notable exceptions—and some
notable mavericks. Senator Frank Church, for example, is now a
member of the power elite of Idaho. Not that he was born into
it—he was not. But he did marry into it. Nevertheless, he has
shown his independence not only on foreign policy, which, as I
said, does not much interest Boise businessmen, but also on the
question of federal power projects. The point remains that by
and large, Boise's upper-echelon lawyers and businessmen have
always seen things the same way, and it has not mattered if by
any chance the governor has had different views on such subjects
as the regulations governing loans and savings associations or
trading stamps—the interest of the power elite has usually been
upheld.[1]

It was this power elite that, in 1955, went after the homosexuals. This does not mean that every member of the Arid Club,
the exclusive get-together of the elite, helped instigate the operation or even knew about it. But those who decided to push it, and
Jim Brown, who was then the editor of the *Statesman,* belonged

---

[1] As a matter of fact, when the legislature did pass a bill regulating trading-
stamp sales, Governor Smylie vetoed it.

to the power elite. Some thought that they could use the scandal to rock City Hall, which was then in the hands of a fairly decent, reformist administration, the winner of a nonpartisan election. Other elite members aimed rather at the City Council, and specifically at a councilman whose son had been directly involved. And others still were after one of their own elite members, the real "Queen," a man so wealthy that it was felt he was untouchable in any other way. (But again, although the professional investigator who was later called in to carry out the sleuthing did furnish his name to the appropriate office, the "Queen" was never arrested.) Whatever the reason—personal rivalry, political backbiting or economic competition—those members of the "Boise gang" who had been in on the investigation from the beginning were not at all interested in the poor shoe repairman who got sentenced to life in prison, nor even in the banker, whose arrest gave Boise the jitters. Their victims were meant to be people whose names were never made public, people who never suffered from the scandal at all—with one excruciatingly painful exception.

The real client, therefore, was not the man who was never named in all those first reports published in the *Statesman*. The unnamed man was a lawyer, well known and well keyed to the goings on in Boise, and active in the local YMCA. But he was not important in the bigger chess game being played out. Nor, in fact, was Howard Dice, the first private investigator who came up with the evidence against Cooper, Brokaw and Moore. According to Jim Brandon, who was then chief of police, the scandal first broke in the Boise YMCA, a rambling brownstone building on Idaho Street, a few blocks from the Capitol. Brandon remembered in 1965: "Tramps who came into town would head for the Y and we'd go down [to check up]. That brought about publicity and the Y didn't want publicity. They were losing money in their yearly drive with the Community Chest. So the Y hired Dice. Dice started an investigation and didn't find out anything. But Dice got to talking to the youngsters and they told him about the Y's juvenile delinquents. They'd been involved with Moore. The police had suspected Moore of being a homo. Now the Allied Civic Group [a Mormon organization], which is anti-everything [such as liquor, gambling, etc.], went to Blaine Evans and presented statements."

The big, tough but soft-spoken and seemingly easygoing policeman, who in 1965 was working as a probation officer of the juvenile court, thought that the first homosexual that his department had arrested during the 1955 scandal was Joe Moore. In this he was mistaken, but Brandon did remember correctly that it was through the testimony of the kids involved with Moore that other men had been arrested. Because of the kids, Emery Bess, the probation officer at the time, got into the case. How, Brandon was not sure, but Bess suddenly showed up with a "list of seventy-five juveniles."

Continued Brandon: "Bess and Dice had been working together. They notified the police. The Allied Civic Group paid Dice to continue his investigation. Our records show that we were making about ten to fourteen arrests [of homosexuals] a year. The prosecutor then called me and Bess. Bess refused to give any information on his list, though we told him we'd cooperate if he'd tell. The City Council then asked us why we hadn't been doing anything. We started getting together a morals file, had about 130 arrests and photos, complaints and modus operandi. And FBI records. Most of the arrests were of people coming from other towns, smaller towns. You know, they'd come to the bigger town where they were not suspected. Anyway, after the *Time* article appeared, the city officials said we've got to make a cleanup. The City Council and the mayor said, 'Spare no one.' Regardless of position or anything like that. Councilman [let's call him Henry Morton] was hollering for action. That's why we got Bill. Bill had been in the State Department and an undercover agent in Washington, Europe, the Mountain Home Air Base. He had just broken up a ring of homos at the Mountain Home Base. Got a lot of guys court-martialed, got well acquainted with the techniques in this kind of operation. In this business you've got to know what's going on. We said we'd furnish some men from the police and the prosecutor agreed to go along. The prosecutor, the city and the county hired Bill jointly."

Bill was indeed a professional. Since he is still involved in undercover work, let's call him Goodman, Bill Goodman. He knew his trade. A tall, easygoing chap, he could talk to the homosexuals in their language, to the kids in theirs. He had a way of extracting information without using coercion, a way of implying possibilities without making promises, and a facility for catching slips without any formal psychological training. Goodman's biggest claim to fame had been his investigation of homosexuals in the State Department during the McCarthy era, but he had also worked on interstate robbery and embezzlement, and in Boise he had investigated a fantastic swindle involving a loan-shark outfit that had supposedly gone bankrupt, leaving the stockholders broke but the company officials rich. Since some members of the "Boise gang" had been involved on the profitable end of that operation, Goodman was not too popular with many of them, but by the time he was hired Blaine Evans was desperate—he needed quick convictions to salvage his political career.

That, too, was another factor in the continuing scandal. Blaine Evans was not responsible for the first three arrests, although he prosecuted them. But he had to try hard to appear as if he had played an active role. The way the scandal had broken, the fact that a probation officer had issued sweeping accusations to the press and that a private client had hired a private detective to uncover the improper goings-on at the YMCA tended to make the people of Boise question the efficiency of the police, the sheriff's office and the prosecuting attorney. To the ordinary, uninvolved citizens of Boise to whom I talked, the first three arrests and the editorial outcry in the *Statesman* were considered ample cause of embarrassment to regular law-enforcement officials.

In 1965, Blaine Evans denied this. Interviewed in his elegant office, right next door to that of his partner, Carl Burke, who masterminded Senator Church's campaign, he was friendly, jovial, witty—and extremely careful. A plump, white-haired, cigar-smoking charmer, he joked about the fact that his office overlooked the Capitol. "I can see everyone who's going in or out," he smiled, pointing to the Capitol's main entrance, which was behind a pleasant, well-manicured park, a block beyond his office in the Bank of Idaho Building. Pursuing the jocular introduction, he said: "I can tell when the governor's in and when he's out. Isn't that better than being inside?" In the same vein I replied, "You're also towering above him," which he thoroughly enjoyed.

Blaine Evans had previously refused to see me, and now, despite his outgoing warmth and sophisticated manner, he was very careful to tell me nothing that he thought I didn't already know. The case began, he said, "during my second term as prosecutor. When you're prosecutor, you've got to prosecute for the crimes you know are going on, don't you? In my first term of office, we prosecuted some other homosexual cases." I pointed out that although this was true, so much fuss had never been made about such cases, nor had the sentences handed down been so harsh. Why, I asked, did these cases get blown up to such an extent? "Well," he answered, "I guess we didn't know that there were so many of them in the community. You know, when it's going on in the basement of the Public Library, and in the hotels, and these guys are soliciting business all over town, you've got to do something about it, don't you? We limited ourselves to adults who were involved with minors."

This was not true. I already had the documentation on a certain Eldon Halverson, who was not a minor and who fingered some of the homosexuals who were convicted. I asked Blaine about that, and about the fact that Halverson himself was never prosecuted. "Halverson was one of our best informers," Evans replied. "He pinned a lot of the guys." As for the prosecution of the adults who were not involved with minors, he said, "Well, it's the law, and we've got to prosecute, because it's on the books. Now, if you want to change the law, you can go to the legislature and get them to change the law. That's the way to do it. But if it's on the books, you've got to prosecute."

I then pointed out that there are different ways of prosecuting and that I knew for a fact that other prosecutors had treated the homosexuals much less harshly. Furthermore, I went on, Idaho, like many states, has on the books a law that makes oral-genital copulation between anyone, including husband and wife, illegal. "If you're going to prosecute the homosexual," I said, "why don't you prosecute a man and his wife? It's the law, it's on the books."

Evans smiled mundanely. "Well, it's very difficult to get testimony or evidence."

"Suppose I came in and gave you such testimony," I persisted. "Would you prosecute such a case?"

Evans pondered for a second, then answered: "No, I wouldn't do it. But you've got to get these guys [the homosexuals] because they strike at the core of society, I mean the family and the family unit. And when you get these guys crawling around the streets, you've got to prosecute to save the family."

The interview did not end there, and I will come back to it, but that was all that Evans was willing to say on how the case began and why he prosecuted the homosexuals. It was enough. It confirmed the fact that he did not start it, verifying the fact that there had been tremendous pressure on him to prosecute once the scandal broke. It also showed me that the strength of the Mormons (a strength we will analyze later) was such that once an issue revolves around the family or the breaking of a family, there's not much that a prosecutor in Idaho can do but be harsh.

My own impression is that Evans, although he is a Mormon, did not want to prosecute the homosexuals the way he did. He must have known, especially after Dr. John Butler and Dr. Dale Cornell had offered their psychiatric findings on the cases and after it was made perfectly clear that many of the so-called minors involved were male prostitutes, that family units were not at stake at all. But that is the way Boise interpreted the scandal, and that, as we have seen, is the way the *Statesman* read it. The *Statesman* had, and has, enormous power—especially in electoral campaigns. And Blaine Evans, although he was not a prime mover in what took place, simply reacted to his environment. Meanwhile, the prime movers remained behind the scenes. Members of the "Boise gang," they were after the scalp of the city administration, and the

"Queen." But the "Queen" was too rich—and too secure. Before they could get him, more small fries and medium fries would have to be convicted. With the mayor, the City Council and the prosecutor demanding action, Brandon's police force, the sheriff's office, and an as yet unknown special team headed by Bill Goodman were coming up with results.

4

THE BOYS

IT WAS A COOL, brisk day in Boise, on November 24, 1955, and a few snow flurries gave a clean white coating to the well-manicured lawns of the city's residential area. It was also Thanksgiving Day, and the *Statesman* announced in a front-page article that Boiseans were set to "give thanks for the 'good things of life.'" Those good things included "turkey with all the trimmings" for the 23 prisoners in Ada County jail, "similar fare" for the 512 inmates of the Idaho State Penitentiary, "a 'substantial' meal of roast beef" for the 6 inmates of the Boise city jail, and a College of Idaho–Whitworth football game at the Bronco Stadium at 1 P.M. for anyone who wanted to go.

But the main headline on that Thanksgiving Day issue of the *Statesman* had nothing to do with the good things of life. It read: "Ada Prosecutor Files Four More Morals Charges." The four were a varied lot: a very prominent attorney, a local store buyer, a liquor salesman, and a hospital attendant. The key sentence in the article, which otherwise gave no details or explanations, came at the end of the second paragraph. It reported that "the four men were arrested after investigations conducted by [Prosecutor Blaine] Evans' office, Police Chief James Brandon and Sheriff C. L. House." Gone were all references to Howard Dice, Emery Bess or the unnamed "client." Obviously the scandal generated by these three men had forced regular law-enforcement officials to take over the investigation of the homosexuals—and to follow it through.

In line with the *Statesman*'s "new" approach to the problem, however, was another article, also on the front page. Under the heading "Idaho Aid to Deviates Is Planned," the article said: "The State Board of Health announced Wednesday [November 23] it was setting up a mental health program to deal with medical and psychiatric aspects of sex offenses involving men and teen-age boys." The article went on to say that Chairman Paul Boyd claimed that "the board had been at work on the situation before the first of a series of recent arrests in Boise." Boyd was reported as having said, "This is not merely a Boise valley problem."

Toward the bottom of the long column on page 1, there were the following paragraphs:

> Dr. Dale Cornell, state director of preventive mental health services, was named to head the board's mental health division temporarily, in addition to his present duties, pending appointment of a mental health director.

> State Health Director L. J. Peterson discussed prospects for this and other positions and was instructed to conduct an interview with a prospective mental health director in the near future.

> Boyd said he and Peterson had met with Gov. Robert E. Smylie and Budget Director James Young Wednesday morning and received approval of necessary salaries to put the mental health program into effect.

It was therefore quite a coincidence that precisely on that Thanksgiving Day, Dr. John (Jack) L. Butler arrived in Boise. His wife, Marjorie, had family in Boise, and the psychiatrist and his wife had innocently come home for a visit after three years in Europe, where he had worked on deviations. It just so happened, too, that Marjorie's family had contacts with the state Republican organization, and since Jack Butler was technically unemployed at that moment, a few strings were pulled so that Jack was appointed as consultant to the Board of Health almost immediately. A few weeks later, he became acting director of the Division of Mental Health.

But Butler was no opportunistic pussyfooter who would take

on a job thanks to contacts and then sit back and collect his pay. Nor was he the kind of man who minced words or held back the truth just because it hurt. In fact, he was the very opposite. Handsome, well-trained and sophisticated, Jack Butler was no stranger to the area. Born and bred in the Mormon country of Utah and southern Idaho, he had been a Mormon himself until he had rebelled against the rigid conservatism of his church and its teaching. For one thing, he could not accept the Mormons' view of racial inequality. Mormons believe that the black race is the fallen race, that it was banished from Israel and is therefore evil in its essence. For another, Jack was a trained psychiatrist and thus knew very well that the Mormons' strong taboos tended to build up resentment, frustration and even neuroses and psychoses. It was bad enough, he told me in 1965, that Mormons strictly opposed liquor, smoking and coffee, but it was inexcusable, in modern psychiatric terms, that they also refused to discuss sex—in any aspect—with their children.

"Boise was a very lonely place for nonconformists," Butler explained. "Liberals, for example, had no one to talk to. I don't just mean political liberals, but any kind. Just to find people who were interested in the arts, in music, people who read novels of quality and essays, was almost an impossible task. Like every narrow-minded, proper town, Boise had its Peyton Place aspects, but oh my God, if anyone dared to say so publicly . . . I think the greatest characteristic of towns like Boise is their hypocrisy. Everybody goes to church, sends their kids to Sunday school, and all that, and of course violently condemns any and all aberrations or deviations from the norms, but then, when they can get away with it, they tend to practice what they do not preach as much as people anywhere else.

"Of course, in Boise there's the extra element of the power of the Mormons—although I guess each town has its equivalent. Still, the Mormons stick together so much that they have forced Boise to separate into distinct groups, and these groups are so isolated from each other that they tend to be intimate among themselves. The result is that Boise is a very segregated city, in fact if not in theory. The atmosphere is stifling, and the pressure to conform is enormous. The city fathers or bigwigs take it upon themselves to impose standards for everyone else."

I asked Dr. Butler how these strict standards of behavior affected the kids. He answered with the obvious: "Just as you would expect." He paused, smiled, then went on: "You know, when I was a kid—and I was raised a Mormon—nobody ever discussed sex at home. There were only three ways of breaking out of the vise then. Talking to an older brother or, rarely possible, an older sister—and that of course assumed that they had somehow broken out themselves. Or rebelling, leaving home, the church and all the rest. Or finally the easy way, being a hypocrite at home and letting go at school. That's what most of us did. If anyone had recorded our conversation, I'm sure they would have concluded that we were obsessed with sex. Well, we were.

"You know, shortly after I started working for the state of Idaho in 1955, I was asked to interview the kids at the Boise High. I don't remember exactly how this came about, but part of my job or jurisdiction was under the Board of Education. In any case, I got a list of some sixty or sixty-five kids, and I tried to talk to each one. But the law required that I get permission from the parents. I told them that it would be a routine interview, that I was just trying to help the police control juvenile delinquency and that no names would be reported to the police, just graphs and statistics. Nevertheless, the expected happened. Of the sixty-five kids, thirty-five were Mormons, and I only got permission to interview two of them. All the other parents, the non-Mormons, agreed. The Mormon parents refused, insisting that they would take care of their own."

Butler did interview thirty-two of the sixty-five kids who were thought to have been involved in some way with the homosexuals. "I don't think that there was one among them who grew up to be a homosexual. Most of the kids who had participated had done so for a combination of kicks and rebellion against parental authority. Some did it for money—they got paid by the adults anywhere from a low of twenty-five cents to a high of ten dollars.

Others did it for power. That's right, power! I remember very well one child telling me how it made him feel important to stand there, with his arms crossed, while an 'old man,' as he called him, got down on his knees in order to—to—as the boys put it, 'to blow me.' But don't think that all the kids knew what they were doing. Many of them just told me that, well, everybody else was doing it. And then there were the sharpies, those who realized just how profitable such an adventure could be. They were the ones who blackmailed the adults.

"Don't misinterpret what I'm saying," Butler suddenly warned. "Some of the adults were very sick guys. There was one, for example, who went around with a red wig, drilled holes in the stalls of the Public Library toilet in order to put his penis through the hole and have a kid masturbate him—for money, of course, which he passed under the stall—yet not be seen. He didn't do that because he was afraid people would know who he was—most of the kids did—but because *he* didn't want to know who was acting *on him.* This kind of depersonalized sex reveals something very typical of Boise. Even when the moral code is completely broken down, indeed flouted in its most abhorrent manner, guilt remains in a perverted shape."

In 1965, the kids who had been involved in the homosexual scandal of 1955 were old enough to understand why they had done what they did. I interviewed many of them, men twenty-five to twenty-nine years old. Only two admitted that they had been involved themselves, and then only after I told them that I knew and made it clear that I would never reveal their names and that I did not condemn them for having done what they did. These two men then told me their story. Although I saw them separately, it was basically the same.

One of them was fifteen when he had his first contact with a homosexual, the other was sixteen. Neither of them had ever had any sexual relations with a girl. Both of them had seen and had occasionally taken part in mutual masturbation sessions at school —a ritual not only at Boise High but common to every high school, prep school, and boarding school in the country, not to mention colleges. Sometimes, not for personal gratification but only because it was part of the fun, one boy masturbated another for a few seconds.

As boys, both of these men had participated in such adventures. Then one day, one of the older boys told them that if they went to the YMCA and were willing to do that to some adult, they could get five dollars for it. Eventually, both did, though in one case it wasn't at the Y but in the public toilet of Julia Davis Park. Finally, these adventures led to oral-genital copulation.

"But remember one thing," one of the two men told me. "I was the one getting blown. I never did it to the queer. Sometimes I masturbated him, but I never blew him. I didn't think it was evil. Oh, I knew a 'good boy' wouldn't do such a thing. But all the other guys said they did it, and all the other guys said that they had slept with girls and that it's just about the same feeling. I didn't know they were lying. I thought I was just being left out of the fun. Anyway, I always closed my eyes when the queer worked on me, and I imagined it was a girl that was doing it to me."

The other young man told me the same story. He too had never had intercourse with a girl. The farthest he had gone had been heavy petting, but even on those occasions, the girl never reciprocated, never put her hands "between my legs." "I thought of myself as a failure. Not consciously, but still . . . I remember once after a dance I took my girl home and managed to kiss her French-style and feel her breasts a little; then I went home pretty happy with myself. I had gone out with her four or five times, but that was the first time I had gotten that far. I was feeling really good. And then I met my buddy, and he had taken to the dance a new girl, a girl he had never dated before. And he told me he had laid her. On the first date! Boy, that broke me up. I got so worked up over that that by the time I got home I was crying. And you know, my buddy had lied to me. He told me so later. He told me that all the other guys who had gone out with older girls had bragged that they had gotten laid, so he told me the same thing. They were all lying. But, boy, what a complex I had until I finally got laid myself—with a whore—when I went to college."

The story is not unusual. In 1965 I interviewed twelve other young men who denied that they had had contact with the homosexuals but probably did.

My basis for believing each boy was involved with the homosexuals is purely circumstantial: slips during the conversation, the way they talked about the others, the way they described their own fears when the investigation started, the way they were all so positive that such experience did not lead to homosexuality in adult life—none of them being, to my knowledge, homosexual today—and so on. All admitted that they used to tell their classmates that they had had affairs with girls when in fact they never did. I recorded the following statistics on these twelve men:

Average age in 1955: 16.7
Range: 14 to 17½ (There were others who were 18 or over, but I considered them adults.)
Number involved in athletics: 11
Number who could have passed for 18 according to height, weight, beard: 10
Number who had had intercourse with women: none
Number who had experienced reciprocated petting: 2
Number who could talk honestly to their parents about sexual problems: none
Number who claimed that they knew of other classmates involved with homosexuals: 12
Number who I thought had performed oral-genital copulation on others: 0
Number on whom I thought oral-genital copulation had been performed: 12
Number who had children in 1965: 8
Of the 8 who had children, number who claimed that they would bring up their children so that they could talk frankly about sex: 8

Since all of the eight were convinced that no harm was really done by the *others'* involvement with homosexuals, that it was "something anyone can go through," I would tend to disbelieve their liberal pretensions. In fact, of the twelve I talked to, nine were willing to let me know how they had voted in 1964. Six had voted for Goldwater.

All the young men I talked to who had been in Boise High (enrollment in 1955–56 was about 1500) at the time of the scandal (twenty-eight in all) were convinced that the figure bandied about by Emery Bess was exaggerated—unless Bess's "100 boys" were meant to include all the kids who had participated in mutual masturbation sessions. This was confirmed by Dr. Butler, who estimated that no more than sixty-five had been involved in any kind of homosexual act (including, mutual masturbation) and that no more than a couple of dozen had practiced oral-genital copulation.

"There was one teacher at school who was probably queer," one of the twelve in my statistical study told me. "We all knew it. He was a nice guy, and some of us even kidded him about it. He used to come down to the locker room and play around—you know, snapping towels and stuff like that. So he liked to see us naked, so what? We laughed about it. He never tried anything that I know of, and *I would have known*. But boy, did he get scared when the scandal broke. He ran out of town. Now if you figure that all the kids that kidded him were in on it, sure, then you'd get a figure of one hundred—easy."

A great many of the kids didn't know a thing about what was going on, but when the scandal broke they tried to sound knowledgeable. David Underhill, a Harvard graduate who was with the *Southern Courier* when I spoke to him in 1965 and had been at Boise High in 1955, told me: "I heard friends of mine making mysterious references to this affair. Almost everybody made believe they knew all about it—but didn't."

In fact, only four or five youths were deeply involved. They knew who the homosexuals were, how to contact them, and how to profit from their contact. They were juvenile delinquents, not homosexuals, and one phase of their delinquency was male prostitution. These youths were the ones who got paid ten dollars per assignation, as *Time* magazine put it, and they were also involved in a little blackmail. One of these juvenile delinquents, whose testimony was later used against one of the homosexuals, approached that same homosexual and asked him to "use me" for money. When the homosexual refused, the boy supposedly said, according to sources both within the police department and among his own friends: "Well, if you don't I'll spread it around that you did anyway, and since everybody knows that you're queer, they'll believe me."

"I heard the same story," Dr. Butler told me, "and I tend to believe it. That hard core of kids supposedly seduced by homosexuals was actually made up of tough gang members. Technically, they were minors, and the law had to prosecute the adults as the responsible lawbreakers. Of course the adults should not have been incarcerated in a penitentiary, but that's something else again. As for the kids, they were fully aware of what they were doing. They may have been only fifteen, sixteen and seventeen, but they were much too developed to be considered children. And, as it turned out, some of them became regular criminals. Not that they too should not have gotten some kind of medical care. One of the boys later killed his father, who had beaten him and mistreated him all his life. There were ample causes for the boy's delinquency, and he should have been forced to undertake some kind of professional care. But he wasn't. Either the police didn't bother to think of it, or the probate court didn't know what to do with him, or else there just wasn't the facilities. Although a Youth Rehabilitation Act had been passed by the Idaho legislature in 1955, the means were not available."

The Youth Act was part of general health laws enacted by the thirty-third session of the Idaho legislature. These laws reorganized all the departments bearing upon health and created a new Board of Health with two divisions—Public Health and Mental Health. The latter placed under one administration the two mental hospitals of the state (North at Orofino and South at Blackfoot), the Nampa State (Industrial Training) School for the mentally retarded, community mental health (both treatment and preventive), and the Youth Rehabilitation Program.

Under this program, social workers were meant to have the responsibility of supervising the paroles, placements and discharges of youths from the State (Industrial Training) School at Nampa and indeed of all juvenile delinquents committed by the probate courts to the Board of Health. But in 1955 there was only one social worker working in this capacity. There just was not enough money allocated for the practical aspects of the program. "Idaho's mental-health laws have long been extremely progressive," explained Dr. John D. Cambareri, the co-director of Idaho's Comprehensive Mental Health Planning Program, "but rarely has there been enough money to put these liberal laws into practice."

The result, in 1955, was that none of the minors involved were given psychiatric care. Yet the Youth Rehabilitation Act, since it was on the books, became a bone of contention between the police and the people in the Division of Mental Health. That bone was publicly picked at a luncheon on Thursday, December 1, 1955, sponsored by the Boise Senior Youth Council and the Ada County Mental Health Association. The guest speakers included Police Chief Brandon, Sheriff C. H. (Doc) House, Probate Judge John Jackson, Prosecutor Evans, and Federal Probation Officer Harland Hill.

It was Chief Brandon who spoke most frankly. He said that more disrespect then existed among Boise's juveniles toward law and order than he had seen in his thirty years of law-enforcement work, and he blamed part of this disrespect on the misinterpretation of Idaho's new Youth Rehabilitation Act by Boise's youth, "who think they are beyond the law." Many youths had told officers, "You don't have any authority to arrest us," Brandon complained. He went on to blame many parents for delinquency, saying that about 2 percent of the parents called to police headquarters during the early morning hours to pick up their children "give old-fashioned" spankings. The other 98 percent "berate us for calling them to the station."

Judge Jackson agreed indirectly. He insisted that his court went as far as it could to back up officers in the enforcement of the law, but by the Youth Rehabilitation Act could only parole the juvenile to his or her family or else turn him or her over to the State Board of Health. Under the new law, he said, the courts could not commit a child to the industrial school, but had to let the board decide whether or not this should be done.

Harland Hill then tried to smooth over matters a bit by pointing out that juveniles and adults had been treated differently in Idaho for the previous fifty years, and so should have been, since "they were not as emotionally or physically matured as adults and that 'adult' treatment of juveniles could complicate their lives seriously." He pointed out, however, that no juvenile was "beyond the law" within the provisions of the act. "The probate court is Idaho's juvenile court, and it is up to the courts to decide if the juvenile is to be treated differently than an adult or if he should have adult treatment."

Since there seemed to be a discrepancy between the interpretations offered by Hill and Jackson, I checked out the law and found that although the board was indeed given broad powers, it received jurisdiction over juveniles only when the court so decreed. Furthermore, the court could sidestep the board altogether. "If the petition concerning a child shows facts which would constitute a felony if committed by an adult," read the law (Section 16-1806), "and if the court after full investigation deems it contrary to the best interest of the child or of the public to retain jurisdiction, the court may in its discretion certify such child for proper criminal proceedings to any court which would have jurisdiction of such offense if committed by an adult."

The law and its correct interpretation notwithstanding, most people attending that luncheon on December in the Boise Hotel were in no mood to think progressively about treatment of minors. Mrs. A. B. Jonnasson, president of the Youth Council, wanted "firm action by the police, a good follow-up by the courts, and public information through the press" to teach juveniles that "they are not beyond the law." And Victor Clemmons, a Boise resident, rose from the audience to advocate "more spankings" and less psychiatric treatment for juveniles. "We are creating a shroud of cotton around our youngsters and we are taking the backbone right out of them," he said, "and if the parents don't spank their children, then they should allow the police to do it on occasions when the need arises."

One thing was clear enough: The townspeople were very much alarmed. Some wanted spankings. Others wanted more publicity. Others still hoped that everything would just disappear. But everyone was upset. In Seattle, I talked to Earle Calvin Underhill, who in 1965 was president of the People's National Bank there but in 1955 had been an officer of Boise's First National Bank. This is the way he put it: "The homosexual scandal took me by surprise. I couldn't believe it. In my opinion such people should be put away and the less said the better. If people don't know about such things they won't get interested. Publicity is bad. Such things didn't exist when I was a boy. I can tell you exactly when the moral degeneration of America began: It began with the election of Franklin Roosevelt. Boise is a nice town. It is growing. Such scandals were bound to hurt it, and the pressure to wipe it clean is understandable."

Except for the publicity—the *Statesman* continued to report each arrest, often on the front page—Mr. Underhill's view was typical. The pressure continued, and "such people" were indeed put away.

5

FROM WHORES TO ADULTS

WHEN *Time,* in its issue dated December 12, 1955, reported that there was "a widespread homosexual underworld that involved some of Boise's most prominent men and had preyed on hundreds of teen-age boys for the past decade," it grossly exaggerated. There was, and had long been, a homosexual underworld. The trouble with the word "underworld," however, is that it implies an organized crime syndicate. Without too much flair for fantasy, one could visualize a central headquarters with files on all the homosexuals of Boise—the underworld—as well as long lists of available teen-age boys, with price tags next to their names. One can even understand how the people of Boise, reading about their town in a tight little story in *Time,* could think that wealthy millionaires from all over America, indeed from all over the world, were flying into Boise because only there could they select fresh young boys for their favors. I even heard one woman tell me very seriously that there was so much homosexual traffic into Boise that United Airlines (which is the main airline covering Boise) "had put special flights into operation during the busy season—the summer."

How the busy season turned out to be the summer is easy to understand, for most of the homosexual cases occurred after June 1, 1955. But, of course, there was no underworld in this sense. And although Boise began to be known as "Boysy" or "Boys' town" around the Northwest, even as far as San Francisco, it was due to the publicity that the cases received, not to the facts. Naturally there were homosexuals in Boise, but no more so than anywhere else. Simply according to population there should have been at least 700, if the Kinsey report is correct, and if Jess Stearn is to be believed the figure rises to 4,000. With 100,000 people in greater Boise today, Stearn's estimate that "one out of every six adult males" [1] is a homosexual would mean that there are now more than 7,000. Whatever the statistics, Bill Goodman's investigation rapidly led to 500 names, and if Blaine Evans had wanted to prosecute them all he would have had to get a special penitentiary just for them, since Idaho's only pen was pretty well crammed with only 512 inmates.

Operating out of an innocent-looking house on 16th Street on a pleasant residential block on the northern side of town, Goodman did his job thoroughly. He used the living room for his interrogation sessions and made it as comfortable as possible. There was usually a fire going in the fireplace, there were a tape recorder and a telephone, there were cigarettes—and witnesses, generally in civilian clothes. As an employee of the county, the city and the prosecutor's office, Goodman had access to the best policemen in town. One was Chief Brandon, another was Sheriff Doc House. There was also House's deputy, Wilbur C. Shideler, known as Willy, who in 1965 was chief of police of Garden City, a conglomeration of bars, factories, depots and new residential projects so close to Boise (on the west) that the cities have no actual demarcation line.

"We'd bring in the suspected homosexuals," Chief Brandon remembered, "and we'd just talk to them. We always advised them of their legal rights, and pointed to the telephone if they wanted to call their lawyers. Bill was great. He'd talk along about anything, get them to relax, and then he'd say, 'Look, we know about you,' and before long the homos would sign a confession, or talk a confession into the tape. Then we'd turn them over to Blaine Evans. But, boy, would they talk. Like women."

[1] Jess Stearn: *The Sixth Man* (Macfadden-Bartell, New York, 1965), p. 16. (The 1960 census gives Boise's population as 34,481, but with its many suburbs, greater Boise included about 50,000 people in 1955, about 100,000 in 1965.)

"That's just it," Goodman told me when I reported to him my conversation with Brandon. "They *were* like women. Look, we didn't have arrest warrants. Nobody had to come into the house if they didn't want to. We didn't force anybody to say anything, or even to come. But think a second. What would you do if a cop comes to your door and says, 'Would you be kind enough to come with me, there's some people who would like to talk to you'? Well, you would say: 'Where's your warrant?' And if the cop didn't have one, you wouldn't even let him into the house, right? Now, suppose you're not home, and the cop says the same thing to your wife. What do you think she'll do? Chances are she'll say, 'Just a minute,' and go put on some makeup. Then she'll go with the cop, and when presented with the facts, she'll talk. More than that, she'll start gossiping. Before you know it, she'll tell all about her friends and neighbors. Well, homosexuals are like that, perhaps more so. They tend to exaggerate those feminine qualities they admire, like cleanliness, primness, hospitality. My God, these homosexuals would sit in our house and tell us about every guy they could think of. 'Have you talked to so-and-so?' they'd ask. So we had another name to investigate. By the time we were told to stop the investigation, we had so many names—with evidence—we could have probably gotten convictions on all of them."

Goodman would not tell me who called off the investigation, even though he knew that I knew. "There was only one guy we didn't get," he went on, "and that wasn't because he refused to see us—he came to the house all right—but because he refused to confess. He was a lawyer and knew how to stick to his denials even when presented with overwhelming circumstantial evidence."

I had heard what that evidence had been. Goodman and his helpers had the boy that this lawyer had supposedly seduced. The boy was brought into the room. The lawyer was asked if he had ever seen him. He said no. The boy then described the lawyer's office, detail by detail, and insisted that it was in that office that the two of them had committed the homosexual act. The lawyer still refused to concede, insisting that someone else must have previously described the office to the boy. (Incidentally, the boy, who was over eighteen, had been involved in a previous case when he was only fourteen, at which time the adult was found guilty and jailed for ninety days.)

After talking to him many times and at length, I became convinced that Bill Goodman was basically honest, despite the unsavory character of his work. "I'm an investigator," he said. "I don't make the laws, I don't prosecute." There was a kind of detachment that reminded me of an atomic physicist I had once heard insist that he was simply a researcher, not a bomb dropper. I told Goodman that I had concluded, after carefully evaluating the records, that there had been great injustices perpetrated in Boise. "Maybe," he said, "but that's not my doing. Maybe the law should legalize homosexuality, I don't know. That's up to the experts—the psychiatrists and legislators. I only investigate." What about the double crosses, I asked him—the fact that he had told some of his cases that they would probably get psychiatric care, although they were then sent to jail. He answered: "Some did get psychiatric care, remember! But I did what I was told, and I was told that in certain cases, if the homosexuals pleaded guilty, they would get psychiatric care. I'm not responsible if they didn't. Besides, I always said that I was not authorized to promise anything or to make deals. And that's on the tapes." I then asked him why he never appeared in court. He answered: "All my findings were turned over to the prosecutor's office. The convictions were not based on my tapes—they weren't even played in court. All those who pleaded guilty signed statements, and I never countersigned them as a witness. What good would my appearance achieve, except to ruin my anonymity?"

A good investigator, Goodman was also a good observer. He told me about the bars where the homosexuals congregated and about their various habits. Some I knew already, like the wearing of a ring on the little finger of the left hand. Others I didn't, like the smoking of Pall Mall cigarettes, in the red pack whose motto reads: "Wherever particular people congregate." He told me about the "Queen," who is usually the richest homosexual in town, although sometimes the most important or even the prettiest. "After a while," he remembered, "some of Boise's homosexuals became pretty sharp. There was one fellow, for example, who got himself a radio on which he could pick up our frequency. He was on the drag, that is, he was out cruising, trying to pick up companions. So he'd listen to our broadcasts, find out the guys we were suspecting, wait until we either called off our surveillance or else stopped it, and then he'd drop in on the guy. There was another who used to watch the cars that drove up to the house on 16th Street, then check out the license plates, and try to make contact that way. Of course, we learned about these guys and outfoxed them—by catching them."

I asked Goodman why the big "Queen" was never picked up. He laughed good-naturedly and said, "I don't know. I turned in a report on him." He paused, then smiled mischievously and added: "Maybe no one could get corroborating evidence." When I snickered, he said, "Wait, don't think we won every case I investigated. Before I was hired to work on the homos, I did some work, also for the prosecutor, on the local whorehouse. We had a stakeout on the place from across the street and we kept pretty good tabs. We were sure we had the right place. Then we sent in a guy with marked money. But the madame was pretty sharp. She spotted it, and we lost our case. Actually, we weren't after the prostitutes at all. We were looking for the drug pusher. We never caught him—or her."

I had already heard about that whorehouse incident. A friend of Bill's was a Boise lawyer and had worked on that case, and he told me about the great day when they finally thought they had a lead. "The way we had it set up is that we all had special flashlights, with different colors. We had guys posted at all the corners. I was at one of them. My job was to see who came out of the place and then give the signal to whoever was at the appropriate corner so he could tail him. Anyway, I suddenly got a signal to follow a guy who was walking right toward me. Well, I followed the guy until he got to where he was going, which was—you guessed it—to Bill. The guy I had followed was our own plant. What a laugh we all had over that one."

But nobody laughed much over the homosexual cases. Bill's agents were experienced men, and they made few mistakes. "We used to watch these guys in the YMCA, in the toilet of the bus depot, in Julia Davis Park," Brandon said. "You've seen that park. There are roads going through it, and the homos would cruise around waiting for a kid to go into or come out of the toilet. They'd stop him, start a conversation, offer to drive him home, then hand him a drink. In one toilet, which had no partitions between johns, we caught a guy sitting on one john reaching over for the genitals of a boy sitting on another. It wasn't very nice work, believe me."

But it got results. On November 26, a high school teacher was arrested by Brandon. On December 3, Brandon and Sheriff House arrested a high school janitor. On December 6, another Boise man was picked up. The next day, a man from Parma, which is about forty miles west of Boise. On December 10, a pianist. On Sunday, December 11, Gordon R. Larsen, a clothing salesman. Thus by the time that the *Time* issue of December 12 hit Boise's stands, there seemed to be good reason to suspect that a whole underworld of homosexuals had indeed been preying on hundreds of teen-age boys.

There was also good indication that the courts were going to punish these homosexuals harshly. On December 2, Judge Merlin Young sentenced Charles Herbert Gordon, charged with lewd and lascivious conduct, to an indeterminate term not to exceed fifteen years, and on December 9, Judge M. Oliver Koelsch handed out another fifteen-year sentence to Gordon's half brother by adoption, Reginald Shaffer. "As I remember," Koelsch said to Shaffer, "you made an extended plea and indicated an intense desire to secure medical treatment. You said sending you to the penitentiary would do you no good." However, the judge said that he had come to the conclusion "that rehabilitation in your case is out of the question." Recalling that Shaffer had spent "some time" at the State Hospital South in Blackfoot and that he was paroled on recommendation by psychiatrists to the State Board of Pardons, Koelsch said, "Instead you reverted to your former practices."

Knowing the conditions that existed at the time in that hospital, it is amazing that Shaffer did not go completely crazy. But this, apparently, was no argument to the judge. Besides, he had another formidable justification for being so harsh: "You made no attempt to live with your wife, and that doesn't indicate a desire for rehabilitation that you profess." Let that be a warning to all men who, after being locked up in an insane asylum, come home feeling they cannot live with their wives: Don't go to Idaho! [2] This incredible *non sequitur* was upheld (Shaffer had no attorney and had pleaded guilty). Shaffer went to jail.

Amidst all the furor, the publicity and the punishments, however, a simple fact went by unnoticed. All these "damn fairies" were being picked up supposedly for having committed infamous crimes against nature or lewd and lascivious acts with minors. The outcry, the *Statesman*'s fiery editorials, the moral indignation, all were justified on the grounds that "our youth" were being corrupted, that poor little boys were being ruined for the rest of their lives by these "monsters." And yet, the record began to show otherwise: The high school teacher, the prominent lawyer, the pianist and Larsen were all charged with having performed these acts with men eighteen years old or older. Obviously the persecution had gotten out of hand. It seemed as if all homosexuals were being rounded up.

On the other side of the ledger, the day that Shaffer was sentenced to fifteen years was also the first day that solid evidence was introduced in court on behalf of one of the homosexuals by a psychiatrist. The homosexual was Charles Ray Brokaw, who was among the first to be arrested. Represented by Pete Leguineche, a fine lawyer, Brokaw pleaded guilty to lewd and lascivious conduct with a teen-age boy and earned a recommendation of leniency from Prosecutor Blaine Evans because of his "cooperation and help in other cases." Leguineche added that he was

[2] In 1965, Koelsch was a Federal judge in California.

convinced that his client (who had broken down on the witness stand, saying he "was not looking for it" and was not the "aggressor") would be very receptive to psychiatric care. And Dr. Dale Cornell, then acting head of the Division of Mental Health for Idaho (Butler had not yet been appointed), supported the defense attorney. "I feel that basically [Brokaw] is a passive type of individual," Cornell said, adding that he wasn't able to find "anything that would make me think he was a real danger to society."

On the stand, Brokaw claimed that he had actually resisted sexual relationships with boys but that in cases where he was approached he had been afraid not to go along because of possible trouble later on with those who knew of his activities. Brokaw also revealed that his first experience had been at the age of ten in a warehouse in Wilder, due west of Boise on the Oregon border. A boy forced him to commit an indecent act on another boy, he said. "I found it hard to make friends. I was afraid they'd find out about that instance." Then he admitted having had other such experiences in high school. "I would do everything in my power to help myself," Brokaw cried. "I hope I'm not too far gone."

It was a moving performance, and I have no reason to doubt that what he said was true. But it seemed almost too pat, as if a deal had already been made. Brokaw certainly did not deserve a term in the penitentiary and could have benefited from psychiatric care. But then so could the others. However, so far only three men had been sentenced: Cooper, Gordon, Shaffer. All three had a previous record, though in the case of Gordon and Shaffer that record was not criminal in the layman's sense of the term, since their crime had been the same as now. All three had, during the preliminaries to their trials, been promised psychiatric care, and all three had pleaded guilty. But they were technically ex-cons, so they got stiff sentences—life for Cooper, fifteen years for Gordon and Shaffer. None of the other arrested homosexuals had previous records. All but one pleaded guilty. All asked for psychiatric care. Some brought in formidable testimony from psychiatrists and medical researchers for their defense. Brokaw had the testimony of Dr. Dale Cornell, a very fine gentleman whom I got to know well and to like very much. But, by his own admission, his experiences with homosexuals had been rather limited until then, whereas some of the other homosexuals got psychiatric testimonials from doctors who had studied the problem longer and deeper.

What was the difference between their cases? Brokaw had, to put it crudely, served as a stool pigeon for the prosecutor. Would that make a difference with the courts? Should it have made a difference?

If the criminals had been regular felons, yes. That, at least, has long been the practice in American law. But in the case of the mentally disturbed, no. That, at least, is what every psychiatrist I have talked to has insisted.

6

HIGH EAGLE

"IT WAS bad enough before," a store executive told me in 1965, "when all you had to do was be careful not to be seen with teen-age boys. But after they arrested that pianist fellow and Larsen, both of whom were charged with indecent acts against adults, well, let me tell you, every bachelor became jittery. I was a buyer then, so I had to travel a great deal. Everywhere I went, people started making jokes. I use to wear my school ring on the third finger of my right hand. Well, I had to stop that. I remember talking to a guy in Denver, a buyer from Salt Lake, a guy I had gotten to know quite well. And all of a sudden, he starts kidding me about *Boys*-y, and then he looks at my hand and says, with the goddamnedest sarcastic smile, 'Hey, I see you're wearing a ring these days. . . .' Boy, I felt like punching him in the nose. He had seen that ring ever since we first met, three years before. Well, anyway, that's the way it went. It got so bad that everytime I left Boise on business I was sure some dirty gossiper was spreading the word that I was going to see my boy friend who had left Boise not to get arrested."

One lawyer told me that the good old "night with the boys" disappeared. "You never saw so many men going out to the bars at night with their wives and girl friends," he said. "I remember we used to have poker games once a week. Well, for a few weeks we canceled them, then one of the guys got an idea: "We'd invite a girl to play with us. You know, it's not very pleasant to play poker with women, not when you're in a serious game. But that's what we had to do. After a while, one of the guys found a chick who was willing to be present at the games without playing, and that helped, although we still had to watch our tongues—and it isn't the same thing, playing without cursing."

Sandor Klein, the *Statesman*'s chief editor in 1965 (James L. Brown having retired), told me that he was in the East for a conference when the scandal broke, but the news traveled fast. "I was city editor of the paper then," Sandy said, "and so I guess people thought I knew all about what was going on in town. Well, I didn't, but I sure got a lot of ribbing." John Corlett, whose "Politically Speaking" column in the *Statesman* is one of the most widely read sections of the daily, added: "Everybody was being suspected. There were rumors about people from the top of the state officials down to the highway people." As a Republican, Corlett did not make the analogy that comes naturally to a Democrat, namely to the panic created by Senator Joseph McCarthy, especially in small towns. But that's how it was. In the early 1950s, thousands of people were calling the *Statesman* or the police or the local FBI office to denounce an acquaintance, a neighbor, an enemy, even a friend, as a Communist. In 1955, they were denouncing homosexuals.

"We didn't pay too much attention to those calls," Goodman told me, "unless one of the homos already had dropped the same name in his general confession. For one thing, very few people knew of my operation, and they certainly didn't have our phone number. We worked very quietly, and we didn't bother to follow up denunciations that were reported to us unless the people who had called them in had given their own name and address. Then we'd talk to them first, and if we thought their suspicions were well grounded, we'd check them out." Police Chief Brandon confirmed this. "Actually, Bill didn't do any of that stuff. He knew where to get stoolies. He was a pro, and he didn't need anonymous phone calls. So, since the calls came into other offices, not his, we usually didn't even bother Bill with them. But we sure got a lot of calls."

I asked Brandon what the calls said. "Mostly they were from

women. They would say, 'I've just seen so-and-so sitting by the high school practice field with a funny look on his face.'" He paused, then added: "But I remember one case where such a report did lead to something. We got a call from somebody working at the school, telling us that they had seen a man sitting on a bench, talking to the boys, and that he was there almost every day. So we put a stakeout on the guy and found out that he had his car nearby. We traced down his license plates. He was an out-of-towner but the police suspected him in his home town. One day he offers a kid a lift home. We stopped the car and asked what the hell he was doing. He said, taking the boy home. We told the kid not to take lifts from strangers, then we sort of warned the old man—without being specific. He got the hell out of town fast."

But Brandon readily admitted that for every serious lead, they received hundreds of phony ones. "The pressure was fantastic," he told me. Judge Merlin Young, a pleasant, soft-spoken, gentle man with a nice, clean-cut look and a deeply reflective, serious approach to his job, also said that the pressure had been great. "Everywhere I went during those first few weeks of the scandal, people would say things like, 'I hope you really let them have it.' It was a difficult atmosphere. And I was caught off guard. I didn't know much about such things. I had to do an awful lot of homework."

Dr. Butler told me that Young really did do his homework. "I've never seen anyone study a subject so deeply. I used to recommend all sorts of books, and by God he read them all. I don't think I ever met a judge who, by the time the whole mess was over, knew so much about homosexuality—and the problems involved for society." But Judge Young learned these things slowly, whereas the cases came at him quickly. "I don't think I could ever send a homosexual to jail again," he said in 1965, "but with kids involved and all that, at the time, well . . . it was a nasty business."

Perhaps the biggest shock to the community came on December 15, 1955, for on page 1 of that day's issue of the *Statesman* a headline reported that Moore had pleaded guilty to the charge against him. That immediately polarized sentiment against all homosexuals, whether they had been involved with minors or only with consenting adults. A respected banker, after all, is a pillar of society, people said. Very few tried to understand what was happening or even listened to the brilliant defense put up for Moore by his lawyer—John A. Carver, Jr.

The Carver name was well known in Idaho even then. His father, also named John A. Carver, had been blinded at the age of five but had managed to stick to his education (his wife later became his "eyes") in Preston, Idaho. It was there that John Jr. was born, in 1918. In 1928, John Sr., a graduate of the University of Idaho, brought his family to Pocatello, where he became prosecuting attorney. With seven children, "we never had much money," John Jr. recalled in 1965. "Life was pretty much a subsistence proposition. I don't mean we ever went hungry. Food used to come to us in sacks from my mother's family on the farms." In 1933, the Carver family moved to Boise, where John Sr. was U.S. attorney for twenty years.

Meanwhile, John Jr. had gone to Washington when he was eighteen. He worked as a messenger for Senator Wheeler's Committee on Railroads Financing while finishing his sophomore year at George Washington University, returned West to get his B.A. at Brigham Young University, studied law at the universities of Montana and Idaho, then returned to Washington to work as a federal Civil Service personnel specialist. He rose from Grade 4 in July 1940 to Grade 13 in May 1943, when he entered the Air Force to serve both in England and Japan. After the war he went back to Washington and finished his law studies at Georgetown. He received his LL.B. in 1947, the same year he decided to go back to Boise to launch his own practice.

"I guess a person would have to be crazy to have done what I did," he said. "I had a good job in the Defense Department, but I decided I didn't want to be a personnel clerk, no matter how well paid. I had a little money saved, enough to eat for six months, and I used about all of it in Boise before I really got going." He also became assistant Idaho attorney general for eighteen months, during which time his boss, the attorney general, was Robert E. Smylie. Appointed in 1947, Smylie was elected for a full term in 1950 and quit only after winning the election for governor in 1954 (taking office in 1955).

In the next few years, Carver built a very successful law practice. But in 1957 he left Boise to go back to Washington, this time as administrative assistant to the newly elected Democratic Senator, Frank Church. "He quickly demonstrated that he had the intuition to locate the jugular vein of a difficult problem, that he could organize an office staff, and perhaps most of all, that he was dedicated to the public welfare," said Church in 1965. Meanwhile, after the election of 1960, President Kennedy appointed Carver an assistant secretary of the Interior Department, where he supervised the bureaus of Land Management, Indian Affairs, and Outdoor Recreation and the National Park Service, the Office of Territories and the Alaska Railroad. As his reputation grew, he won many honors and many titles, including "Tch-aa," which means High Eagle, when he was made Bear Prince of Alaska's Eagle tribe.

Carver did such a good job that he eventually became Under Secretary of the Interior, the only Idahoan ever to attend Cabinet meetings in an official capacity (whenever Secretary Udall was absent). At the time of this writing, John A. Carver, Jr., was still in Washington, still Under Secretary. But few people who knew him thought that his rise had stopped. He was being talked about either as Udall's successor (if Udall retired) or as a most likely candidate to oppose his old boss, Governor Smylie, in the fall of 1966. The Lewiston (Idaho) *Morning Tribune* insisted that "he would be a superbly qualified candidate for governor," while Pocatello's *Idaho State Journal* predicted simply that "Idahoans and the Nation are bound to hear a lot more of John Carver in the years to come."

In 1955, however, he was still just a Boise lawyer, but a good one, very dedicated to his office. And he took the defense of Banker Joe Moore most seriously. There was no doubt that

Moore was guilty. Two boys had signed statements against him and were willing to testify. But those statements, as legal as they were, are nevertheless highly peculiar. The first is in longhand. Some of the words are illegible, but I shall quote it as I read it again now from a certified photocopy. I have inserted parentheses around the words I cannot identify for sure, and I have not corrected the misspellings.

November 3, 1955

My name is Lee Gibson. I am 15 yrs old. I live at 2913 Hazel Boise. I first got acquainted with Joe Moore [another, longer name had first been written in, then "Joe" was written on top of the other first name and "Moore" above the other crossed-out last name] about June 1955. I do not know what date in June. I know it was a Sunday, about 2:00 p.m. I was in Julia Davis Park next to tennis courts. He asked me where I was going when he stopped his 1954 Cadillac which was some shade of green, next to me. I told him I was going over to my girl friends. He asked me to ride which I did. On the way over he asked me if I drank I said 'yes'! He had Sagrams 7 (pint) in (jockey) box he got it out and handed it to me. He asked me if I would rather get drunk then go over to my girls. "I said I guessed so." He drove to the shack across the street from Riverside in the negro section. He asked me how much he should get. I told him I did not know. He went in and returned with two gallons jugs half full of whiskey. Did not taste good. We drove around town, went to the show (ada) around 4:00 oclock We got into show and he started playing with me. unbuttoned first top button. We got out of show around 6:00 ock. Asked me if I had ever been blowed as we were driving around. We then went to Bagus Basin Road, then turned to our left. He parked on top of a hill and started playing with me. He put his mouth over my penis and worked it up and down until I come. I was feeling my liquor and after he got through going down on me he had me drink some more whiskey. I do not remember how long we stayed there. On the way home I passed out on the way home. As we entered town he woke me up. Took me to Junction station cafe HiWay 14 and 44 and had me drink some coffee. He took me to 3113 (Alturas) and let me out. He said be quiet about this. (arrived) there about 12:00 midnight. This is a true & correct statement made by me. I have corrected any mistaked and initialed them while reading this.

The statement was signed by Lee Gibson and witnessed by Howard Dice and Emery Bess. Next to the "Joe" there was an "L.G." and next to the "Moore" there was an "L.C.G." Basically, what disturbs me about his statement is (1) that it sounds as if it was written by a very shy, or at least pliant, juvenile, when in fact Lee Gibson was a tough kid, and (2) that there is no satisfactory explanation for what happened between 6 P.M. and midnight, with no food and only one sexual act performed when the car was parked on top of a hill. Also, of course, there can be no doubt from the document that when Lee Gibson first wrote it, he did not refer to Joe Moore, but to a different person, someone whose last name ended with a *d,* which is clearly visible under the cross-out marks.

The next statement is not dated. It is typed and has two handwritten corrections of no consequence (although the initials W.H.B. are handwritten above them). It reads (with misspellings):

Statement

This statement is taken under oath swarn by James C. Hunt, Criminal Investigator U.S. Army Fort Carson, Colorado.

My name is William H. Baker, I am now 17 years old, I am now in the U.S. Army at Fort Carson, Colorado. When I first got aquainted with Joe Moore I was 16 years of age. This was in the month of January 1955, Joe Moore came out to the roller rink at Gowen field in his green and white Cad. 1955 model. He came inside and waited until 12:00 midnight when it let out. I run outside to catch Clyde Harris and he had already left for town. Then I went back inside Joe was still there. I got a coke and went back outside to see if the bus had left, I found out that it had gone so I stayed outside with the idea that the boys would be back after me. They did not show up, then about that time Joe Moore came out and asked me if I would like a ride home, I said "yes," We got into his Cad. and went back to Boise. He asked me if I wanted to stop by someplace and get something to drink I said no that I had to get home, he took me home the address if 414 East 42 st. Garden City. I did not see him again until about a week later at which time I was walking down the street around 16th and Main when Joe Moore came by and stopped and asked me if I wanted a ride home. I told him OK, then he asked me if I wanted some beer, I told him yes that it would taste good, We then went out to a place out on Hi-Way 30 across from Harbert Electric. He went in and brought it back to the car. We drank it in the car on the way back to town, then he asked me if I wanted to go out. I told him it would be a good idea because I had just got paid, (I was working at Shoetorium at the time) then he asked me if I wanted any whiskey. I told him I did not much care for any, then he told me that he would go and get a fifth anyway. He drove to Liquor store across from employment office and got a fifth of whiskey. We rode around town for about a hour then to Riverside Ball Room. We stayed there until it closed. This was on a Saturday night. Then we drove outside of town. Then is when he started to play around with my penis without direct contact with it because I had my pants still zipped. I then told him to cut it out and take me home. He took me home, before I got out of the car he told me he would see me around. I saw him again the next Friday, He came out to the skating rink. He saw me there and asked me if I would like to go out with him and get a jug. This we did. He bought it at the same place. We drove around town and drank it until around one oclock, he drove out Harrison Blvd then out on a dirt road and he parked then we killed the rest of the bottle. Then he started playing around. He unbuttoned my pants and played with my penis until it was hard then he put his mouth over my penis and worked it up and down until I came off. When we got ready to leave he put a ten dollar bill in my pocket and told me to keep still about it. I saw him again the following Wednesday. I was up to the Greyhound Bus station. He drove by slow and motioned me out. I got into the car and Joe Moore gave me several drinks while he was driving around. We saw Lee Gibson on the street. I yelled at him, we drove around the corner and stopped Lee Gibson got into the front seat next to me. Lee was handed the bottle and he started to drink. Joe drove around town and got some more liquor at liquor store in the west part of town. We drove around for about an hour and a half and then Joe drove out in the back of the Vets. Housing project. He parked and I got into the back seat with Joe Moore.

He unbuttoned my pants and played with my penis until I was hard then he put his mouth over it and worked it up and down with my penis in his mouth. I went off. I put my penis back into my pants and he gave me a ten dollar bill. Lee Gibson was in the front seat and saw this. I got back in the front seat with Lee, we drank some more liquor and I went to sleep. Joe was still in the back seat. The next thing I know someone was shaking me trying to get me awake and then I noticed that we were at my home 414 East 42 street. Garden City. Lee Gibson and I stayed alnight at my place. The next time I saw Joe was about two weeks, It was on a Friday night along toward March 1955. My sister and I was out to Bings dance hall, Joe Moore walked in. I walked over to where he was and we talked for a little bit. He asked me who I was with and I told him. He asked me if I would like to go with him. This I did, We got some beer at Save-on Food store. Joe bought it. We then went out and parked off Bogus Basin Road. We drank all the beer which consisted of six quarts. He started playing around with me in the mean time. He then went down on me again. He then payed me ten dollars again and then took me home. I never seen him since.

I certify that the above statement, was voluntarly, no force, threats or promises were made to me to obtained this statement.

Since the statement takes two pages, William Harvey Baker signed it twice, once at the end of the first page, then at the end of the text. There are two other signatures: Howard Dice's and James C. Hunt's. Under Hunt's signature his name is typed out, followed by "CID US Army Authority of Oath (Art 136 para 4b)."

There are many things wrong with this statement, such as going to buy liquor after liquor stores are closed. Also the statement is supposely dictated ("taken under oath"), but it is so badly written, with so many misspellings and errors of grammar, that it is obviously made to look as if it were written by Baker himself. Also Baker, like Gibson, is made to look like a stupid but innocent kid who at first doesn't like the idea of a man "playing around" with him but eventually succumbs, when in fact he was a tough juvenile delinquent who knew the score.

But these are details, as is the discrepancy of date on Moore's Cadillac. There is a very important error, however—an error so crucial that had Moore pleaded innocent he should have won. And that is that whereas Gibson claims to have met Moore for the first time in June 1955, Baker insists that they were all well acquainted in January 1955, or, at the latest, in February. Baker's chronology is: meeting Moore in January, on a Saturday, then again the following Saturday, then the next Friday, and finally the next Wednesday, when they met, Gibson. Obviously, one of the two kids was lying, and it is quite clear that if the prosecution had tried to base its case on the statements of these two boys, no jury, or certainly no appeals court, could have sustained a guilty verdict.

But Moore *was* a homosexual. Although he was married and the father of a well-brought-up son, he had uncontrollable urges for homosexual relations and needed help. So Carver, who was not just a lawyer bent on winning a case (after which his client might have fallen back into similar affairs) but was an honest, decent human being who wanted to help his client, decided to fight cleanly. He admitted his client's guilt, but hoped for a sentence of probation, during which his client would undergo psychiatric treatment. Thus he made a three-hour plea to the court, by which he hoped not only to help his client but also to help Boise in general. "I am not attempting to minimize the seriousness of the charge," Carver said, but "I have a duty to promote an understanding of the type of activity involved so it will be judged in an atmosphere of understanding."

Carver proceeded to read a fifty-six-page research paper that he had conscientiously and meticulously prepared in order "to secure for the court the benefit of informed thinking and writing on the subject." He quoted the Illinois commission on sex offenders as saying, in a 1953 report, that "sexual conduct of the socially distasteful kind characterizes such a large portion of the population that if the law were enforced effectively there likely would be more people in jail than out." He called for a "setting aside of prudery" in dealing with the problem. "Understanding sexual deviation requires the burying of a number of ghosts, born of our prudery and ignorance."

Carver cited Benjamin Karpman, chief psychotherapist at St. Elizabeth's Hospital in Washington, D.C., who had written that a "homosexual is not a pervert but the victim of a constitutional development which gives him a sexual orientation that is different from the established social pattern." Unfortunately, this fact does not affect the popular view, which is the product of "unreasoned emotions" rather than "rational thinking." A homosexual, Karpman's statement said, "may be a wise and cultivated gentleman or he may be a fool, just as any herterosexual may be either one. He may be the highest representative of honesty and integrity or he may be a crook, just as any heterosexual may be either one."

Carver also pointed out that every typical American community has a vast underground of sexual behavior that is illegal and antisocial. He quoted Kinsey and cited other researchers in the field to show that there is no uniform approach to the classification of sex offenders. There are twenty persons convicted for each six million homosexual acts, Carver said. "Probably a large percentage of men who are legally prosecuted have not been involved in behaviors basically different from those widely practiced in the real culture, although they are proscribed in the ideal culture and by legal codes." Carver added: "A vast underground of these illegal sex practices goes on constantly. The law is invoked only on those whose behavior comes to public notice as a result of accidents and other attendant circumstances. . . . Violators who keep their behavior from view are accepted." Carver concluded: "Prison does not solve the fundamental problem. . . . Jails are not suitable for treatment, but clinics are."

Carver then tried to show that his client, Joe Moore, was no ogre, but a responsible member of the community who had this one important problem, which he wanted to cure and which could be cured. Carver called various character witnesses, including an employee of the *Statesman* who had known Moore since school days, a real-estate man who had dealt with Moore for years and an attorney who had known him for forty years. The Rev. William C. Johnson, a Boise Episcopal minister, testified that he was Moore's pastor and that Moore had exhibited great stability in his personal adjustment to his arrest and particularly had shown remorse, repentance and a strong tendency toward reformation and rehabilitation. Johnson said that he had been a chaplain for longshoremen and seamen on the waterfront in New York City, was familiar with problems of homosexuality and was convinced that Moore was adjusted and stable enough to take treatment successfully.

Joe Moore's son also testified, saying that his father had always been very considerate and understanding, a man to whom he could and did take his problems, and that he was aware of the responsibility that would devolve upon him and other members of the family should the defendant be given probation. Moore's son said he would willingly accept such responsibility. Moore's nephew and daughter-in-law, who also testified, were also willing to accept responsibility. Moore's wife insisted that her husband had always been loving, thoughtful and considerate, attached to his family and home. Dr. Dale Cornell, the psychiatrist, then took the stand, supported Carver's research, and stated that he had treated Moore and considered him a good risk for probation.

Judge Koelsch decided that it would take him a week to come to a conclusion. He thus postponed Moore's sentencing until December 23 and took Carver's research paper home to study. But most other Boiseans remained unimpressed. They did not even exhibit temporary doubts. To them, the fact that Moore had pleaded guilty only justified their fear and increased their rumormongering. As one housewife told me in 1965—and she felt just as strongly then as she had a decade earlier—"If a banker can be guilty of such sins, anybody can. I realized I couldn't trust anybody. I had two boys, one was twelve and the other fourteen. Did I worry! I wouldn't let them alone with the postman or any man, not even a policeman. To tell you the truth, I didn't stop worrying until both my boys got married, which was last year for the younger one. I know' marriage doesn't prove anything, but now my boys are no longer my worry. That banker was married, wasn't he? And had a boy too! Disgusting. They should have put him away for life—I don't care what those fancy doctors say."

7

THE CURTAIN FALLS

CARVER'S DEFENSE, as reported in the *Statesman* on December 15, 1955, must have stirred up a lot of people, even if it did not convince them, because that night hundreds of Boiseans showed up for a meeting to discuss the problem. Held at the South Junior High School, the meeting featured five main speakers, including L. E. Clapp, who was the warden of the penitentiary, Jim Fowler, who was boys' counselor of West Junior High School, and a young Boise lawyer named Frank Church who, ten years later, was Idaho's Democratic Senator, and an equally young psychiatrist, Dr. John Butler, who had just been retained by the State Board of Health to conduct psychiatric interviews and give psychiatric assistance in the homosexual problem.

Jack Butler was fairly candid in his remarks. He said that homosexuality was neither a disease nor an illness, but a symptom of disorder in a person's character and personality. Like Carver, he cited Kinsey's figures that 4 percent of the male adult population is homosexual and that 46 percent have a predisposition to become homosexual. But unlike Carver, he focused most on the kids, saying, in effect, that their participation in these incidents was no accident. "The homosexual activity involving teen-age boys is only a symptom of many difficulties facing youth in Boise," he said. What had happened was that youngsters who had reached the age of "revolt" had formed a social system of their own. "They got to exploring forbidden things and a few of them became involved with Boise's 'closed homosexual society.' " That society, Butler said, "opened its doors and before long more youngsters were involved." Daringly, Butler was trying to show that the parents' hate is misdirected. Not all the blame should fall on the adult homosexuals.

"Here in Boise," Butler continued, "when a boy gets to be fifteen or sixteen the sledding gets tough for him." The 6-4-2 division of grades in the Boise school system was one major cause; with junior high school four years long but senior high school (or what is usually normal high school) only two years long, adjustment was hard and too many cliques would arise, causing many kids to feel lost. "I am told that some youngsters have dances that other youngsters can't attend," Butler said. "Many boys feel they don't have adequate recreation facilities. Many don't get square breaks in finding part-time jobs." He insisted that the answer to the problem was prevention, which is impossible without understanding by the parents and by the community, by the schools and by the church. Butler then stunned the audience when he said: "The answer has to be in the preventive field because there is no hope of success in any kind of therapy."

That was the last thing the parents wanted to hear. They were still convinced that if you jail all the homosexuals, the problem will disappear—although as parents they were concerned enough to try to do something for their kids. Jack Butler told the audience what that something should be: "You have to live closer with your child. You have to understand that there are these things in the world. You must take the realistic view that homosexuality is here and a little bit of it is probably in all of us." Then he exhorted his audience to "go to work and build your community supports and forces. This is a big challenge, but it is up to you."

Warden Clapp basically agreed with Butler—without sounding the same. "There is the lack of a program to keep our young people occupied," he said. "By working they get spending money of their own. They like to be a little self-supporting and know they are accepting responsibilities. The great majority of youth-

ful offenders who come to the penitentiary never accepted responsibilities. You can't treat the kids like babies until they are
eighteen and expect them to be men and women overnight."
But whereas Butler pointed out that there were only three psychiatrists in the state in the preventive field, including himself,
and that there should be more funds allocated to bring in more
medical help, Warden Clapp fell back on strictly old-fashioned
prevention: The family knows best. "Each case is a personal
problem," he said, "and parents, who should be close to their
sons, should be able to help. I am not sure that this entire burden
should be carried by the taxpayers. Parents should handle their
own individual problems. Each parent should make decisions in
this matter for his children." Then, to soothe Butler, he added:
"Only when parents refuse to accept responsibility should the
public enter into the problem."

Thus did Warden Clapp have the best of both worlds. He
backed the expert in criticizing parents, though much more
gently, for insufficient interest in their children, but he also indirectly supported Boiseans' natural aversion to public spending
and state-sponsored mental health. He also managed to amuse
the audience with a joke, which many people who know him
have assured me was strictly unintentional. After talking to him
in 1965, I tend to think that he knew exactly what he was saying.
Someone had asked him from the floor how they treated the
homosexuals in the penitentiary. Clapp replied: "Well, you can
be sure that we're certainly not going to turn our backs to them."

Jim Fowler then made a few remarks in defense of the "kids
who don't get into trouble," insisting that "youth is better
today physically, morally and mentally than at any other time in
history." But he added that these good boys "come from closely
knit families where the parents have confidence and faith in
youth and from a home where boys can confide in parents." Since
such confidence is quite rare in Boise (or anywhere else where
a large proportion of the population is Mormon) his argument
was not too sound. Unfortunately, most parents did not realize it.

Frank Church, always an able politician, then smoothly sum-

marized the various speeches. He won over the audience by prais-
ing Fowler's perspective "because the problem does concern a
small portion of the population." But he also did his best to
help end the panic and rumormongering that had gripped Boise
by warning that "we can't be the prosecutor and we can't deter-
mine the sentence of these people. But we can stop the gossip and
rumors we unintentionally circulate; rumors that can do a lot
of damage." Then he gave Butler a small pat on the back by
adding: "What we can do is to learn more about this problem
and welcome expert advice." And finally he supported Warden
Clapp by insisting that "we can find ways to keep our kids active and occupied and to find jobs for our youngsters. Basically
the problem rests on all of us as parents. We should take an
interest in our children so we can lick the problem at its source."

Few parents left that meeting any wiser. Butler had antago-
nized them. Though he had been raised in the area, he was an
outsider, a foreigner who had dared to tell them that prevention,
not therapy, is the issue and that they, as parents, were so bad
at prevention that they should get more professional help. Boiseans were not prepared to accept such criticisms. They viewed
themselves as good, clean, wholesome, patriotic Americans, who
went to church regularly, who upheld law and order, who had
a natural and justified distrust of eastern intellectualism—which
is cynical, corrupt and permissive. During the McCarthy era,
many Boiseans became convinced that intellectuals are more apt
to betray the nation than nonintellectuals and that all the new
talk on mental hygiene, eugenics and preventive medicine was
basically part of an over-all Communist plot. Few of these Boiseans had changed their mind by 1955, or indeed by 1965, when
another Communist plot was added to the list: fluoridation.

"Considering what Boise was like—and still is—Butler's recep-
tion was no surprise," said Irene Wilcox, a social worker who had
long fought for better youth programs and better adoption pro-
cedures. "I remember that we had once invited a prominent
Canadian psychiatrist to talk to some group or other. He was a
liberal and said a few things about treating people who were

mentally sick, not locking them up. He pointed out that some criminals behave the way they do because of deeply rooted neuroses which date back to their childhood. Well, everyone accused him of being a Communist. People were very angry and very suspicious of his high-fangled ideas. I think one of the worst insults you can use in Boise is the word 'expert.' It's amazing how many people automatically think of experts as enemies."

Don McClenahan, a lawyer who in 1965 was partner in the firm of McClenahan & Greenfield, commented: "You must understand the atmosphere in Boise at the time. Such things had never happened before—that is, no one had ever been aware of them. We were used to looking upon Boise as a fairly model city, relatively free of crime or juvenile delinquency. Of course, specialists like Irene here knew that an awful lot of tension underlaid the surface, but you couldn't convince ordinary people about that. And then the whole lid blew. There was both hysteria and moral indignation. And don't forget that the judges, as elected officials, could not ignore that indignation, even if they tried to be as fair as they could." McClenahan, whose firm in 1955 had been headed by John A. Carver, Jr., added: "And the publicity in the *Statesman* could not but help increase the hysteria."

That publicity was finally condemned in court by another lawyer, J. Charles Blanton, on December 16, 1955. Defending Vernon H. (Benny) Cassel, who had pleaded guilty, Blanton charged that "sensationalism in the local press has gone far afield and has caused fear to those who would themselves testify" on behalf of his client. "Fear and hysteria has gripped the community," Blanton said, adding that the situation was "kindled by the press." He said that he was also concerned because people apparently considered the attorney who represented the defendant in such cases "as guilty as his client."

Cassel, a fifty-one-year-old clothes salesman, took the stand on his own behalf that day. He explained that he was first introduced to homosexuality in a high school in Nebraska when he was a freshman—his principal had promised him a passing grade in mathematics if he would engage in an indecent act. Cassel admitted that he had performed a similar act on a sixteen-year-old Boise boy in the basement of the men's clothing store where he worked. Prosecutor Blaine Evans pointed out that there was another boy involved, a seventeen-year-old juvenile delinquent who had been charged with a burglary felony but whose case had been dismissed to allow him to join the Army. The boy in question was William Harvey Baker, the same Baker who had signed an accusation against the banker, Joe Moore. But Cassel denied the content of Baker's new affidavit, which claimed that the incident had occurred in Cassel's car. Cassell insisted that he does not own a car and has never driven one in Boise.

After Blanton produced a character witness to support this fact, Cassel went on to say that no money had ever been exchanged in any of the acts described and that he felt he could "overcome" his trouble "with medical help." Dale Cornell, the psychiatrist, then testified that Cassel "should have treatment in a hospital or a closely supervised home setting. A penal institution would do no good and would stimulate the desire. I'm not in favor of it."

Neither Judge Koelsch nor Judge Young rendered any decision that day, continuing all cases until December 23. At least five homosexuals would be sentenced then: Brokaw, Cassel, Moore, Charles Pruett, and Willard Wilson. Wilson was thirty-nine years old and his case was very similar to Moore's.

Charles Pruett was twenty-four years old. He was not represented by a lawyer and had admitted picking up boys in the park. On December 16, Judge Koelsch had told him that "you're not required to answer any questions, but it would help me if you did." Whereupon Pruett volunteered that he had come to Boise in 1953 from Fort Worth, Texas, where he had finished the ninth grade. He told the court that he had received an honorable discharge from the Air Force as a staff sergeant and that he had an unblemished service record and no prior trouble or conviction. He explained that his father had committed suicide when he was one year old and that he had been placed in a children's home until 1942, ten years later, when his mother had taken him back. He described life under a stepfather as "not too good" and said that his first homosexual experience was when he was seven, at the orphanage. He insisted that his meetings with teen-age boys in Boise were not prearranged but accidental, and that no money was involved. Thus, in honestly revealing his life history, which had all the classical characteristics of the typical homosexual's, he admitted various homosexual incidents—probably to his detriment.

Meanwhile, on December 17, L. J. Peterson, the Idaho health director, appointed Dr. Butler to head the Mental Health Division, effective the twenty-seventh. And on the nineteenth, Wilson's lawyer asked for a continuance of the case so that Dr. Butler could, in his official capacity, examine and evaluate Wilson's attitude so as to be able to recommend or not recommend probation under psychiatric treatment. David Doane, one of Wilson's two defense attorneys, began the hearing by reading a prepared speech, which read, in part:

> We recognize that though we are representing Mr. Wilson, as attorneys we are also officers of the court. Therefore, in addition to the duty we owe our client, we have a duty to the community and to society to assist the court in arriving at the best available solution of the problem as opposed to a mere postponement of the problem.
>
> We feel that this case and other similar cases before the court are particularly amenable to the establishment of a pattern of disposition which will alleviate as much as possible the reoccurrence of the offenses. The character of these cases appears to require a greater medical and sociological understanding of human behavior than more common criminal matters; hence the necessity for the evidence we are about to present.

First, of course, it was established just what crime Wilson had committed. According to the prosecuting attorney, Blaine Evans, the crime was that Wilson had gone to a trailer house in Boise where he had had homosexual experience with a fourteen-year-old, a student in junior high school. Evans admitted that the boy in question had been involved in several other such affairs, whereas Wilson, who was married and had two children, was not known to have had any other involvements. With that firmly entered in the record, Doane began to call his battery of witnesses.

The first was Warden Clapp, who, under questioning by Doane, said that the prison had "quite a few" homosexuals and that homosexuality was "not confined" to those men who had been sentenced for such offenses. Clapp admitted that the prison had a limited facility for treatment of homosexuals and that inmates might, in some cases, be transferred to the State Mental Hospital South at Blackfoot. Clapp added that homosexuals were one of the largest problems at the prison, because other inmates resented them. "They resent eating and working with them," he said. Thus, he went on, homosexuals became extremely nervous, making therapeutic treatment difficult, however limited such treatment might be. Finally, Clapp told the court that he would like to see complete segregation of homosexuals in prison. He said that after any man was sent to prison, for any offense, the chance of rehabilitation lessened because of the stigma of being an ex-convict.

Herman Fails, director of probation and parole and secretary to the board of corrections, followed Clapp, testifying that he did not think incarceration had any effect whatsoever in rehabilitating a homosexual offender. Mark Maxwell, vice chairman of the board of corrections and the official in charge of rehabilitation at the prison, said that the facilities at the penitentiary were inadequate for treatment of homosexuals and that confinement, in his opinion, did not help rehabilitation and "constitutes a hazard toward it."

L. J. Peterson also took the witness stand on behalf of Wilson. He said that the Board of Health was planning a program that would help the current situation and that he was convinced that prison was a waste of time for homosexuals. "I cannot see any way where a prison sentence has a deterrent effect on a person mentally ill," he said. Peterson was followed by the Rev. William Spofford, Jr., an Episcopal minister who had earned an M.A. degree in social work from the University of Michigan, had served as a psychiatric caseworker for Wayne County in Michigan, had taken a special course offered to chaplains at the Menninger School of Psychiatry, and had spent two years at Cornell University medical school. In 1955, Spofford was also in charge of a Town and County training program for his church in Idaho. He stated that incarceration "per se" was not a solution to the homosexual problem but would only add a "burden" to treatment.

Dr. Dale Cornell took the stand and said that an isolated homosexual experience did not cause the person to become homosexual nearly as much as a "disturbed child-parent relationship early in life." If the "soil" was good, he said, the experiences were not as damaging to adolescents, in the long run, as it was generally assumed. Dale tried to point out that distinguishing the difference between the crimes of larceny, for example, and homosexuality requires a psychological evaluation of each case. "We have to individualize rather than generalize," he insisted.

Judge Young obviously felt he had heard enough. He did not delay Wilson's case long enough for Butler to furnish his evaluation. He postponed sentencing to December 23—which, by then, already had gained the aura of the Day of Reckoning.

In anticipation of that day, the people of Boise continued to work themselves into a frenzy. On the 19th, the Boise police set an 11 P.M. curfew for all youths sixteen and younger, and an old retired farmer named Forrest D. Turner came up with another suggestion. After having called Governor Smylie Sunday night (waking him up) and Mayor R. E. Edlefson, Warden Clapp, the judges, and various business leaders to tell them about his plan, farmer Turner released it to the public. His plan was to rehabilitate Boise's corrupted youth by putting them in camps similar to those established by the Civilian Conservation Corps during the Depression. What the youngsters would do, Turner, who was semiparalyzed, explained, would be to work—and read the Bible.

Then, on December 22, 1955, the City Council issued a lengthy statement that not only reflected the hysteria of the people—and its own—but also did much to undermine all the diligent, meticulous educational work that such conscientious lawyers as Carver and Doane had undertaken. The statement read:

The mayor and members of the Boise City Council have held several special meetings in which many interrogations were conducted relative to conditions as they are known in Boise today. Namely the apparent lack on the part of some citizens, of a respect for law and order, both governmental and moral.

Also in these meetings it has been our intended purpose to find out why the degree of such disrespect has assumed its present proportions.

Also to ascertain certain definite moves which the Boise city government can make to improve and aid local law enforcement. We have come to several definite conclusions, some of which we herewith wish to make public.

We find that law enforcement has not been as efficient as it should be, this we find has been due to several conditions, such as certain inequities in our civil service code, lack of sufficient pay and a general lack of administrative ability. Also a serious lack of the proper tools for good law enforcement, and most certainly a need for new legislation on the state level.

We intend to make a complete study of the civil service code, and to follow suggestions of the civil service board which have already been made known to us.

At the next budget time in May, we intend to look very thoroughly into the matter of pay, commensurate with ability, time and position of our police force.

We intend to provide our police department with the tools needed for better law enforcement, and will make it part of our responsibility to see that they are used to the fullest.

We have come to the obvious conclusion that Boise city problems are not exclusive. Many of our problems are also problems of every city in Idaho, and in this light we would like to make certain observations.

The Boise city government is glad to offer any assistance it can give, to those individuals, groups or associations who have been advocating the state legislature to call for a Constitutional amendment that would allow the setting up of juvenile courts. We feel there is a great need for this as well as need for a better juvenile law.

We also would like to suggest to those interested, and most especially to the state Legislature, that enactment of an adequate parental responsibility clause be included in a new juvenile law.

We believe that Ada County and Boise city should go together and pay for a well trained investigating officer to deal primarily with the homosexual problem, and that this said officer should be permanent, to see to it that we are never again in the position we now find ourselves. It is also our suggestion that the state employ such personnel on a statewide basis.

The state should provide a valuable department of law enforcement, which no city can now afford by itself, but which should be available to all of Idaho, and that is a "crime laboratory and central record" department.

In this respect a local business concern stands ready to buy a lie-detector for use by such a laboratory, and Boise city is willing and anxious to help pay for the training of a man to operate it.

Such a laboratory would be a great help to all of Idaho. As it is today, a known criminal, for the most part, is only known primarily in one city, whereas, with information and records being centralized from the county levels to the state center, known criminals, perverts, etc., would not be as free to ply their trades as they now are. But most important, a central laboratory, with proper facilities and experienced personnel, should help to solve all sorts of crimes much more rapidly and with much less expense of the total tax dollar.

There has been considerable interest generated along the line of a separate place of incarceration for homosexuals in order that they might receive special psychiatric treatment. This we heartily endorse and urge that the state bend every effort along these lines.

In conclusion we feel that Boise will be a much better place for our children if those guilty of molesting our youth and committing immoral acts against them, are not only convicted and sentenced, but also that all those who live outside the law are vigilantly watched and rigidly prosecuted for any felonies in the future.

This cannot be accomplished to the fullest, unless the above suggestions are brought to fruition by the joint efforts of the state of Idaho, its counties and its cities.

Besides being a panicky, ridiculously worded, often contradictory statement, this shameful "declaration of conscience" by the City Council members contributed much concrete harm. Not that there is anything wrong with a laboratory and records center from which all the towns and cities of Idaho might profit. Indeed, such a center would have been most useful had an effective, efficient one been set up. Nor was it wrong to suggest that Idaho get juvenile courts. And it was not even too hypocritical to suggest that Bill Goodman, who was already operating in Boise, be given legalized status, although the paragraph that made such a suggestion was couched in vigilante terminology with the smell of a witch hunt.

What was extremely harmful, however, was that the statement implied most directly (1) that homosexuality would not exist if law enforcement was more efficient, (2) that psychiatric care for homosexuals, which was up to the state, not the city, to obtain, should take place in "a separate place of incarceration," and (3) that all those who had been caught should be convicted and sentenced. This last point, which appeared in the *Statesman* on the morning of December 23, the very day that at least five homosexuals were to hear the judges' verdict, surely had a tremendous influence—if not directly on the court, certainly on the atmosphere in which the judges, elected by popular vote, had to proceed. In fact, it is surprising that no defense attorney moved for misjudgment just because of that statement, which was heralded by the *Statesman* in three-column headlines across page 1.

Like the people of Boise, the mayor and members of the City Council were scared. They reacted to their fear without the calm that the situation and their positions required. As events will show, some of these men paid dearly for such rashness.

8

THE FIRST DAY OF
RECKONING

ALL DAY LONG, on December 23, 1955, the brick, block-wide, rectangular building that houses the Third Judicial District Court, with jurisdiction in and for Ada County, buzzed with activity, excitement—and surprises. Five men were sentenced that day: Moore, Cassel, Pruett, Brokaw and Wilson.

Brokaw was lucky. After his lawyer, Pete Leguineche, said that his client had ceased his activities some time before he was arrested and that his parents would help him conform to a rigid program, Judge Koelsch began his allocution. "All statements made on your behalf have been considered," he said. He then sentenced Brokaw to five years. But he added: "I viewed the fact of your cooperation as a commendable step forward toward your own self-rehabilitation." And he commuted Brokaw's five-year term to six months in the Ada County jail. Thus Judge Koelsch went on record as believing in rehabilitation for homosexuals, and he interpreted Brokaw's cooperation with the prosecutor as a step toward that rehabilitation. Brokaw had been a stool pigeon—and it paid off.

But Judge Koelsch forgot about rehabilitation when he sentenced Cassel—perhaps wisely. After all, Cassel was fifty-one years old, and, in Koelsch's words, "you've been afflicted with this condition for your full adult life. You have been involved primarily with younger people. I feel you have had a damaging influence on their future conduct. You have had a hand in helping a number of youths to deviate." Although he used the word "afflicted," which seems to reveal that Koelsch himself looked upon homosexuality as a disease, he nevertheless decided to ignore the testimony of psychiatrists and penal experts who had insisted that the penitentiary not only does not cure homosexuality but tends to reinforce it. Koelsch sentenced Cassel to ten years in the pen.

When he faced Charles Pruett, the twenty-four-year-old victim of ten years of an orphanage and an unhappy home, he could not very convincingly talk about "your full adult life." Pruett had willingly and voluntarily testified in court that he had engaged in homosexual acts with minors, but legally he was charged with only one "crime against nature," performed on November 23, 1955 (a month earlier)—*with an adult.* Pruett learned that day that it does not pay to be honest. For after Judge Koelsch stated that "you attempted to establish yourself, but you were unable to cope with the situation," which again would seem to indicate the importance of medical or psychiatric help, he concluded: "That does not excuse or minimize the potential." And so he ordered Pruett to nurse, probably increase, that potential in the state penitentiary—for five years.

The case of Joe Moore, of course, attracted the most attention —and took the most time. Since Moore's defense attorney, John Carver, had prepared such a brilliant brief not only in defense of his client but also in trying to make the court understand the nature of homosexuality, Judge Koelsch felt compelled to answer with equal authority and aplomb. This was his allocution:

"The task of determining what disposition to make of a man once he has been found guilty of the commission of a crime presents an unusually difficult problem to a trial judge; one for which I am frank to say no entirely satisfactory answer can generally be found.

"The criminal law, of course, is designed and intended to apply to all persons alike and to prescribe a minimum standard of conduct for the entire social group.

"Thus, when a particular person must be dealt with, the interests of society in general as well as those of the individual himself are at stake and necessarily must each be the subject of considerate treatment. The ideal solution, of course, is one that would benefit not only the person himself but the group as well. Unfortunately, however, the situation is extremely rare when such a solution is possible.

The criminal law is not primarily concerned with the individual; its concern, and properly so, is welfare of the state, the common good. That individuals may be injured in the process is perhaps inevitable. Although the individual must be considered, the state is supreme, for, in the words of Oliver Wendell Holmes Jr., in his brilliant treatise on Common Law, "the dogma of equality makes an equation between individuals only, not between an individual and the community. No society has ever admitted that it could not sacrifice individual welfare to its own existence."

"Modern thinking seems to indicate that the considerations which should control the imposition of punishment are:
"1. Protection of society;
"2. Deterrence of the individual and the public generally;
"3. The possibility of rehabilitation;
"4. Punishment or retribution for wrongdoing.
"It does not necessarily follow that simply because an individual has violated a law he must be punished or even that he should be; only when one or some of the purposes for punishment will be clearly served [should] punishment be invoked. In other words, some impelling reason and worthwhile object must exist before punishment should be meted out. This, of course, is true of punishment for any one of the numerous kinds and grades of criminal offenses. But it is strenuously urged by many that, particularly in what are commonly regarded as unnatural crimes, such as the crime against nature, punishment in the form of incarceration of the so-called offender lacks justification on any grounds advanced.
"Benjamin Karpman, psychotherapist at St. Elizabeth Hospital, and a disciple of William A. White, perhaps the most distin-

guished of American psychiatrists, has culled from his experience with thousands of criminals the following conclusion: 'Criminal behavior is an unconsciously conditioned psychic reaction over which criminals have no conscious control.' His thesis, in common with many people, particularly psychologists and sociologists, is that no rational justification can be advanced for punishment as such; indeed he holds that fundamentally punishment is wrong:

> We have to treat them as physically sick people, which in every respect they are. It is no more reasonable to punish these individuals . . . than it is to punish an individual for breathing through his mouth because of enlarged adenoids, when a simple operation will do the trick;

but even granting the hypothesis that the individuals referred to are sick in the medico-psychiatric sense, nevertheless [the individual]

> is first a social unit and . . . although he may ultimately be handed over to the doctor, the demands of society ought first to be met. He does not have cancer or flu or dyspepsia; he has committed a crime, has injured someone, has damaged society according to his own definition. Because of this and irrespective of any moral trait, the criminal is obligated and must answer to society;

and Dr. Karpman also says that punishment neither protects society nor rehabilitates the criminal

> . . . and that sending [him] to prison is the wrong thing to do, both from the moral, professional and a practical standpoint. Everyone of them comes out of prison as bad as he went in, *if not worse,* except in the comparatively few cases where the prison is equipped to offer psychotherapeutic treatment, and how many prisons are so equipped. The law which offers the protection of society as an excuse for its attitude fails to accomplish the very thing with which it professes to be most concerned, for society is *not* protected except temporarily so long as the sexual offender carries within himself the same emotional reactions that were the cause of his arrest and which, upon his release, will continue to operate precisely as they did before. The sexual offender must either be sent to prison for life or he must be

placed in an institution where his warped emotional patterns can be corrected by psychiatric means. A prison sentence for so many months or so many years does not solve the fundamental problem;

and lastly he says punishment does not deter; we punish

thus adding hate to hate, which grows, as it were in geometrical proportion. . . . Punishment, therefore, is not a deterrent of crime; on the contrary, it is a most powerful stimulant for further crimes.[1]

"But these conclusions are primarily based on a consideration of the interests of the socially maladjusted person; if we consider the matter from the perspective of society itself, punishment finds ready justification, not as it relates to the individual, but as it affects the remainder of these individuals comprising the entire social group. In dealing with people we must necessarily take a realistic and honest attitude and recognize that society as a whole is not above reproach and that we have a long way to go before all persons abide by the same code of morality.

"The sad fact is that there is a basic antisocial drive in all of us; parenthetically, the psychiatrists say as to the particular type of crime involved here that the per cent of potential deviates is high.

"This whole problem has become hopelessly confused with social prejudices that have little or no relation to scientific facts. Every human is bisexual. There is some homosexuality in every so-called normal man, just as there is some potential sadism, exhibitionism, voyeurism, or other paraphiliac (perversive) manifestation. Students of sex psychology have long accepted the view that during adolescence, all of us go through a homosexual state of development and there are many youths who had a few homosexual experiences here and there, yet later developing into perfectly healthy normal men and women. Because of such experiences it is quite possible for any so-called normal man to regress to a homosexual level under certain conditions. There is no positive guarantee against development of homosexuality in any human being just as there is no positive guarantee against the development of any other form of mental or emotional disturbance.

[1] Karpman, *The Individual Criminal* [1935], pp. 292–299.

"And Dr. Alfred Kinsey in his testimony before the California Assembly Subcommittee on Judicial System and Judicial Process 1949, App. 109, confirmed this when he said:

> Let me draw your attention to this, since you have mentioned the homosexual. You have at one end of the population males who are exclusively heterosexual throughout their lives. Males who are exclusively heterosexual throughout their lives constitute about half of the population and not more than half. Males who are exclusively homosexual constitute about 4 per cent of the population. That means that you have about 46 per cent of the population which has some combination of heterosexuality and homosexuality in their histories. . . . Now the persons who lie in that other 46 per cent, you see, are persons who might be modified. Their behavior might be thrown one way or the other.

"In short, the justification for punishment for any crime and particularly for sexual offenses is that it deters not primarily the individual who has once committed a crime from repeating, but rather the great bulk of the population who know and fear that their own misconduct would subject them in time to like treatment as that meted out to the offender.

"As was well said in a monograph in the *Columbia Law Review* entitled "Crime Without Punishment" (Vol. 52, June 1952, No. 6):

> There is, however, another function of legal punishment which concerns the entire psychological equilibrium termed justice. Given the occurrence of crime there must follow the administration of punishment—be it at the hands of parent, teacher, society, law or superego (moral conscience). It is this balance of criminal punishment which provides the basis of the common concepts of justice and morality. Right begets wrong: wrong begets punishment. The simplicity of the expression is deceptive; its profundity must obtain recognition. When it is realized that "wrongs" are impulses whose satisfaction is desired by the individual but denounced by parent and society and as a consequence renounced by the individual it is clear why an individual cannot tolerate a "wrong" in another without that other's paying for it through punishment. The individual has sup-

pressed certain anti-social impulses because he expects compensation. The child is taught to suppress his wrongful desires by the infliction of pain and withdrawal of love; he learns that if he abstains from wrong doing he will be compensated by the withholding of punishment and the receipt of parental love. If, however, the compensation is not forthcoming, or if the wrongs of another are not greeted with punishment, a feeling of injustice is provoked. A man who has agreed to bargain away his instinctual desires at no small psychic cost to himself is incensed that another man pursues his anti-social impulses without being punished. Here indeed is injustice.

And the author goes on to say, speaking of the 'superego,' or in more familiar terms, the moral conscience:

Most adults deviate to some degree from the morality prescribed by society due to the presence of a faulty superego structure. . . . The superego being somewhat out of line with the social morality, the sanction of punishment is necessary to subdue the license given to antisocial impulses not condemned by the superego. . . . The importance of these criminal potentialities is their prevalence in the majority of the populace. If the psychiatrist would maintain that punishment is unnecessary as a deterrent to crime, he must be held to demonstrate the presence in most individuals of a superego strong enough to deny all criminal impulses irrespective of any threat of punishment. The evidence is contrary to such a contention;

and the writer concludes with this question:

Here, then, is a psychiatric answer to the psychiatric critics of criminal punishment. Here, then, is justification in a most realistic form for the punitive-retributive theory of punishment. Who would dare gauge the mass conscience deterioration and the increase in crime which would follow public awareness that the criminal goes unpunished? Who would dare to calculate the spread among the public of the criminal edict, 'If he does it, why should not we?' were criminal punishment abolished? And who could contemplate the resulting social disorder if not only the public conscience were thus abused, but the external threat of criminal punishment were removed?

"What I have just said is, of course, but a brief and general rationale of the pros and cons of punishment and an extremely brief consideration of its functions and aims. Punishment alone is not the full answer, and if it were not so true it would be trite to repeat the saying that an ounce of prevention is worth a pound of cure.

"It recognizes, of course, that crime will never be completely eliminated from human conduct, but I am fully convinced that the number of law violations can be reduced and kept to a minimum under an enlightened program of education and enforcement.

"I am always bitterly disappointed when a man of your background, talents and former reputation [Moore] stands before me as a common criminal. You have stood high in the esteem of the community and should be expected to do more than simply measure up to the required standard of ordinary moral and ethical conduct. Instead you have let us down. How can younger and less fortunate people be expected to have respect for the dignity of the law if persons of your caliber allow their talents to be warped into antisocial channels?"

That was Judge Koelsch's reasoning and his justification for his sentence. It was fairly well researched and calmly delivered, and it revealed that he had obviously been impressed by Carver's defense, enough to deem it worthy of a lengthy and scholarly rebuttal. But did it, in fact, rebut Carver's basic arguments and those of the other defense attorneys in the homosexual cases on which Koelsch had to pass sentence?

Carver's arguments, in summary, were the following:

1. Homosexual experiences between consenting adults hurt neither society nor the individuals and therefore should not be a crime.

2. Homosexual experiences involving minors must be judged according to these facts:

    a. The adults involved are sick, not criminal.

    b. They cannot help what they do.

    c. They might disturb the minors, therefore they should not be allowed to continue.

    d. Jailing the adults will not cure them of their illness (unless they are jailed for life and segregated in jail).

    e. They should be probated and treated by psychiatrists or recognized competent specialists.

    f. The minors are often the aggressors, because sexual deviation does not follow age lines.

    g. Punishment cures neither the adults nor the minors.

3. Incarceration tends to harden all criminals and, in the case of homosexuals, most positively reinforces their deviations.

4. Once in jail, homosexuals tend to cause the deviation of other criminals who are not homosexual or who have managed until then to keep their homosexuality in check.

5. Society will be served by curing the homosexuals, which can only be accomplished without incarceration.

6. If all sexual deviates are jailed, there will be more people incarcerated than free.

7. In judging the "crimes" of homosexuals, generalizations must not apply. Rather each case must be "individualized," and the only proper authority capable of doing so is not a judge but a psychiatrist or other recognized competent specialist.

8. In the cases brought before the court in Boise in 1955, such psychiatrists and specialists testified that in most cases treatment would succeed while incarceration would have deleterious effects.

Judge Koelsch did not choose to answer all these arguments. As a judge sworn to uphold the law it was not his business, and indeed should not have been, to question the soundness of the law, which defines "crimes against nature" as any and all forms of sexual intercourse that are unnatural, with the word "unnatural" defined as that which does not normally lead to procreation. Nor did he challenge the law that makes it a "lewd and lascivious" act to fondle a member of the same sex or a minor.

Basically Koelsch had only one argument. He conceded that 4 percent of the population may be homosexual, which is contrary to the standards set by society, and implicitly admitted that these 4 percent, since they cannot alter their ways, should all be in jail. As for the other 46 percent of the population, which can and does deviate from the standard, the judge's point was that the deviation should be stopped. That can be accomplished by punishing those who are caught. Such punishment, he said, citing other authorities, will have two effects: On the one hand it will serve as a deterrent to those who can still manage to control their impulses, and on the other hand it may teach those who are bisexual and are convicted for violating the norm that when they come out of jail they should work harder to control those impulses so that they are not jailed again. On the moral question of whether punishment is justified when there is no chance of rehabilitation, Judge Koelsch used the simple argument that if violators of the law are not punished it would be an injustice to those who do *not* violate the law.

Judge Koelsch's allocution raised various questions that fall outside the scope of this study. But let us at least pose those questions and describe the positions that they entail.

1. Is punishment a deterrent to crime? Statisticians would answer no. Despite all our "deterrents," the crime rate has increased in the United States faster than the population. Such statistics have convinced most of the world—at least in the case of capital punishment, since more nations have banned it than not. In the United States, too, these statistics are aiding the trend to outlaw capital punishment. Furthermore, sociologists and psychologists insist that the increase in crime is directly related to upbringing, security, personal experiences, financial status, examples by others in nonillegal activity (such as ruthlessness in business and police brutality), wars, impending disasters (the crime rate always soars whenever a large segment of the youthful population becomes convinced that an atomic war is imminent or that it will soon die in Korea or Vietnam or whatever), and so on. On the other hand, many legal experts argue that if there were no punishment the crime rate would be much higher still. This was, fundamentally, the line of reasoning taken in the *Columbia Law*

Review article cited by Judge Koelsch. What would keep most, perhaps all, of us from committing crimes if we thought we could get away with it? Nothing. Although individual acts can be statistically studied when they are first made a crime or first made legal, the general argument is not statistical and is not verifiable, since presumably we shall always have laws that punish criminals. It is based on the assumption that man's superego is developed by law, not by instinct. It is a fair assumption—but an assumption nonetheless.

2. Are all deviations from the sexual standards established by society considered equally criminal by the nondeviates? There seems to me little doubt that most people in the United States today think a sex offender is a criminal in much the same way that they think a robber is a criminal. This is not true in New York or San Francisco or other major cities, where most people are constantly in contact with deviates. How many New Yorkers would want to fill the jails with the young transvestites who parade up and down Times Square? Most New Yorkers would undoubtedly say that these kids and young men (and some adults too) are "disgusting." Perhaps many might even ask, "Why the hell don't the cops get rid of these bums?" But if pressed for a concrete opinion, most would certainly admit that it is ridiculous to jail them. But in Boise, Idaho, both in 1955 and 1965, the vast majority of the population considered these offenders criminals—worse, perhaps, than common criminals because they "preyed on our young." And America is full of Boises. I think it is fair to say that most Americans, brought up as they are on a more or less rigid sexual standard (which they violate in secret), would want homosexuals jailed.

But this attitude toward deviates does not necessarily have to remain so inflexible. Education and exposure *can* destroy prejudice. The anti-Semite from the Midwest who comes to an eastern liberal-arts college might become more hardened as he discovers that anti-Semitism is fashionable in the East, but if he shares a room with a Jew he learns to like, meets many Jews in class, respects his Jewish professors, he may abandon his anti-Semitism. Through education a man can change his values, even his politics.

Take Byron Johnson, for example. When I met him in Boise in 1965, I found him to be one of the most progressive, forward-looking young men around. He was twenty-seven then, a leader of of the Young Democrats, a good lawyer and a fighter for what he considered to be most lacking in Idaho. Despite its unpopularity, he was in favor of the new, increased tax bill, because through it the state could provide more needed services. He supported the transmission of more public power into southern Idaho to pave the way for greater economic development. He was in favor of abolishing capital punishment. And he wanted to reform the state's mental and penal institutions. Yet only a few years earlier, he had been a die-hard Republican conservative, as had been his family. In fact, he was such a rightist that in 1956 he considered Eisenhower too liberal and deserted him to support T. Coleman Andrews, a right-wing candidate who favored repeal of the federal income tax.

What had happened to him in between? Byron had gone to Harvard Law School and learned that, as he said, "Idaho is the Mississippi of the West in its inadequate support for education, its lagging economic development, and its antiquated state government." If education can broaden the field of vision in matters of economics, prejudices, principles and general attitudes, it can certainly do so in matters concerning mental health—and deviation.

The question of justice for the innocent—"if *he* is not punished for his crimes, it is unfair to *me*"—is much too loaded to use as a criteria for law and order. What would stop me, for example, to use that argument as follows: Rockefeller did not work for his money but inherited it, I word hard but I'm poor, it's unfair, and Rockefeller's money should be taken away from him and distributed to us poor. I'm sure that the *Columbia Law Review* would not like to see its argument used to promote socialism.

Besides, Judge Koelsch did believe in rehabilitation, since he showed himself quite flexible when dealing with Brokaw. Ah, but Brokaw had cooperated with the police! Under this light, Koelsch's principle becomes ludicrously simple: Commit any crime you want and if you then cooperate with the law, the court will be lenient. But would he apply such a syllogism to murderers? Of course not. What is the difference? Homosexuals are not really criminals, they're sick, and Brokaw was curable because he squealed, but Moore and the rest were not curable because they didn't—or because they didn't have anyone to squeal on. When it came to Moore, Judge Koelsch found no cause to be understanding. He sentenced him to serve seven years in the penitentiary.

Judge Young saw no flaw in his colleague's reasoning. Telling Wilson that adults who engage in homosexual practices must "expect more than the prospect of psychiatric tretament," he sentenced Wilson to five years. Young said that he had read Koelsch's statement and concurred with it. "The act upon which you are particularly charged," Young told Wilson, "is activity with a boy of the age of fourteen years. As an adult you have an obligation to the youth of the community, and no matter what the boy involved may be himself, or your own desires, you as an adult have the duty to discharge and not engage in such activities with him or similar boys."

In other words, even if Kinsey, Karpman and the other specialists and psychiatrists are correct, homosexuals must be punished. Young insisted, in effect, that a drug addict, if he is an adult, must refuse to buy his fix from a pusher if the pusher is a minor. Adult addicts must learn to be responsible—even if their addiction makes them irresponsible.

But the crucial question remained to be clearly answered: Is homosexuality so strongly rooted in character and personality as to be deemed an addiction?

9

THE HOMOSEXUAL AND
THE ANALYST

THE ONLY STATEMENT that can be made with absolute certainty about homosexuality is that it has always been around—and will never disappear. In fact, our first records of homosexual associations date back to ancient Egypt, Greece, Rome and Palestine, where they often had a religious significance. In northern Africa, female homosexuality was sacred, and in the Far East and Middle East, lesbian rites were a basic part of the religions. During the Middle Ages there were numerous Satanic cults in Europe that practiced homosexuality as a blasphemy, and in the twelfth century the Knights Templar, founded to protect the Holy Land, became almost exclusively homosexual. Later, during the Inquisition, the Knights Templar were accused of having incorporated homosexuality into their initiation rites and were condemned—one of the great homosexual scandals in history. This has led many homosexual societies to claim that the Knights were their "direct spiritual and ideological ancestors." [1] One of these societies, OTO (Ordo Templi Orientis), had a chapter in New York City as recently as 1930, when it was disbanded because the members seemed more interested in sex than in the occult powers they were supposed to derive from it.

The most famous homosexual society was the Greek, mainly because it was the only highly civilized culture that not only ap-

[1] R. E. L. Masters: *The Homosexual Revolution* (Belmont Books, New York, 1964), p. 41

proved of homosexual love but also advertised its virtues. *Time* magazine has claimed that the Greek example has been misinterpreted: [2]

> The homosexuality that Socrates and Plato knew rose only with the development of a slave culture and the downgrading of women to the level of uneducated domestics. This resulted in a romantic cult of the beautiful young boy—but not to the exclusion of heterosexual relations—much as the restriction of women to purdah led to a high incidence of pederasty in the Middle East, which is now abating with the growing emancipation of Moslem women.

This, of course, is an oversimplification, due, most assuredly, to the fact that *Time*'s article was bent on condemning homosexuality, as is obvious by its conclusion: Homosexuality

> deserves no encouragement, no glamorization, no rationalization, no fake status as minority martyrdom, no sophistry about simple differences in taste—and, above all, no pretense that it is anything but a pernicious sickness.

Very few psychiatrists, psychologists, sociologists, physiologists or biochemists would render such a harsh condemnation. Although there is some agreement today on what homosexuality is not, there is plenty of disagreement on what it is. A century or so ago, the prevailing view was that homosexuality was hereditary. Then a few researchers refined that explanation into the theory of physical bisexuality. What happened, it was thought, was that all human beings had both male and female characteristics, and either through traumatic experiences or through some derangement of hormones, the wrong characteristic could become dominant over the right one. When the female characteristic dominated the male in a man or the male dominated the female in a woman, the result was homosexuality.

Sigmund Freud, the inventor of psychoanalysis, destroyed that theory once and for all, replacing it with a dual hypothesis that became generally accepted before World War II. Basically, Freud explained that each human is born *psychically* bisexual—that is,

[2] Issue dated January 21, 1966, p. 41.

each of us has the tendency to *express* both male and female characteristics. Freud thus contradicted the physicalists and insisted that sexual impulses were divorced from their object. In other words, although it may occasionally be experience and conditioning that allow one tendency to dominate the other, both tendencies are perfectly normal. As a result of his new concept, homosexuality in men, for example, no longer was considered a desire for other men but rather a desire to experience both maleness and femaleness. With this approach, Freud could deal with the Greek phenomenon in a less simplistic manner than *Time*—yet more convincingly. Freud wrote: [3]

> Among the Greeks, where the most virile men were found among inverts,[4] it is quite obvious that it was not the masculine character of the boy, which kindled the love of man, but it was his physical resemblance to woman as well as his feminine psychic qualities, such as shyness, demureness and the need of instruction and help. As soon as the boy himself became a man, he ceased to be a sexual object for men and in turn became a lover of boys. The sexual object in this case as in many others is therefore not of the same sex, but a union of both sex characteristics, a compromise between the impulses striving for the man and for the woman, but firmly conditioned by the masculinity of body (the genitals).

Freud does not deny that experiential factors can either accentuate or repress man's inherited psychic potentials. However, he maintains that the existence of homosexual tendencies is permanent. A boy's first love is narcissistic, since his first love object represents himself. It must therefore possess the male genital. Fear of loss of that organ—the castratation complex—necessarily follows, and it is fortified by the discovery that the female has no penis. Girls are therefore shunned because they represent the embodiment of that fear—they are considered inferior precisely because they lack the male organ.

[3] Sigmund Freud: *Three Contributions to the Theory of Sex* (in *Basic Writings of Sigmund Freud*, Random House, New York, 1938), p. 560.

[4] "Invert" is the proper psychoanalytic term for a homosexual, and it is much more acceptable than either "deviate" or "pervert," both of which are insulting.

But, Freud continues, since the mother is the first donor of love and security, an unconscious incestuous desire develops, and the father appears as a rival. The boy unconsciously seeks a method to eliminate the rival—and the best method is castration. The rivalry between father and son for the mother's love (commonly referred to as the Oedipus complex) thus tends to fortify anxiety over castration. An unconscious and symbolic equation takes place: the boy's anus is like the mother's vagina. If the boy identifies more with his mother than with his father, the homosexual impulse may lead the boy to a passive role. If the reverse is true, then the boy's homosexual drive will take a more active turn. In either case, homosexuality is one way of coping with the rivalry while still gratifying sexual urges.

Freud ingeniously develops explanations for all forms of deviations, or inversions, fitting them into the over-all pattern of the human personality like jigsaw-puzzle pieces. Perhaps the best known of these speculations—and certainly one of the most fascinating—is his analysis of Leonardo da Vinci's homosexuality, in which Freud brings to bear his vast knowledge of mythology, history, languages and, of course, psychology. Historians have always considered Leonardo a homosexual, but very little proof has ever been brought out. Freud bases much of his study on a single passage in Leonardo's scientific writings, in which the Renaissance master made an aside, while talking about the flight of the vulture: "It seems that it had been destined before that I should occupy myself so thoroughly with the vulture, for it comes to my mind as a very early memory, when I was still in the cradle, a vulture came down to me, opened my mouth with its tail and struck me many times with his tail against my lips."

Freud first showed why the tail represents the penis, then said: [5]

The desire to take the male member into the mouth and suck it, which is commonly considered one of the most disgusting of sexual

[5] Sigmund Freud: *Leonardo da Vinci—A Study in Psychosexuality* (Random House, New York, 1947), pp. 39-40.

perversions, is nevertheless a frequent occurrence among women of our time—and as shown in old sculptures was the same in earlier times—and in the state of being in love seems to lose entirely its disgusting character. . . . Investigation then teaches us that this situation, so forcibly condemned by custom, may be traced to the most harmless origin. It is nothing but the elaboration of another situation in which we all once felt comfort, namely, when we were in the suckling-age ("when I was still in the cradle"), and took the nipple of our mother's or wet-nurse's breast into our mouth to suck it. The organic impression of this first pleasure in our lives surely remains indelibly impregnated; when the child later learns to know the udder of the cow, which in function is a breast-nipple, but in shape and position on the abdomen resembles the penis, it obtains the primary basis for the later formation of that disgusting sexual phantasy.

Freud goes on to retrace the known facts of Leonardo's life and concludes that Leonardo, whose birth was illegitimate, long repressed his infantile fixation on his mother. But, "thanks to his early preference for sexual inquisitiveness, the greater part of his sexual needs could be sublimated into a general thirst for knowledge and thus evade repression." [6] Leonardo was therefore not an active homosexual, says Freud, but a passive one. That is, Leonardo transformed his libidinal (sexual) drive into his artistic production. Freud's psychosexual analysis confirms what everyone had thought—that Leonardo was homosexual—but it maintains that this homosexuality, traceable to and explainable by a very concrete fantasy, was channeled into a highly respected activity. This did not happen because of Leonardo's superior talent, Freud insists—it was caused by his infantile experiences, over which he had no control. The over-all implication, therefore, is that a homosexual cannot help being a homosexual, but, as Leonardo's magnificent creativity demonstrated to the world, being a homosexual does not mean being ill. Indeed, in 1935, Freud stated just that, clearly and unequivocally, in a letter to a worried mother: [7]

[6] *Ibid.*, p 112.
[7] *American Journal of Psychiatry*, No. 107, p. 786.

April 9, 1935

DEAR MRS.———

I gather from your letter that your son is a homosexual. . . . Homo-sexuality is assuredly no advantage, but it is nothing to be ashamed of, no vice, no degradation, it cannot be classified as an illness; we consider it to be a variation of the sexual function produced by a certain arrest of sexual development. . . .

By asking me if I can help, you mean, I suppose, if I can abolish homosexuality and make normal heterosexuality take its place. The answer is, in a general way, we cannot promise to achieve it. In a certain number of cases we succeed in developing the blighted germs of heterosexual tendencies which are present in every homosexual, in the majority of cases it is no more possible. It is a question of qual-ity and the age of the individual. The result of treatment cannot be predicted.

What analysis can do for your son runs in a different line. If he is unhappy, neurotic, torn by conflicts, inhibited in his social life, analysis may bring him harmony, peace of mind, full efficiency, whether he remains a homosexual or gets changed. . . .

Sincerely yours with kind wishes,

FREUD

Not all psychoanalysts agreed with Freud, and even fewer do so today. Sandor Rado, for example, strongly criticizes the theory and posits his own: that homosexuality is caused by fear of the opposite sex and is, therefore, treatable psychoanalytically.[8] Rado, however, does not consider homosexuality evil, which Dr. Bergler (and *Time*) implicitly does: [9]

The entire personality structure of the homosexual is pervaded by the *unconscious* wish to suffer; this wish is gratified by self-created *trouble-making*. This "injustice-collecting" (technically called psychic masochism) is conveniently deposited in the external difficulties con-fronting the homosexual. If they were to be removed—and in some circles in large cities they have been virtually removed—the homo-sexual would still be an emotionally sick person.

[8] Sandor Rado: "A Critical Examination of the Concept of Bisexuality," in *Psychosom. Med.* (1940), pp. 459–467.
[9] Edmund Bergler: *Homosexuality: Disease or Way of Life?* (Hill & Wang, New York, 1956), p. 9.

Few responsible psychiatrists or psychoanalysts take Dr. Bergler's declamations too seriously. But the findings of Bieber and his aides are something else again.[10] Although Bieber tends to come to the same conclusion as Bergler, Bieber's research is based on extensive experiments, which are explained and evaluated in a calm, rational manner. Specifically, the experiments amount to a systematic study of 106 male homosexuals (both exclusively homosexual and bisexual) and 100 male heterosexuals in psychoanalytic treatment with members of the Society of Medical Psychoanalysts. The study began in 1952 and lasted more than eight years. The results, published in 1962, are the following:

1. Of 106 homosexuals who undertook psychoanalysis, 29 became exclusively heterosexual; 14 (out of 72) had been exclusively homosexual at the beginning of treatment and 15 (out of 30) had been bisexual (4 are unaccounted for in Bieber's study)—proving that it's easier to change bisexuals than exclusive homosexuals.

2. The 29 who became exclusive heterosexuals included 2 out of 28 who had less than 150 hours of analysis (7 percent), 9 out of 40 who had between 150 and 349 hours (23 percent), and 18 out of 38 who had 350 hours or more (47 percent)—proving that the longer the analysis the better the chances of result.

3. The homosexuals who stayed under analysis the longest had one or more of the following:

    a. Admiration for mother.

    b. Brothers and/or sisters.

    c. A sense of rivalry with brothers and/or sisters.

    d. First heterosexual contact by age sixteen.

    e. Desire to conceal homosexuality.

4. The homosexuals who abandoned analysis soonest had one or more of the following:

    a. Parents who spent little time together.

    b. No brothers or sisters.

    c. Homosexual but not heterosexual contact by age sixteen.

[10] Irving Bieber, Harvey J. Dain, Paul R. Dince, Marvin G. Drellich, Henry G. Grand, Ralph H. Gundlach, Malvina W. Kremer, Alfred H. Rifkin, Cornelia B. Wilbur and Toby B. Beiber: *Homosexuality—A Psychoanalytic Study* (Vintage Books, New York, 1965).

    d. Never attempted heterosexual genital contact.

    e. No desire to conceal homosexuality.

Bieber and his associates then state that their study

> provides convincing support for a fundamental contribution by Rado
> on the subject of male homosexuality: A homosexual adaptation is
> a result of "hidden but incapacitating fears of the opposite sex." A
> considerable amount of data supporting Rado's assumption has been
> presented as evidence that fear of heterosexuality underlies homo-
> sexuality, e.g., the frequent fear of disease or injury to the genitals,
> significantly associated with fear and aversion to female genitalia;
> the frequency and depth of anxiety accompanying actual or con-
> templated behavior.[11]

And they concluded that

> in our opinion a heterosexual shift is a possibility for all homosexuals
> who are strongly motivated to change. We assume that heterosexual-
> ity is the *biologic* norm and that unless interfered with all individuals
> are heterosexual. Homosexuals do not bypass heterosexual develop-
> mental phases and all remain potentially heterosexual.[12]

This study by Bieber *et al.* is fascinating, detailed and, within
its scope, quite complete. But it does not prove its conclusion
except as explicitly stated, namely, that heterosexuality as the
biologic norm is an assumption. The reasons for this are: (1) All
the patients, both the homosexual and the heterosexual, *desired*
analysis, thus might not have been well adjusted to begin with.
This does not prove that the homosexuals who do not seek analysis
are not well adjusted. (2) Not enough time has elapsed to be sure
that those who were changed from homosexuality or bisexuality
to exclusive heterosexuality were changed permanently. Just as
there are cases of men who behaved heterosexually for most of
their lives—the banker Joe Moore did not begin to feel his homosexual desires until middle age—so too there are many homosexuals who are changed to heterosexuality, but years later, under
a specific strain or after a singularly frustrating experience, revert

---

[11] *Ibid*, p. 303.
[12] *Ibid.*, p. 319.

to their old habits. (3) Although Bieber and his associates define homosexuality operationally—that is, anyone who has only homosexual experiences is an exclusive homosexual and anyone who has both homosexual and heterosexual experiences is a bisexual —there are good indications to believe that most of his patients, perhaps *all* who were changed, were bisexual nonoperationally— that is, by their own desires to change, their fantasies and so on. Just as it does not mean that a thirty-five-year-old bachelor who has never had a sexual experience of any kind does not *want* to have any, so too it does not mean that a man is exclusively homosexual because he has not had a heterosexual experience. (4) The assumption that "heterosexuality is the *biologic* norm" is contradicted by zoological comparisons. The physiologist Rollin Denniston has found that in the various species of lower animals he has studied, bisexuality or "ambisexuality" is normal: "It occurs in every type of animal that has been carefully studied [and] has little relation to hormonal or structural abnormality." [13] Dr. Judd Marmor, a psychoanalyst, has witnessed homosexual behavior among primates even when heterosexual opportunities were available.[14]

Nevertheless, most psychoanalysts today tend to believe that homosexuality is pathological—that is, an illness that can be cured. But most psychoanalysts come to this conclusion because patients claiming to be exclusively homosexual have *asked* to be cured. This fact alone broadens the chances of a change, for it indicates that the so-called homosexuals in question were unhappy or uneasy in their society. A nonpsychoanalytic study, however, might reveal that homosexuals who do not seek professional help and do not want to change are perfectly well adapted. Perhaps the best research on this subject has been carried out by Dr. Evelyn Hooker, a research associate in psychology at the Univer-

[13] Rollin H. Denniston: "Ambisexuality in Animals," in *Sexual Inversion —the Multiple Roots of Homosexuality*, Ed. Judd Marmor (Basic Books, New York, 1965), pp. 27–43, specifically p. 42.
[14] Judd Marmor: "The Role of Instinct in Human Behavior," in *Psychiat.* (1942), pp. 509–516.

sity of California (Los Angeles).[15] She has found no "demonstrable pathology" among homosexuals. In one experiment, she matched thirty homosexuals with thirty heterosexuals of the same age, intelligence and education, making sure that the homosexuals were well-adjusted members of the community. She then had all sixty tested extensively and intensively and handed the results to judges who did not know which test had been taken by whom. None of the judges, who were all experts in psychological testing, could tell the homosexuals from the heterosexuals. But let us be careful: The conclusion that therefore there is no difference psychologically between a homosexual and a heterosexual does not necessarily follow. What does follow is that all homosexuals cannot be considered sick. That would be equivalent to a psychoanalyst whose patients are all heterosexuals (and all emotionally disturbed) concluding that all heterosexuals are sick.

An earlier medical study anticipated Hooker's findings: [16]

> We are reluctantly driven to the conclusion that there is, so far, no evidence upon which any reliance can be placed that there is any endocrine difference between "normals" and homosexuals. This is in accordance with the clinical finding that castration does not cause a man to be homosexual, nor does it even, in all cases, cause cessation of heterosexual intercourse. Moreover, injection of female hormones fails to make a man behave homosexually if he has previously been normal.

And there is at least one recent serious study which, convinced that homosexuals are not sick, has tried to draw implications from this—the Wolfenden report. After three years of research, a British panel of experts and lawyers headed by Sir John Wolf-

[15] Evelyn Hooker: "Male Homosexuals and Their 'Worlds,' " in *Sexual Inversion—the Multiple Roots of Homosexuality*, pp. 83–105. See also her "A Preliminary Analysis of Group Behavior of Homosexuals," in *J. Psych.* (1956), pp. 217–225, and "The Adjustment of Male Overt Homosexuals," in *J. Proj. Tech.* (1957), pp. 18–31, and "Male Homosexuality in the Rorschach," in *J. Proj. Tech.* (1958), pp. 33–54.

[16] Clifford Allen: *The Sexual Perversions and Abnormalities—A Study in the Psychology of Paraphilia*, 2d ed. (Oxford University Press, London and New York, 1949), p. 119.

enden reported to the British Parliament that "evidence leads us to the conclusion that a total reorientation from complete homo-sexuality to complete heterosexuality is very unlikely indeed," [17] and that therefore British laws should be changed so as to legalize homosexual activity between consenting adults. Published in 1957, the report was finally incorporated into law in 1966, after pressure had so mounted that Britain's Labour government allowed time in Parliament for consideration of a bill to reform the law on homosexuality. At that time, Dr. Arthur M. Ramsey, the Archbishop of Canterbury, came out in favor of the Wolfen-den report and said that he hoped it would be incorporated into new legislation.[18] In the House of Lords, the Earl of Arran, a Liberal and a columnist for the *Evening News and Star,* stated that "nothing and nobody can change a man's erotic make-up." He added that there was "no ultimate standard on unnatural behavior" and that homosexuals needed compassion and tolerance "although our instinct is often to try to stamp them out."

It is true, however, that England has had a much freer climate for the debate over homosexuality than America. It has had its share of scandals, to be sure, including the case of Oscar Wilde, the poet and author who was jailed at the end of the last century for immoral conduct. Other homosexuals have been jailed since, and one, Peter Wildeblood, a topnotch journalist, has written a book about his experiences. Perhaps the most important point of his book came out of the conversations he had with other homo-sexuals in jail. He wrote:

> I have never met a homosexual who has resolved to mend his ways as a result of being imprisoned. The laws under which these men are prosecuted appear to them so flagrantly unjust that there is no question of their feeling any remorse or shame for what they have done.[19]

[17] *Report of the Committee on Homosexual Offenses and Prostitution* (H.S.M.O., London, 1957).
[18] *The New York Times,* May 13, 1965.
[19] Peter Wildeblood: *Against the Law* (Julian Messner, New York, 1959), p. 183.

Wildeblood insisted that he was still heterosexual when he began to "think of myself as a homosexual" and that he had never been seduced—refuting, in his case, the theory that homosexuals make converts.[20] This caused Max Lerner to state, in the preface of Wildeblood's book, that "the British and Americans stand almost alone, in the modern world, in their archaic legal prohibitions in the area of homosexuality and their fitful spells of intensity in carrying them out.

But in 1966, Lerner's comments could apply only to Americans, for the British finally made adult homosexuality legal. In 1960 a bill to do so was defeated in the House of Commons, 213 to 99. In 1965, after the May debates, the Commons again turned back such a bill 178 to 159. But in 1966, the House of Lords approved the bill and the churches lent their support. Labour's Home Secretary, Roy Jenkins, testifying as an individual and not as a Cabinet minister, stanchly commended the bill. He said: "The great majority of homosexuals are not exhibitionist freaks but ordinary citizens. Homosexuality is not a disease but is more in the nature of a grave disability for the individual, leading to a great deal of loneliness, unhappiness, guilt and shame." [21]

The bill, which was introduced by a Conservative, was voted on by conscience—that is, the Labour government did not make it a question of party policy but permitted a free vote. It was passed 164 to 107.

[20] *Ibid.,* p. 21.
[21] *The New York Times,* February 12, 1966.

10

THE GAY WORLD

AT THE TIME OF THE SCANDAL IN BOISE, all states in America had
some kind of rigid law against "unnatural crimes." (By 1965,
probably because of the influence of Kinsey and his researchers,
one state had changed its laws and another was contemplating
doing so.) Most of the state laws used the word "sodomy" or the
phrase "crime against nature." In either case, the "crime" was
generally defined as to "carnally know or have sexual intercourse
in any manner with any animal or bird or . . . any male or
female by the anus (rectum) or with mouth or tongue." These
laws applied to everyone, including married couples. What's
more, all that a prosecutor had to prove was penetration, not
emission.

Few states enforced these laws—if they had, more than 80
percent of the population would be in jail. But some—besides
Idaho—have tried. In North Carolina, for example, one particular
case attracted nationwide attention, mostly because of an article
in the *New Republic*.[1] That case began in January 1962 when a
grand jury handed down an indictment against two men for
having committed an act of fellatio. The first man pleaded no
contest, received a five-year sentence and served part of it. The
other defendant pleaded not guilty, was tried by jury, lost, and
got twenty to thirty years.

The North Carolina law under which he was tried was first
enacted in 1533 in England, with the approval of Henry VIII.

[1] Issue dated December 12, 1964.

That law made "the vice of buggery" a felony. In 1837, North Carolina copied that law into its statutes, but changed the word "buggery" to "the abominable and detestable crime against nature, not to be named among Christians, with either mankind or beast." It prescribed "death without the benefit of a clergy." A few years later the reference to Christians was eliminated and the sentence was reduced to a maximum of sixty years. That law was still on the books when the defendant won a new trial, in 1964, because he had been deprived of "the effective aid and assistance of counsel." But the judge who reversed the original verdict also had a few things to say about the law, namely that "most doctors who have studied homosexuality agree that prison environment . . . aggravates and strengthens homosexual tendencies and provides unexcelled opportunity for homosexual practices."

There is little doubt that the laws condemning consenting adult homosexuals are unfair. Such people are often deprived of their civil liberties, as when they are fired from government jobs because the manual of regulations of the Civil Service Commission makes "immoral conduct," which is defined as any "action not within the sphere of conformity with generally accepted standards," an unchallengeable cause for dismissal. The Veterans Administration has a similarly sweeping definition of immorality. (Are beards within the sphere of conformity? Are wigs? Are poets? Are liberals?) For example, it has refused to give veterans who were discharged for homosexuality ("blue discharge") their GI Bill of Rights benefits, even though in some cases the veterans were heroes and Purple Heart winners and had not been convicted of any specific homosexual act.

Just as arbitrary has been the Senate investigations subcommittee of the Committee on Expenditures in the Executive Departments (81st Congress, 2d Session, June 7, 1950). This subcommittee stated categorically that

there is no place in the United States Government for persons who violate the laws or the accepted standards of morality, or who otherwise bring disrepute to the Federal service by infamous or scandalous personal conduct. Such persons are not suitable for Government positions and in the case of doubt the American people are entitled to have errors of judgment on the part of their officials, if there must be errors, resolved on the side of caution. It is the opinion of this subcommittee that those who engage in acts of homosexuality and other perverted sex activities are unsuitable for employment in the Federal Government. This conclusion is based upon the fact that persons who indulge in such degraded activity are committing not only illegal and immoral acts, but they also constitute security risks in positions of public trust.

Why are they security risks? Because they can be blackmailed.[2] Why can they be blackmailed? Because if it is revealed that they have committed an act of fellatio, for example, they are violating the law and can lose their positions. Would they be liable to blackmail if they were not acting illegally? Of course not. Another thing: Are not Senators as liable to blackmail as federal employees? Yet, if the statistics apply, at least four Senators are homosexual and eighty (out of one hundred) commit or have committed cunnilinctus with women, or women commit or have committed fellatio on them, which is just as illegal as homosexuality.

Laws against "perversions" have also been attacked on the grounds that homosexuals have long contributed knowledge, insights and aesthetic works to society. It has been pointed out that some of the world's greatest men have been homosexuals, including Alexander the Great, Caesar, Napoleon, Socrates, Plato, Pindar, Marlowe, Shakespeare, Francis Bacon, Leonardo da Vinci, Michelangelo, Tchaikowsky, Rimbaud, Verlaine, Baudelaire, Goethe, Wagner, Whitman, Byron, Shelley, Wilde, Proust and Gide. Havelock Ellis has even insisted that "there cannot be the slightest doubt that intellectual and artistic abilities of the highest order have frequently been associated with a congenitally

[2] On March 3, 1966, a *New York Times* reporter (Jack Roth) reported that a nationwide blackmail ring preyed on all sorts of prominent personalities who were homosexuals (pages 1 and 25).

inverted sexual temperament." [3] And Gide claimed that homosexuality "is indispensable to the constitution of a well-regulated society." [4] Even the Army found that homosexuals topped the average soldier in intelligence, education and rating—although, of course, the Army proceeded to kick such homosexuals out of the service despite the fact that many "performed admirably" and "tried to be good soldiers." [5]

But this argument begs the question. Many murderers and madmen have been very talented and have contributed to society. Should all murderers and madmen be allowed to go free? In America, the problem is rather whether, if homosexuality between consenting adults were legalized and accepted, the talented homosexuals would feel freer to express themselves—and whether that freedom would make their works better. The first question must surely be answered in the affirmative, but the second remains doubtful. Is Great Homosexual Playwright X as great as he is because he is a homosexual? Would he be greater if he were not homosexual or if he could admit his homosexuality? Such questions can never be answered. But the fuss made over 1966's "homosexual playwrights," both in defense and in attack, would disappear if the laws were changed. As critic Stanley Kauffmann wrote in 1966:

> The homosexual dramatist ought to have the same freedom that the heterosexual has. While we deny him that freedom, we have no grounds for complaint when he uses disguises in order to write. Further, to deny him that freedom is to encourage a somewhat precious esthetics that, out of understandable vindictiveness, is hostile to the mainstream of culture. It seems to me that only by such freedom can

[3] Havelock Ellis: *Studies in the Psychology of Sex*, 3d ed. (F. A. Davis Co., Philadelphia, 1928), p. 26.

[4] Andre Gide: *Journals* (Knopf, New York, 1959), p. 117.

[5] *Newsweek*, June 9, 1947, p. 54. The article reports that "once this abnormality was detected, the man was usually evacuated by the unit doctors to a general hospital where he received psychiatric treatment while a military board decided whether or not he was reclaimable. A good number begged to be cured, but doctors usually doubted their sincerity and recommended discharge. At least half of the confirmed homosexuals, one psychiatrist estimated, were well-adjusted to their condition, and neither needed nor would respond to treatment. The majority, therefore, were released."

our theater be freed of homosexual "influence"—a misnomer for
the stratagems that homosexuals in all branches of the theater are
now often forced to use in order to work. . . . Homosexual dramatists
need the same liberty that heterosexuals now have. If this is too much
for us to contemplate, then at least let us all drop the cant about
homosexual "influence" and distortion: because we are only complaining of the results of our own attitudes.[6]

To return to antihomosexual laws, a much more telling argument, it seems to me, is the statistical argument. Consenting adult
homosexuals do no harm—why should so many of them be dis-
criminated against? But then, just how many are there? Dr. Irving
Bieber claims that there are not so many. Interviewed at his
home on East 72d Street in New York, the small, round-faced
psychiatrist told me that "after thirty years as a clinician and
analyst, including four years in the Army, where my sampling
was huge, I have the impression that there are very few homosexuals, though because they tend to concentrate in specific areas,
like Manhattan's West 72d Street or Lexington and Third Ave-
nues along the Fifties, people tend to believe that there are many.
I did a case study of one company in the Army—211 men. Not
one was a homosexual." The Army backs up Dr. Bieber. According to Defense Department records, only one out of each
10,000 draftees during World War II was rejected for homosexual activities. But, having gone through the induction process
myself, I'm not very impressed by the Army's figures. My session
with the psychiatrist, for example, lasted less than a minute.
He asked me my name, what I did in life and whether I liked
girls. I answered that I was married. And he shouted, "Next!"

It is true, however, that I came across very few soldiers that I
thought were homosexuals. But there was one man in our unit
in Japan who openly admitted to three of us that he was a homosexual. We had the kind of job that required us to be on call
most of the time, yet also allowed us to be free during long
stretches during the day—but we had to be able to call each other
and have a car pick us up on very short notice. We couldn't

[6] *The New York Times*, Sunday, February 6, 1966, Section 2, p. 1.

conceal our off-barracks activities from each other, especially since all of us had "civilian" homes out of camp. Anyway, this man told us that he was living with a Japanese homosexual, and as we got to know him better—and as he learned to trust us—he told us how he had managed to go undetected in the Army. "The first and most important rule," he said, "is never make a pass at another soldier, even if you think he's gay. Also, you've got to fake it. Talk tough, tell dirty jokes, occasionally about 'fairies.' Brag about seducing women. And always be the first to shout 'Disgusting!' when you hear or learn about somebody being a fairy." His tactics had obviously worked, despite the fact that, because we had to have top security clearance for our work, we had been investigated by the CIC, the CID, and other outfits. (Like James Bond—except it was before we had ever heard of him—we used to leave hairs across our desk drawers to see how often someone went through our stuff. It happened about once a week—and our desks were locked.)

That soldier's tactics in concealing his homosexuality fortifies Dr. Gordon Westwood's statement that "an aggressive, vitriolic attitude to homosexuality may be a defense against these tendencies." [7] It also explains how homosexuals may fool people who know them well for years. Jess Stearn, for example, reports that

> often a community is the last to suspect that it may be a harborer for homosexuals. Long before a stunned citizenry of Waukesha, Wisconsin, was aware of what was going on regularly in one of its most beautiful parks, the homosexual underground was fully alert to the situation. After the arrest of ten men in a series of raids on the park, which was also frequented by families on innocent outings, flabbergasted Waukesha police learned that in public washrooms as far as Milwaukee and Detroit, was scrawled this advice for the knowledgeable: "Try Frame Park, Waukesha." [8]

Stearn, however, tends to exaggerate his figures. He claims that "one out of every six adult males" is a homosexual,[9] which would

[7] Gordon Westwood: *Society and the Homosexual*, cited in Peter Wildeblood: *Against the Law* (Julian Messner, New York, 1959), p. 22.
[8] Jess Stearn: *The Sixth Man* (Macfadden-Bartell, New York, 1965), p. 39.
[9] *Ibid.*, p. 16.

mean that almost 10,000,000 American men are homosexual today. Since he thinks that there are almost, but not quite, as many lesbians, the over-all homosexual population in America would be about 17,000,000. Stearn, of course, may be right, but he does not reveal how he went about gathering his statistics. The more scientific survey was undertaken at Indiana University by the Institute for Sex Research, Inc., headed by Dr. Alfred C. Kinsey. After years of research, Kinsey and his associates found that at least 4 percent of the adult population is exclusively homosexual throughout its adult life, and that 46 percent "engages in both heterosexual and homosexual activities, or reacts to persons of both sexes, in the course of their adult lives." [10] Kinsey devised a rating system for the 46 percent, which ranged from 1 to 5 (0 being exclusive heterosexual and 6 being exclusive homosexual). This 1–5 rating has been questioned by some. They point out that Kinsey included mutual masturbation as homosexual activity—a practice that is very common but which psychiatrists claim is not a factor leading toward permanent homosexuality. Kinsey included mutual masturbation because his definition of sexual activity is simply "physical contact to the point of orgasm," but he classifies males involved only in mutual masturbation sessions in rating 1.[11] Kinsey found that 10 percent of the homosexuals in ratings 4 to 6 are married,[12] that the homosexual tendency defines itself between the ages of five and fourteen years,[13] and that there are at least 6,300,000 confirmed homosexual males in the U.S.[14] He also concluded:

> When it is recognized that the particular boy who is discovered in homosexual relations in school, the businessman who is having such activity, and the institutional inmate with a homosexual record, are involved in behavior that is not fundamentally different from that

[10] Alfred C. Kinsey, Wardell B. Pomeroy, Clyde E. Martin: *Sexual Behavior in the Human Male* (W. B. Saunders Company, Philadelphia and London, 1948), p. 656.
[11] *Ibid.*, pp. 615–623.
[12] *Ibid.*, p. 631.
[13] *Ibid.*, p. 658.
[14] *Ibid.*, p. 665.

had by a fourth to a third of all the rest of the population, the activity of the single individual acquires a somewhat different social significance.[15]

The judge that dismisses the homosexual case that has come before him, or places the boy or adult on probation, may find himself the subject of attack from the local press which charges him with releasing dangerous "perverts" upon the comunity. Law enforcement officers can utilize the findings of scientific studies of human behavior only to the extent that the community will back them. . . . It is not a matter of individual hypocrisy which leads officials with homosexual histories to become prosecutors of the homosexual activity in the community. They themselves are the victims of the mores, and the public demand that they protect those mores. . . .[16]

There is no evidence that the homosexual involves more males or, for that matter, fewer males today than it did among older generations, at least as far back as the specific record in the present study goes.[17]

If all persons with any trace of homosexual history, or those who were predominantly homosexual, were eliminated from the population today, there is no reason for believing that the incidence of the homosexual in the next generation would be materially reduced. The homosexual has been a significant part of human sexual activity ever since the dawn of history, primarily because it is an expression of capacities that are basic in the human animal.[18]

Many psychiatrists, including Bieber, and many penologists reject Kinsey's statistics on the ground that his questionnaire naively assumed that people would tell the truth. But one homosexual who supports Kinsey's statistical method is Donald Webster Cory:

The psychiatrist can never hope to meet a cross section of homosexuals, for his patients are only the frustrated and the maladjusted.

[15] *Ibid.*, p. 665.
[16] *Ibid.*, p. 665.
[17] *Ibid.*, p. 631.
[18] *Ibid.*, p. 666.

In the same way, the experience of the penologist is limited to the homosexual who runs afoul of the law." [19]

Cory was outraged not only by the laws against homosexuals, but by their justification as well:

Faced with constant sexual frustrations and paradoxes, restricted by a sexual morality which is self-imposed but which cannot be enforced, humanity finds some source of joy in the lower position it can assign to the invert. The man-on-the-street, teaching his children continence while practicing infidelity, believing he was a sinner when he masturbated, secretly desiring to cohabit with almost every female passerby while condemning in the harshest terms the victim caught in the flagrant act, protecting the virginity of his daughter yet condoning sexual activity on the part of his son, bored and dismayed by his wife's frigidity and by his own inability to arouse and to satisfy her—this man, not at all atypical, is anxious to believe that there is some poor miserable creature who is sexually more a misfit than himself. He laughs at the eunuch, and his laughter gives him greater faith in his own potency. And, finally, the "fairy" becomes the victim of his anguish. He substitutes invective for reason, ridicule for logic. His ego is boosted, and by an unconscious comparison he becomes good, normal, righteous, manly—hence superior! His is the better way; therefore he is the better person.[20]

Cory then analyzed the laws and found that "crimes against nature," "sodomy" and the other legal terms referring to homosexual acts are all defined by the word "unnatural." He asked whether the rhythm system of birth control was natural, then said:

The heterosexual society is enmeshed in its own contradictions when it contends that homosexuality is unnatural, for it not only fails to prove this charge, but by the force of its own argument demonstrates how completely unnatural are the heterosexual activities of most people. . . . If certain sexual behavior must be banned because it is unnatural, why not ban the telephone as an instrument of unnat-

[19] Donald Webster Cory: *The Homosexual in America* (Greenberg, New York, 1951), p. xiii.
[20] *Ibid.*, pp. 19–20.

ural living? And what shall be said of the unnatural release of the energy imprisoned by nature in the atom? [21]

He added:

Punishment is no deterrent. It may make some homosexuals angry, others bitter, others ashamed, but it has never made a straight person out of a gay one. It has at times—for better or worse—succeeded in preventing the fulfillment of a homosexual desire, but it has never displaced that desire. And even the thwarting of the fulfillment is rare.[22]

He concluded:

What the homosexual wants is freedom—not only freedom of expression, but also sexual freedom. By sexual freedom is meant the right of any person to gratify his urges when and how he sees fit, without fear of social consequences, so long as he does not inflict bodily harm or disease upon another person; so long as the other person is of sound mind and agrees to the activity. This means that both on the statute books and in the realm of public opinion all sexual activity is accepted as equally correct, right, and proper so long as it is entered into voluntarily by the parties involved, they are perfectly sane and above a reasonable age of consent, free from communicable disease, and no duress or misrepresentation is employed.[23]

Few psychiatrists, sociologists or serious jurists would disagree with Cory or would deny him and all homosexuals the rights he demands—with the stipulations that he himself insists upon. Whether homosexuality can or cannot be treated, the law should be changed so that homosexuality among consenting adults is not punishable. From a human, logical, moral and biological point of view, those who were convicted of homosexual acts with consenting adults and were sent to jail by Judge Koelsch and Judge Young in Boise, Idaho, in 1955, were punished unfairly. They

[21] *Ibid.*, p. 31.
[22] *Ibid.*, p. 32.
[23] *Ibid.*, p. 232. See also René Guyon: *The Ethics of Sexual Acts* (Knopf, New York, 1948) and *Sexual Freedom* (Knopf, New York, 1950).

were convicted and sentenced within the law—although with variances that are hard to justify. And so the law should be changed.

But what about those guilty of having committed homosexual acts with minors? Cory insisted that such cases should be considered no differently than when adults commit heterosexual acts with minors:

> The very real problem of sexual acts conducted by an adult with an adolescent or child, and the possibility of such acts having a permanent influence on the life of the younger person, affects the homosexual and the heterosexual, one not more than the other.[24]

The eight big homosexual societies in America take the same position. The Mattachine Society, which is perhaps the biggest (and which derives its name from the medieval court jesters, or fools, who, because of their status, could get away with telling the truth), has long fought to legalize homosexuality—but only between consenting adults. In its various publications (including the *Mattachine Review,* the *Dorian Book Quarterly* and *Interim*), the society, which has chapters in most major American cities, specifically and repeatedly condemns activities with minors and extravagantly manneristic behavior or dress. One, Inc., which is the most militant of the homophile groups in America and which has a staff of top-drawer lawyers to fight against blatant and brutal violations of homosexuals' civil rights, also denounces every form of activity involving minors. But my opinion is that the Mattachine Society, One Inc., and the other homosexual organizations condemn acts with minors only out of tactical logic. They know very well that it will be hard enough to get homosexual acts between consenting adults legalized without enraging the general population by talk about minors.

And yet there is much to say about minors. Most sexologists agree that sexual tendencies are defined in the human being at a very early age. Iwan Bloch, the pioneer European sexologist, was convinced that the direction of sexual instinct is clear long before puberty. Kinsey and his associates said that homosexuality becomes dominant between the ages of five and fifteen. Freud

[24] Cory, *op. cit.,* p. 33.

thought it was even earlier. The Institute for Sex Research also found that the "homosexual offender vs. children is the least oriented toward his own sex" of all the sex offenders that they studied—in two out of three cases his interest is youth, the young, more often than boys as such.[25] Furthermore, many of the kids are indeed the "aggressors"—they are older, developmentally, than their age would indicate, and they know very well what they are doing. Two experts put it thus:

> The truth of the matter is that those sixteen and seventeen year old "boys" about whose libidinous orientation the journalistic fraternity expresses such great alarm with such great regularity . . . are really long past their sexual boyhood: if they are presently engaging in homosexual behavior, it is quite likely that they have been doing so almost since the onset of puberty—at which time they were not so much *led* "astray" by others as *propelled* into the homosexual situation by forces within their own psyches: conversely, if they have not by age sixteen consciously experienced homosexual desire, chances are extremely slim that they ever will.[26]

In their study, the Institute for Sex Research found that homosexual offenders against children almost never used force (whereas many of the heterosexual offenders against children did), that half the time they were friends with the children, and that in half of the cases, according to the court records (therefore, presumably, much more frequently in fact), the boys encouraged the offenders.[27]

Interviewed specifically on the question of homosexual child molesters, Dr. Wardell P. Pomeroy, who worked on both Kinsey reports, as the findings of Indiana University's Institute for Sex Research are called, told me: "Any man who is attracted to children, male or female, is a problem. Legally a minor may be eighteen or twenty-one. Actually, many children sixteen, or even

[25] Paul H. Gebhard, John H. Gagnon, Wardell P. Pomeroy, Cornelia V. Christenson: *Sex Offenders* (Harper & Row and Paul B. Hoeber, Inc., Medical Books, New York, 1965), pp. 282–285.

[26] John S. Yankowski and Hermann K. Wolff: *The Tortured Sex* (Holloway House, Los Angeles, 1965), pp. 187–188.

[27] Gebhard *et al., op. cit.*, pp. 280–296.

fourteen, or twelve, are adult enough to know exactly what they are doing. Frankly, if it were up to me, no man involved with a minor where no compulsion or force was used would ever be punished. I don't believe it hurts either party. But if compulsion is used or if the male seeks out children repeatedly I would place him under the charge of a psychiatrist or psychologist."

Bieber put it to me this way: "Neither law enforcers nor society should be interested in homosexuals who are both adults and consenting. We know that punishment is not a deterrent. All adults have certain desires and responses towards minors [with heterosexuals, these desires are now commonly called the Lolita complex]. But the responsibility is theirs, not the minor's, even if provoked. Anyone habitually involved with minors, either homosexual or heterosexual, should be separated from society—not imprisoned, but separated."

In a paper presented at the annual meeting of the American Orthopsychiatric Association in New York in March 1965, Dr. D. E. J. MacNamara, a criminologist, gave the results of an experimental study (carried out during 1960–1963) of 103 male prostitutes in seven American cities. He found, as one would expect, a very high rate of broken homes, alcoholism, brutality and unemployment in the boys' backgrounds, but no family immorality. He and his associate (a sociologist with psychological training) concluded that although nearly all the prostitutes were neurotic, probably none were psychotic or psychopathic. With little education and few vocational skills, they had found in prostitution a relatively satisfactory survival activity—an activity that is less destructive than suicide, narcotics or alcoholism and much less antisocial than other crime, which is what kids of similar backgrounds resort to most often.

In another study [28] it was found that sexually dangerous per-

[28] Carried out by Harry L. Kozol, Director of the Center for the Diagnosis and Treatment of Sexually Dangerous Persons (Bridgewater, Massachusetts) and Director of Psychiatry, Department of Mental Health, Commonwealth of Massachusetts; Murray I. Cohen, Associate Professor of Clinical Psychology at Boston University; and Ralph F. Garofalo, Senior Mental Health Coordinator at the Bridgewater Center.

sons are curable. Over a five-year period, of 141 patients who had been committed for crimes much worse than those committed by the homosexuals in Boise, 35 had been released on parole. Although 9 of these had been recommitted on technical violations of parole, none had committed a similar "dangerous" sex act again. The implication is clear: Whether or not "normal" homosexuals can be changed by psychoanalytic treatment, homosexual offenders against children certainly can. Dr. Dale Cornell, in Boise, was convinced of this. Many times he told me that homosexuals cannot be changed unless they want to be, and then "they are usually bisexual in the first place. But if they go after children, they can—and of course must be—guided into channeling their sexual desires towards older people."

Dr. Jack Butler told me the same thing. "My general conclusion, professionally," he said in Portland in 1965, "is that everyone has the tendency to go after kids. The Lolita complex is more or less universal. One generally controls this impulse or even hides it from oneself, except at moments of strong depression, when one drinks heavily or, in general, when controls are down. Thus that the homosexuals went after kids is just as understandable as when heterosexuals go after young girls. Such people should be treated to elevate their object-desires, and they can be. I have treated many such patients successfully. I have not changed a homosexual into a heterosexual—unless he desperately *wanted* to change—but I have succeeded in having him aim for consenting adults."

These conclusions seem incontestable: (1) homosexuality between consenting adults is no danger to society and (2) homosexuality involving minors is an illness, a weakness, a sign of stress and strain (as is heterosexuality involving minors), and is therefore treatable. Child molesters should not be allowed to roam the parks, streets, YMCAs and gymnasiums, but neither should they be put in jail. Although there is good evidence to indicate that molesting a child when that child is willing and encouraging is not dangerous, as long as this is not a proved scientific fact, such activity on the part of an adult should be punished. But is not separation from society other than in prison —in a mental hospital, for example—punishment enough?

However one approaches the problem, what happened in Boise in 1955 and 1956 was wrong—except legally. And when one analyzes how and why it happened it also becomes immoral.

11

THE MURDERER AND THE
WEST POINT CADET

As was to be expected the *Statesman* never understood the problem facing Boise. Instead, it decided to praise the ill-advised City Council for its rancor-laden, bigoted "declaration of conscience" that demanded the conviction and sentencing of the homosexuals. This praise appeared in a *Statesman* editorial on Christmas Eve, 1955. It said, in part:

THE COUNCIL SHOWS THE WAY

The Boise City Council and Mayor Edlefsen have issued a joint statement in respect to law enforcement and control of homosexuals that should be recognized as the most important governmental step in 1955. The statement will be welcomed by every thinking citizen of the community and applauded throughout the state and the nation.

Immediately following the first homosexual arrests in Boise, the council inaugurated a series of closed hearings. We have not understood what took place at these hearings, or who may have been interrogated, and there have been so many rumors in Boise the last several weeks that speculation would have been not only useless but dangerous.

The council and mayor are in agreement that Boise needs more police activities. Furthermore, they are agreed to provide the funds for this expansion. In fairness to the present police administration, it must be recognized that their activities have been limited by the city police budget. Police salary schedules are ridiculously low from top to bottom. This has been one of the controlling factors.

Special attention must be paid to the fact that there is no question as to the integrity of the city police department. . . .

Boise's government is in good hands. Calm minds are in control. Just as it has taken the council several weeks to proceed to the point where it could make a definite announcement of its findings, so will it take another like period to effect its purposes. But effect them the council will. When done, the community will be back to normal ways, purged of a bitter situation it has had the courage to face. Aside from an occasional weakling who has not realized the scope and consequences of this problem, all concerned have measured up extremely well. The crime would have been to sweep this social disgrace under the community carpet to let it continue to ravage children.

Other communities may well take note of the procedure which has been followed by the Boise city government in meeting head-on the challenge of the homosexual. Until it is met in other areas (and it exists in all of them) the problem that has been faced here will one day surely rise to plague them.

Whatever the council and the mayor decide necessary in the way of law enforcement revision, or in law enforcement expansion, must be welcomed, regardless of cost. There is no measure of the value of a safeguard that this community requires in the name of decency and family protection. The council shows the way.

This editorial was not only arrogant, vain and chauvinistic, it was also misleading from beginning to end. It gave the impression that the council and the mayor had actually accomplished all sorts of things to get rid of the homosexual problem, when in fact all they had done was to announce the hiring of Bill Goodman to investigate homosexuals in Boise—which he was already doing. They recommended certain changes in law-enforcement personnel and practices, but nothing concrete was undertaken, and they claimed that by convicting all homosexuals who were caught, the problem would be solved. This, of course, is not true —there are as many homosexuals in Boise today as there were in 1955. The way the Boise council "solved" its problem, rather than being an example to be "applauded" everywhere, showed how prejudice can easily overcome common sense in small (and large) communities.

The *Statesman* pretended that it did not know what had been going on in the council investigation. But it seems most unlikely that the editor had not been well informed. The editorial also went out of its way to praise the police department—which is a sure sign that it was fully aware of the tension existing between the police and the sheriff's and prosecutor's offices on one side and the City Council on the other. That tension eventually led to a confrontation—but not before another crucial arrest was made.

Meanwhile, on December 27, Joe Moore and Willard Wilson filed appeals to the Idaho Supreme Court, and on December 29, William H. Baker, who had testified against Moore and other homosexuals, admitted that he had killed his father.

The murder had occurred ten days earlier, at the Baker home. It had been Baker's mother, Theresa, who had been arraigned. She had insisted that it was she who had killed her husband. But during the preliminary hearing, too many discrepancies had been revealed, so that Blaine Evans, Police Chief Brandon and the defense attorney Carl P. Burke had continued their investigations and interrogations. Finally the story came out: Mrs. Baker had admitted the murder in order to protect her son.

As it was pieced together, the killing was no spur-of-the-moment explosion. William Baker, who, as we know, was in the Army, came home on leave, called some of his friends—including Lee Gibson, who was the other witness against Moore—and told them to come over because he was going to kill his father. The youth then took a pistol from its hiding place in the dining room and shot his father four times from different angles. Baker's mother, who was in another room, heard the shots and rushed out to find her son holding the gun. She took it away from him, wiped off his fingerprints and held the gun so it would bear her own prints. She then told the boys to tell the police that she had fired the shots. At the preliminary hearing, William Baker testified that it was his mother who had killed his father, and Baker's brother and his friends followed suit. After the truth came out, Lee Gibson admitted he had lied because "Mrs. Baker wanted it that way."

After that, the pace slackened temporarily. For a while it definitely seemed as if the atmosphere were becoming less tense. "I can't explain it," one of the defense attorneys told me, "but it was as if there was a general feeling that the cases had gone far enough. Not only the court but also the people of Boise felt this —I think."

A minister put it this way: "As I talked about the homosexual problem, I began to sense a general cynicism. People would tell me: 'So there are a few homosexuals around, why all the fuss?' Everybody agreed that the child molesters should be stopped, but for some reason, people began to wonder just how real was all the talk about the 'homosexual underworld.' "

A garage mechanic gave the reason as the *Time* articles. His feeling was that by bringing national attention to Boise the *Time* articles made Boiseans self-conscious and that they therefore wanted the arrests—and publicity—to end. Lawyers who were familiar with the cases felt the change in public opinion was caused by the indictment of Baker for murder, which, in their eyes, tended to discredit the case against Moore, even though Moore had pleaded guilty and was obviously at least bisexual. Most women, of course, were still outraged. As if the offenses had been perpetrated against their own children, they wanted revenge. "It was no accident," said one lawyer, "that it was the women who packed the courtrooms whenever one of the homosexual cases came up." But the year 1955 ended without a single trial, since each of the homosexuals pleaded guilty.

The year 1956 was going to change all that, however. On December 30, 1955, the prominent attorney—let's call him Mark Rome—pleaded innocent. His trial was to begin on March 6, 1956. And there was going to be another, more important, trial later that year. But before either of these trials began, there was another arrest—and this time it affected the insiders.

The arrest took place on January 7, 1956, when Sheriff Doc

House traveled to San Francisco and brought back Melvin Dir, an actor and director who had left Boise a few months earlier. Dir waived extradiction and once in Boise voluntarily wrote the following statement in longhand:

January 7, 1956

I, Melvin W. Dir, making the following statement of my own free will and without duress, promise of reward or leniency in any manner whatsoever, to Blaine Evans knowing that . . . whatever I now say can and may be used against me now or at a later time in court. I have been advised of my rights to council. . . .

I first met * * * the summer of 1953 and a group of his friends, boys & girls, and offered to drive them all home. When I got * * * to his home he did not want to get out. He said he wanted to drive around for a while because he very seldom got a chance to stay out late. We drove out Warm Springs and eventually parked down a road by the old sanitorium [?]. The conversation got around to Benny Cassel and * * * said he understood I knew him. I said "yes." He said "How well." I said "well enough." He said well you must like to have sex then if you know Benny so we had a mutual oral copulation. He went down on me first then I went down on him. Afterwards we talked about gay affairs that he had had with * * * and * * *. And how much "coming's on" went on at Scout Camp.

I wish to state he is the son of * * * [Councilman Henry Morton].

After the first incident I accidentally ran into * * * twice and we went for drives and had mutual masturbation.

The Dir case is interesting because it reveals two aspects of how law-enforcement officials operated in Boise. The first is how the above statement was used by the law to destroy Councilman Henry Morton's son (let's call him Jim). The incident related above by Mel Dir took place in 1953, three years before Dir was brought back to Boise and confessed. Since the charge was an immoral act with a seventeen-year-old, that means that Jim was fourteen when it took place. In 1956, Jim was at West Point. After Dir confessed, Sheriff Doc House flew East and brought Jim back. "Here his father'd been hollering the loudest," remembered former Police Chief Brandon in 1965, "and his son was in on it."

Jim never went back to West Point—his career in the Army was finished. I asked Sheriff Doc House why he felt he had to do what he did. He interpreted my question as a general one and answered: "I put in extra hours of work to apprehend. I like to think that I was fair. Getting the evidence, backing it up. But I feel I have no remorse. I tried to do it as confidentially as possible. But a record is a record. I didn't have any desire for big news." I then asked House specifically about the councilman's son: Why go to West Point? Why get the kid who was now out of the whole mess mixed into it again? Why ruin his desire to make a career out of the Army? .

Doc House didn't like the questions. We had been having lunch, and while we had talked, my assistant had carefully taken down his words. Doc House paused. "Can I see your notes?" he asked.

My assistant looked at me and I nodded. She handed him the notes and he glanced through them.

"Any objection?" I asked.

He didn't have any, but he did not answer the questions on Jim.

Councilman Henry Morton, who was still a councilman in 1965, was equally uneasy about my questions. A sad, graying man, he almost came to tears while we talked. He was still bitter, still torn about what had happened to his son, yet not very willing to talk about it—understandably. "The whole thing was disgusting," he said. "It was a political witch hunt. What they did to my kid was disgusting. They didn't tell me a thing. He was in West Point and in their investigation they found out that he had had a homosexual experience four years [actually three] earlier. They could have told me about it, and I would have had him brought home on an emergency leave and then we could have gone into the whole thing. Instead, they send this Sheriff Doc House and he gets a confession from my kid, and they boot him out of West Point then and there. It was dirty. In their investigation there were other names, big shots, involved—one very big name. But nothing happened to him."

I tried to press the councilman a bit, asking him why he and his fellow City Council members had been so harsh and blind and unwilling to understand in the first place. But the old man was in no mood to answer. "My son has made another career," Morton said. "He's all right now. Let's leave him alone." I promised I would change his name, and left.

Mel Dir was never tried for his affair with Jim Morton. He was arraigned on March 30, 1956, and on April 13 he pleaded not guilty. Trial was set for June 25, 1956, then reset for August 27. But three days before the trial was scheduled to begin, Dir changed his plea to guilty. A hearing was held on September 13, 1956, and a week later, Dir was granted probation and withholding of sentence for five years.

Mark Rome's trial began on March 6, 1956, to a packed courtroom, mostly women. The prosecutor's case was generally based on hearsay. A police sergeant testified that Rome had freely but verbally confessed to the crime, to homosexual affairs since he was seventeen and to three or four specific acts during the previous year. A Boise YMCA secretary, testifying reluctantly for the prosecution, said that Rome had come to his office for spiritual guidance, admitting his homosexual tendencies. And the twenty-one-year-old man who claimed to have had the affair with Rome one day in the early part of the previous August repeated his allegations on the stand, describing the incident in all its details. But he said that Rome was wearing a heavy flight jacket because it was a rather cool day, and the defense produced a temperature chart showing that it had been in the seventies and eighties during every evening of the first fifteen days of August. On March 8, as he handed the case to the all-male jury for its deliberation, District Court Judge Merlin Young instructed its members that if any crime was committed, the twenty-one-year-old prosecution witness was an accomplice and therefore his testimony could not be accepted without corroboration. Coming on top of the defense's reminder that Rome was "not being charged with a tendency and can't be convicted of a tendency" but only of a specific crime, the jury found Rome not guilty.

Since there was no corroborating evidence against Mel Dir but only the confessions of the participants, it seems to me quite clear that Dir could have won an acquittal. But Dir was in fact a homosexual as the following letter from Dr. Dale Cornell to Judge Young states:

September 17, 1956

This is in reference to Mel Dir. At the request of Mr. Melvin Dir, I am writing this letter. Mr. Dir contacted me about three years ago about a problem, but was unable to clearly define it was [sic] being homosexual in nature. He was considering the possibility of entering pschotherapy [sic] at that time, but did not follow through at that time.

I subsequently examined him here in Boise on March 1, 1956 and March 20, 1956. He was very cooperative during the examination and, I felt, held back no conscious information. It is my medical opinion that Mr. Dir is an overt homosexual with bisexual activities. He appeared to me to be active and aggressive in his relationships with his own kind, and primarily, with individuals about his own age. He has had relationships with minors, however, these were individuals who were also homosexual in orientation.

I feel that he is desirous of changing his orientation at this time. I do not feel that he will be able to change his orientation without quite intensive and prolonged analytical help; hence, I recommended to him that he move to a city where psychoanalysts were available for his medical care. I do not feel that outpatient care with myself or on treatment in a mental institution, as they are at present understaffed, that he would be able to effect this change in orientation.

This patient is quite intelligent and a very talented person who, I believe, would have a good opportunity of being salvaged if he would accept therapy.

Trusting this will be of help, I remain,

Yours sincerely
(signed)
Dale Cornell, M.D.

Dir was probated, jailed in Ada County prison and made a trustee. In January, 1957, by which time Eugene Thomas had succeeded Blaine Evans as prosecuting attorney, Mel Dir's fate was sealed—thanks to the following two statements:

Jack Luther, being duly sworn, upon oath deposes and says:

That I am nineteen years of age; that my birthday is August 21st, and that my home is in Florence, Colorado;

That I was committed to the Ada County jail in Boise, Idaho, on or about November 27, 1956;

That I make the within and following statements to Eugene C. Thomas, Ada County Prosecuting Attorney, and to W. C. Shideler, Ada County Deputy Sheriff, knowing them to be law enforcement personnel; that I make said statements freely and voluntarily and without promise of reward or leniency knowing full well that they may be used against me, and that I am under no duress or coercion as I make said statements, but do so because I wish to cooperate and make a full disclosure as to the within-mentioned incidents in order to get them off my conscience; I understand and have been advised that I do not have to make this statement at all if I choose not to;

That I met Mel Dir shortly after I was committed to jail in November of 1956 when he was a trustee in the jail and came to the cell in which I was confined to serve our meals; that I was in jail for petty larceny involving the theft of gasoline in Ada County; that in December of 1956 I was transferred from my above-mentioned cell to the jail kitchen, having become a trustee;

That on becoming a trustee in December of 1956, I naturally got to know Mel Dir personally because he was a trustee in the kitchen at that time also; that as I got to know Mel Dir better he talked to me about homosexual matters and started making what I consider to have been advances to me; that since December when I became a trustee Mel Dir and I have, as trustees, been living and sleeping in the same cell together during off-work daytime hours and during the nights; that approximately one week ago; that is about the seventh of January, 1957, on the evening of said day, I had fallen asleep in my bunk in the trustees' cell when I was awakened by someone climbing into the bunk with me; that on awakening I discovered that it was Mel Dir; that there was no conversation between us at that time but dir [sic] then and there proceeded to take my penis into his mouth and to suck on it until I had an orgasm, and that I do not know why I permitted him to do this to me nor do I know why I did not resist this act;

That on about the eighth day of January, 1957; that is, on the night following the last-mentioned incident, Mel Dir again climbed into my bunk as he had done the night before and attempted to blow me but that on that occasion I refused him and told him to get out of my bunk, and that he then got out of my bunk but crawled into the one next to mine and tried to talk me into letting him blow me again; that on that night I refused to let him do it and he finally stopped bothering me;

That tonight, January 15, 1957, Dir again crawled into my bunk after I was asleep, this being sometime after 10:00 P.M., and wakened me by rubbing his hands on my back; that the next thing I knew he, Dir, was taking my shorts off; that I did not protest at said time and the next thing I knew after that Dir had taken my penis into his mouth and was sucking on it; that I did not have an orgasm because a flash bulb went off during the commission of the act and we were stopped before it was completed; that I have read the foregoing statement and it is a true and correct statement of the facts therein set forth and I had given the same freely and voluntarily, as is mentioned above.

(signed) Jack M. Luther

Subscribed and sworn to before me, Eugene C. Thomas, Ada County, Idaho, Prosecuting Attorney, this 15th day of January, 1957,

(signed) Eugene C. Thomas

Witnessed—1/15/1957
W. Shideler

The second statement begins the same way, then reads:

Mayo D. Kelso, being first duly sworn, upon oath deposes and says:

That I am a prisoner in the Ada County jail having been committed to the Ada County Sheriff's custody in November of 1956, and that since about December 21, 1956, I have been a trustee in the Ada County jail and that, when not working in the kitchen, I have, since December 21, 1956, been living and sleeping in the trustees' cell;

That Mel Dir has been a trustee living with me in said trustees' cell since December 21, 1956, and that Jack Luther has also been a trustee and in said cell during said period of time;

That about ten days ago I noticed Mel Dir climbing into Jack Luther's bunk, which was above mine, about ten o'clock at night or shortly thereafter after we had turned the lights out, and that at that time I heard a sucking sound from the bunk above me in which Dir and Luther were then and there located; that said incident has been repeated about three or four times altogether during the past ten days; that at about 10:30 p.m. on January 15, 1957, the last of said incidents occurred; that on said night at said time and place I had a camera with flash attachment in my bunk with me and that as I heard the sucking noise commence I got out of my bunk and looked into Luther's bunk to observe what Luther and Dir were then and there doing; that on doing so I observed that Dir had his mouth over Luther's penis and was sucking the same; that I then and there and thereupon used said above-mentioned camera by photographing the said Dir and Luther in the act of committing the above-mentioned act of sodomy; that I turned said camera and the film contained therein over to an Ada County Deputy Sheriff; that the photographic print contained in a sealed envelope which is attached hereto, said print bearing my signature and being dated 1/16/57 and said envelope being sealed in my presence and bearing my signature and like date, is a print of the picture I took and fairly and accurately represents Dir and Luther as I observed and photographed them, as aforesaid; that in said photographic print Dir is the person on his knees and Luther is the person lying on his back;

That I have given the above and within statement freely and voluntarily to Eugene Thomas, Ada County Prosecuting Attorney, and W. C. Shideler, Ada County Deputy Sheriff; that I have given the same without promise of reward or lenience and because I have no use or tolerance for homosexual activity of the above-described character and because I wish to cooperate with law enforcement personnel in the apprehension and suppression of such persons and conduct, and

That the above statements of fact are true and correct to my own personal knowledge.

(signed) Mayo D. Kelso

Subscribed and sworn to before me, Eugene C. Thomas, Ada County, Idaho, Prosecuting Attorney, at 1:30 A.M. this 16th day of January, 1957.

(Thomas' and Shideler's signatures)

That, of course, would convict Dir in any court. It does not matter that there are minor inconsistencies, such as one statement saying that only one homosexual act had occurred before the night in question while the other claimed three or four. Nor does it matter, legally, that the whole thing was obviously a set-up and a plant—a disgusting trap prepared, obviously, by law-enforcement officials. It was all nice and legal. Once confronted by the evidence, Luther, a nineteen-year-old, quickly signed a confession, and there it was: the confession and the corroborating evidence. The photograph was attached to the statement, as Kelso said, and is still (or was in 1965) part of the record. Mel Dir was brought before Judge Young on January 21, 1957, and sentenced to seven years in the penitentiary.

"That was a pretty dirty business, setting up the trap on Dir," I commented to Blaine Evans during our interview.

"Yes," he replied, "but the guy could have restrained himself until he got out of jail."

"Suppose you had been in the same situation, but with a beautiful woman," I persisted. "Would you have restrained yourself?"

Evans laughed. "Well, at least until I got out of jail," he said.

And there was Boise's moral code: Do what you wish, but in private.

But long before the Mel Dir case came to an end, his arrest and his confession—involving the son of one of the members of the city council—helped bring out into the open the animosity existing between the City Council and the mayor and law-enforcement officials. The mayor, of course, was an elected official. So were the sheriff and the prosecutor. Only one top law-enforcement officer was appointed, not elected—the chief of police. James Brandon, who had risen through the police ranks to captain of detectives, had been appointed chief of police by Mayor Edlefsen. Only the mayor could make that appointment, but the City Council had the right to dismiss him by a vote of three-fourths. On March 2, 1956, the council did just that. Although it insisted that Brandon's integrity was not questioned, it claimed that there was "a serious lack of loyalty, cooperation and coordination of police operations." It then unanimously voted to oust Brandon from his position, by which action he automatically reverted to his old post as captain of detectives.

Mayor Russ Edlefsen was furious. "This is a gross injustice to the chief of police," he said. He added that he was convinced that Brandon's dismissal was instigated by people "who want to get at me and at him." He warned that he would "keep this matter open for further discussion," which he did by simply not appointing another chief of police. (By city regulations the captain of police automatically took over as acting chief of police.) Meanwhile, Mayor Edlefsen asked the City Council to appoint more personnel to control the homosexual "threat to our community."

A month later, the City Council replied to the mayor's request by scolding him—in a letter released to the press:

> With reference to your request of March 26 concerning your recommendation to establish a separate department to specifically handle youth problems, we believe that the letter is worthy of consideration at the proper time. However, we are all of the united opinion that you, the mayor, should first fulfill your responsibility as mayor and appoint a competent police administrator at the earliest possible time.

Edlefsen reacted by telling the council, in effect, to go to hell. He did so indirectly by telling a reporter: "Due to the council's past action relative to the former chief, I feel that some qualified persons are hesitant about making application for the chief of police position in Boise."

As a result of this intramural fighting, pressure resumed in Boise to do something about the homosexual problem. Dr. Butler, in an interview, said that he hoped this pressure would lead to positive action. He stated that there was hardly a village or town in Idaho that couldn't use at least one psychiatric social worker —not because juvenile and adult delinquency were so high but simply to help ease problems of marriage, employment and modern living, which could end in crime. He added: "Too many communities, like the people in them, see life too much in terms of black and white and right and wrong. They need to grow up a little."

A few days later, while the mayor and the council were feuding, the executive and social-action committees of the Boise Ministerial Association issued a statement that could only undermine Butler's attempts at launching a mental-health program. The committees praised "the valiant efforts of the prosecuting attorney, Ada County sheriff and the Boise city police in cleaning up our community and safeguarding the welfare of our boys. We request them and their assistants to continue to protect the community by all legal means from known homosexuals who prey on our youth. We assure them our wholehearted cooperation and support."

Finally, on April 9, a week after the City Council had chided him for not appointing a new police chief, Mayor Edlefsen formally replied that he was doing his best to do so. But he again stressed the importance of an antihomosexual squad. He wrote the council:

> The members of the council are aware that an extensive investigation has been carried on during the past several months on the homosexual problems in this area. Much of this work was carried on by the Boise City police department under the direction of Captain Brandon in cooperation with the personnel and facilities offered by the county sheriff's office, the office of the county prosecutor of Ada County, and the office of the attorney general of the state of Idaho. This investigation was as thorough as the nature of the problem would permit, and every effort was made to contact any person in this area who might have some knowledge of the situation. A total of 1,472 persons were interviewed. . . . It is my opinion that the establishment of a bureau within the Boise City police department and in cooperation with Ada County officials to police and handle the existing problem and to safeguard the youth of this area will not admit of further delay. It is my opnion that Captain Brandon is best qualified by experience obtained during those investigations, experience as a detective and police officer, knowledge and stature in the community and character to fulfill this assignment.

The direct result of these conflicting statements—(1) what is needed is psychiatric help, (2) our community has been cleaned up and our youth safeguarded, and (3) a huge problem exists that requires a new department headed by a former chief of police—was that the people of Boise now began to think that the homosexual scandal had only barely begun. An amazingly large number of residents interpreted Edlefsen's statement to mean that there were 1,472 known homosexuals in Boise. As late as 1965, I kept hearing women complain that the homosexuals had been "whitewashed." One woman told me: "It was a known fact —the mayor said so publicly—that there were more than a thousand homosexuals in town, yet look how few were arrested!" In April 1956, it suddenly seemed that only the private detective Howard Dice and the probation officer Emery Bess had been on the ball. Dice had been relieved of his cases. He went on to try to make a business out of swimming-pool equipment, apparently did not do very well and left the state. Bess, on the other hand, had quietly continued as a probation officer until April 10, 1956, when he was asked to resign by Probate Judge John Jackson because of his "general incompatibility in working with other officers."

The next day, Bess came back fighting. He said he had been fired because of "considerable pressure brought to bear against him by groups embarrassed" by the exposure of homosexuals. The new Youth Rehabilitation Act, he added, "provides that the probation officer 'shall be a friend of the child at all times.' If this is incompatibility with other officers, then I've had it."

Emery Bess had had it, and so had many other officials on all sides. Too many people had been hurt, and too many were afraid that they might still suffer. Councilman Henry Morton, who had demanded the jailing of all homosexuals (he had been "hollering the loudest"), was furious at the law-enforcement officers for ruining the career of his son. Police Chief Brandon paid for his part in the investigation with his job. Evans was stuck prosecuting homosexuals whom he no longer wanted to prosecute, specifically those whose "crimes" had been between consenting adults. Dr. Butler was making enemies by telling Idahoans that they were too rigid, too puritanical and too ignorant. The mayor was scaring Boiseans by telling them that the problem would continue. The *Statesman* was awkwardly attempting to salvage its position of leadership, after having praised the wrong people —and after having generated the panic in the first place. And Boiseans, confused and insecure, were desperately hoping they could make the whole thing just disappear—by demanding strict conformity, which did much to cause "the problem" in the first place.

12

PUBLIC POVERTY AND
PRIVATE POWER

"WE GROW THEM TOUGH out here," a Boise Valley farmer told me in 1965, "and that's the way we *want* to grow them. None of this hanky-panky and city stuff for us. Our kids have to be men, just like their forefathers." To this farmer, as to most of the non-Boisean Idahoans I talked to, the 1955 homosexual scandal was not only a shame but also proof that "city ways" were encroaching on their proud history and tradition. Given the chance, such farmers will immediately rattle on about the great fur trappers and Indian hunters who founded Idaho, and the vicious Nez Percé Indians who had to be defeated to the last before Idaho was safe to live in. In this heritage, said one farmer, "there's no room for these queers. We don't want them. They should be run out of the state."

Idaho has indeed had a fascinating history—but not as clean or pure as its people like to claim. Until 1805, the Oregon Country, which included part of what is now Idaho, was a no man's land, claimed by Spain, Russia, England and the United States. That year Lewis and Clark began their attempt to cross Idaho but were turned back by the impassable canyons of the Salmon, which was called the River of No Return by the Indians. They finally made it. They were soon followed by two British fur traders who came down from the north and set up the first trading post on the shores of Lake Pend Oreille. The British controlled most of the fur business in what is now Idaho for the next thirty-five-years, although Americans were trying hard to compete. John Mc-Loughlin, known as the Father of Oregon and the Monarch of the Northwest Country, smashed most attempts by Americans to set up their own business. If he could not buy out his rivals, he exterminated them. In 1834, after he had devastated a large part of the beaver of the north, he moved southward and established Fort Boise (a French word meaning full of trees) to compete with Fort Hall, which had been set up by Nathaniel Wyeth, a Bostonian. Fort Hall eventually passed into British hands.

The year 1834 was also the year that Idahoans first got religion, in the form of services performed by Jason Lee, who had accompanied Wyeth. The next year, the Dutch Reform Church sent in a minister, and then came the Mormons. In 1860, the Mormons founded Franklin, Idaho's first permanent settlement. They dug irrigation canals and founded the first school for white children within the present boundaries of Idaho. Also in the 1860s, gold was discovered in the Boise basin as well as in the western and northern sections of Idaho, attracting thousands of fortune hunters. Idaho Territory was then created in 1863, and Fort Boise became a U.S. military post. Three days later, Boise City was established next to the fort as a service and supply community.

Idaho Territory's first governors were not very commendable. Gilman Marston never showed up at all, nor did Alexander H. Conner. William Wallace was an outright crook, and one governor who called himself Caleb Lyon of Lyonsdale and specialized in ebullient rhetoric died while he was being investigated for misappropriation of funds earmarked for the Nez Percé Indians, a heroic tribe who had fought courageously against outrageous odds before being forced onto reservations. Nor can Idahoans be too proud of their social history. For example, the first legislatures prohibited marriage between whites and non-whites—including Chinese, against whom there could be no historical animosity. The Chinese were taxed four dollars a month just for living in the territory.

As for homosexuality, which Boiseans and other Idahoans find so despicable today, it was quite common in those early days, especially among the trappers and lumbermen. The fur trappers, who often spent months at a time away from female companionship, considered homosexual relationships perfectly normal. So did everyone else.

Idaho became a state in 1890—the forty-third. Most of its valleys were rapidly homesteaded by sturdy midwestern stock. Although railroads had been laid across the territory in the 1880s for shipping out the vast quantities of minerals, Idaho soon became primarily an agricultural state.

There are, of course, semiarid sections of the state, but Idaho has more lakes and more running water than any other state. There are alpine pinnacles where the ice never melts, and there are so many hot springs that some cities pipe the water into homes for heat. In dollar earnings, agriculture ranks first, livestock second, timber third and mining fourth. Of the 53,960,000 acres in the state, 39 percent is forested, 36 percent grazing, and less than 8 percent cultivated—only a little more than half of that 8 percent is irrigated, despite the fact that Idaho is actually sixth in water power among the states and could be first. The Snake River, which cuts across the state, has an annual flow of water greater than the Colorado or Rio Grande.

Idaho is an underdeveloped state. It has the largest expanse white pines in the world, lots of virgin forests and more silver and zinc than any other state. It is second only to Missouri in lead, first in pumice and antimony ore, and holds 85 percent of the phosphate wealth of the United States. Yet despite all these riches, Idaho's main exports are: (1) poles and posts, (2) potatoes, (3) sugar beets, (4) lumber, (5) stone, (6) wheat, and (7) cattle. It imports manufactured goods. The result is that Idahoans are exploited much in the way as are the people of the underdeveloped countries of Latin America and Asia. They are dependent on and are victims of the fluctuation of commodity prices, while they are squeezed by the constantly rising prices of manufactured goods. As a consequence, salaries are low everywhere, despite strong unions in the northern mining areas. Idaho's per capita annual income is less than $2,000—which is $600 lower than the U.S. average. In Boise, which pays the highest scales, average weekly wages are $90–$110 in the food industry, $110–$120 in the construction industry, and $117–$135 in the printing industry.[1]

Financially, the state is not well off. It has a high property tax, which accounts for 29 percent of the budget, and an income tax, and there have been various sales taxes, such as on gasoline (six cents per gallon), until 1965, when a general sales tax was enacted. Governor Smylie, who had opposed the sales tax for most of his twelve years, favored it this time, and although some politicians, both Republicans and Democrats, intended to make its repeal their campaign issue in the fall of 1966, the chances were good that the tax would remain. In January 1965, before the sales tax came up for a vote in the state legislature, Governor Smylie explained his switch: "There are some who have said to me that the course which I here strongly recommend is a course fraught with great political hazard. My answer to that contention is this. True, the course is hazardous, but in my considered view, not as hazardous as failure to act. There may be those who will be tempted to contend that we should tighten our belts and do without many of the things we all know should be done. That, I submit, would be the easy road —easy because it involves no accurate measurement of a course of action. And it permits the unfounded hope that everything will turn out all right. This year I think is different. This, I think, is the year when Idaho is ready to move, and move swiftly. . . ."

A month later—before the legislature faced the problem of the sales tax—the Joint Senate Finance–House Appropriations Committee made its budget recommendations to the Idaho legislature. It trimmed Governor Smylie's request from $134,800,000 to $131,-700,000. What was interesting about the cuts was not the amount, which after all was only $3,100,000, but what they were:

Funds for the State Mental Hospital North (at Orofino) were

[1] *Editor and Publisher's Market Guide* (1965 ed.), pp. 119–121.

sliced by one-eighth of what the Board of Health had requested, which meant that new employees, including twenty nurses that the hospital wanted in order to meet the standards that the state sets for private hospitals, could not be added. Nor would there be any raises to hospital staffers, 31 percent of whom earned less than $3,000 a year, thus qualifying them for aid under the War on Poverty Program.

The budget for the Nampa State School was cut down from the $3,750,000 recommended by the Governor and the $4,000,000 asked for by the Board of Health to $2,500,000, which meant that the school could not hire the speech and physical therapists it had sought. The school would also have to abandon its vocational-training program, reducing the 800 mentally retarded residents to simple boarders.

The Idaho State Youth Forestry Camp on Lake Pend Oreille was eliminated altogether. Costing only $61,000 for two summers (Idaho's state legislature meets every two years, hence the budgets are for two-year periods), the camp had provided work and recreation for 300 boys and had proved its value by cutting the rate of delinquency among its graduates.

But when the session ended (the 38th Idaho legislature), the 3-percent-sales-tax bill was passed. Boise's *Idaho Observer* was jubilant, for it pointed out that the bill would increase the state budget by 35 percent, which was much needed in view of the fact that Idaho ranked last among the fifty states in percentage of increase in school expenditures per pupil over the last ten years.

Ronnie Dugger, the editor and manager of the *Texas Observer*, a liberal weekly in Austin, Texas, reacted by writing to the *Idaho Observer* a letter pointing out that a sales tax is a retrograde tax. "It is the most reactionary, illiberal, and noxious of all tax options," he wrote, because it "is devised precisely for the purpose of taxing the poorest the heaviest, comparable to their ability to pay, and the wealthiest lightest, comparable to their ability to pay." Sam Day, the liberal crusading editor of the *Idaho Observer*, replied that though Dugger was right in principle, in Idaho there was no alternative if money was to be raised for the services the state needed. "We prefer what evil there may be in the sales tax features of a revenue structure based on sales, income and property taxes to the far greater evil of the neglect of a society's just needs."

Both Ronnie Dugger and Sam Day were correct in their arguments. The fact is that Idaho, though potentially one of the richest states in the country, was so poor that there was no alternative but to impose a sales tax if there was to be an improvement in education—not to mention in mental-health services. And the reason that Idaho was, and is, so poor is twofold: not enough people and not enough businesses. These two factors interlock. If there were more businesses, less people would leave the state to find jobs elsewhere. As it is now, Idaho, in the words of one of Senator Church's Washington aides, "is a hatchery for young people who are exported. There's no place to go within the state." Of Idaho's forty-four counties, thirteen have had a boost in population in the last twenty years, eighteen have remained more or less unchanged and thirteen have had a decrease. The five counties with the greatest population increases have been Ada (which includes Boise), Canyon (which is next to Ada and includes the city of Nampa), Bannock (which includes Pocatello, Idaho's second city), Bonneville (Idaho Falls) and Twin Falls (with a city by the same name). All five of these counties are in the southern part of Idaho, and their five cities are the most populated in the state.

To the north of Boise, about halfway up the state, are the counties of Adams and Valley. John Moser, a doctor living in that area, has made a study (mimeographed, dated February 19, 1965) to find out for himself, and various church groups, the socio-economic conditions of these counties. The counties' main population center is in Long Valley, which stretches north-south along sixty-odd miles of the Payette River. Long Valley is entirely surrounded by mountains and has about 4,000 year-round residents. In the summer this is augmented by a fluctuating tourist and vacation population of 2,000 to 4,000, most of whom spend their vacationtime at either Cascade or McCall, two small towns thirty miles apart. The residents of Long Valley, Dr. Moser says, "consider that they are essentially a rural population. This is not so, because the bulk of the population lives in the two towns. The farm population has been steadily declining and will continue to do so. The residents of McCall and Cascade are essentially urban dwellers in the sociologic sense that their problems are much more closely linked to those of city people than those of farm people."

The area's industry consists of logging and lumber processing (the mill owned by the Boise Cascade Corporation), farming and ranching. This has been the situation for many years and will likely so continue. The prospects of new industry are negligible. The number of persons actually living on farms will continue to decline. The area's worker income, whether derived from lumber or agriculture, seldom exceeds $4,000 a year. Unemployment is high but temporary, usually about four months a year. "The general educational level of the resident population is low because most employment requires low-grade skills at best. This is true of mill workers, loggers, and agricultural workers," Moser says. "The few people who aspire to higher educational levels must leave the valley to find employment. The persons who wish to continue here need no further education to become gainfully employed. There is an extremely high turnover each year in the resident population and although this extreme mobility has never been accurately measured it is readily apparent to the few people who do not move. At the end of seven years it was found that 90 percent of the persons who had been hospital patients at one hospital were no longer living in the area."

"This affects the towns in various ways," Dr. Moser finds. "The people consider that at best they are temporary residents of Valley County. They prefer to live in trailers rather than build homes. They take little interest in schools, churches, or community functions and institutions although they utilize available services as provided by the communities. They form no close ties to any organization, to neighbors or to fellow workers. They take little or no interest in local, state or even national government except as it directly and immediately affects them. They are uninformed politically and never function as pressure groups. Their day-to-day interests are on a rather simple level and are primarily concerned with satisfying their material wants and needs." But—and this is an important but—they *can* vote, and when aroused to do so either by local issues, which is unlikely, or because of sympathy for a particular candidate, they *do* vote.

Since Idaho is full of Long Valleys, there is an important minority of voters who will cast their ballots strictly according to personalities. In the 1956 general election, for example, Eisenhower defeated Stevenson in Adams County 842 to 542 and in Valley County 1,285 to 511. But in that very same election, Democrat Frank Church won those same two counties from Republican Herman Welker (the incumbent) 890 to 415 and 847 to 804. In the state as a whole, Eisenhower won by a plurality of 61,111 (out of about 272,000), but Church won his Senate seat by a margin of 46,315—a swing of almost 40 percent. Some political commentators in Idaho attribute Church's election to the fact that Welker was sick but appeared to be drunk. But almost every election in Idaho illustrates similar idiosyncrasies. In 1958, Governor Smylie, a Republican, won reelection by 4,574 votes, but the lieutenant governor, a Democrat, did even better, beating his Republican rival by 6,942. In 1964, President Johnson carried the Second Congressional District, but a Republican won the House seat. In 1960, Nixon defeated Kennedy in Idaho, and the Republican candidate for Senate defeated the Democrat, but both Democratic candidates for the House of Representatives (Idaho has only two) beat their Republican rivals. And in 1962, the Republicans won the elections for the secretary of state, the auditor and the treasurer, but a Democrat won the attorney general's post.

The most famous modern personality in Idaho (since the death of Senator William E. Borah in 1940) is Glen Taylor, a Radical Democrat who was elected Senator in 1944 and in 1948 ran for the Vice Presidency with the Progressive Party. Taylor did not win his Senate seat because he was a Radical. In fact, he rarely spoke on an issue. Instead he campaigned with a guitar, singing, sometimes with his family, shaking hands, making friends, and generally exhibiting his charm and warmth. In 1956, although he blasted Church a few times, he did the same thing to try to take the Democratic nomination away from him, and he almost succeeded.

"Personalities have a great deal to do with winning elections in Idaho," the *Statesman* columnist John Corlett told me, "but don't let it fool you. Idaho is a very conservative state. The Democrats up north are sometimes even more conservative than the Republicans here in Boise. If personalities don't enter into an election, or if both candidates are equally appealing, then the guy who wins is the one who talks most against the federal government. You know, the government owns 63 percent of Idaho's land, and although most farmers would go broke without federal subsidies, everybody in Idaho thinks like the farmers, and the farmers hate the government."

Interestingly, this came through in the Long Valley study carried out by Dr. Moser. The county government there was almost entirely geared to the period of some thirty years ago when most of the people lived on farms. In 1965, all of the county commissioners were farmers or ranchers with little commitment to the bulk of the population, who lived in the two towns, McCall and Cascade. Dr. Moser found that "an amazing wealth of services are offered to the few farm families and almost none outside of educational services to the village residents. There are no social services available to the great bulk of the people. . . . The very small farm population exerts a disproportionate amount of political power through the county commissioners simply because of the persistent idea in the county that it is primarily rural. County officials and state officials, elected and appointive, consider that they must first satisfy the small rural population. The farmers are an unusually articulate group and have no hesitation about making their desires and preferences known. Their entire thinking, however, rests on an economic basis, and on any controversial question the farm response can be predicted. 'We only want it if someone else can pay for it. We cannot possibly meet any increase in taxes as we are already overtaxed.' This has so far been an effective argument even though it does not rest on a valid basis."

Government "control" of Idaho is such a hot issue that few people can discuss it calmly. Even moderates rant and rave against the federal government, and no one seems to know—or they conveniently forget—that for every sixty cents that Idaho pays to the U.S. Treasury, Idaho gets back a full dollar to help it stay afloat. Even Governor Smylie is careful to say the right words when talking about the federal government. Though a moderate who demanded that the GOP disavow the John Birch Society and its support [2] and who claims that "a proper function of the Federal government [is] paying for the Interstate system," Smylie insists that "some of the best merchandise we've got is in the department labeled, 'States of the Union.'" [3]

Naturally, everybody in Idaho accepts federal money when it is offered, but inevitably, *after taking it,* denounces it as still another step toward federal control. Such was the case in education, for example, where, under the 1965 National Education Act, Idaho received $3,500,000. The school system in Idaho is one of the worst. Few good teachers stay there because the pay is so low. Yet no sooner had the money been allocated than speaker after speaker, in clubs, associations and rallies, damned the aid as government intervention that would inevitably lead to thought control and socialism. (One respected politician, the liberal Republican state senator from Bannock County, Perry Swisher, who had opposed McCarthyism, loyalty oaths and Barry Goldwater and had fought for pollution control, state development and the sales tax, did have the courage to answer such charges by calmly pointing out that the antifederalist *Statesman* is a private newspaper using government mail service—yet who would accuse it of being controlled by Washington?)

Very few Idahoans, on the other hand, ever stop to ask themselves how much thought control, indeed sheer brute power, is wielded by private companies. Idahoans, like most Americans,

[2] *The New York Times,* December 8, 1965, p. 38.
[3] *Idaho Observer,* December 31, 1964, p. 3.

take free enterprise for granted to such an extent that they are perfectly willing to let it exert much more influence over their daily lives than the federal government ever could. I don't just mean in terms of elective offices—although it is true that here too the "Boise gang," as Glen Taylor called it, is as powerful and far-reaching as any old-style Tammany political machinery. One Democratic candidate for state representative, Dan Emery, tried to win an election by bringing this out. On October 1964, he ran the following ad: "Mr. Bob Hansberger of the Boise Cascade Corporation made radio, TV and newspaper headlines when he made public his preference for President Johnson, but said he would still support the County and State Republican tickets. I can see why: (1) Larry Mills is a top echelon Boise Cascade Employee. (2) Chuck McDevitt is head of Boise Cascade Legal Department. (3) Bill Roden is associated through Mr. Bill Eberle who is one of Boise Cascade's vice presidents. These three men are candidates for Republican State Representatives and that is just too big a pipeline to our State Capitol. I would appreciate your vote for me November 3rd." What Emery said did not influence the voters.

Much more serious, however, is the way that one Idaho company has been able to forestall progress and exploit the people—with their general approval. That company is the Idaho Power Company. Of course, the company has had allies, many of them formidable, including the governors of Utah and Wyoming and the executives of big corporations in Idaho, Wyoming, Utah, Montana, Washington and California. What's more, the power that Idaho Power wields is legal. But the incredible thing is that many Idahoans want it to have that power. Because of it, they pay higher rates for electricity than any of their neighbors, their taxes are high because the state can find no one else to tax, and their state cannot get new businesses, which means that no new jobs are created. All this because the issue of cheap electric power has been obscured by the false issue of private power versus public power—and most Idahoans, especially the farmers, who would benefit most from cheaper power, apparently would rather go bankrupt than do business with the public—that is, with the government.

The real issue has nothing to do with public power. The Columbia River Basin, which is one of the richest sources of hydroelectric power in the world, has already been tapped. In fact, the Bonneville Power Administration (BPA) has been in business since 1937, harnessing Idaho's huge water resources in a system of dams creating energy that is transmitted all over the Northwest. BPA is not a subsidized federal subsidiary. It is a money-making project that has already returned more than a billion dollars to the government over the tax-supported original costs needed to set it into operation. BPA has tremendous potential. It could send electric power throughout Idaho. But it has not been allowed to. Why? Because the privately owned Idaho Power Company has successfully stopped it from doing so, through its Washington lobbies, its allies and its public-relations efforts in Idaho itself.

Idaho Power Company is not an Idahoan company. It is owned mostly by Middle Atlantic and New England companies—70 percent of the common stock. Only 6 percent of the stock is held by people or firms in the Idaho area. It is a very profitable company, having paid out $6,700,000 in dividends in 1964. It has no interest in providing Idahoans with cheaper service. In fact, its rates are higher than its neighboring equivalents, as the following table demonstrates:

ELECTRICITY PRICES

MONTHLY BILLS FOR RESIDENTIAL CONSUMPTION OF 500 KILOWATT-HOURS
1938 AND 1963

Utility Service Area	1938	1963	Percent Change
Idaho Power Company, Boise	$8.60	$9.95	+15.7
Pacific Power & Light, Portland	8.07	6.40	−20.7
Portland General Electric, Portland	8.07	6.40	−20.7
Puget Sound Power & Light, Renton	7.95	6.79	−14.6
Washington Water Power, Spokane	9.15	7.05	−23.0

Because of Idaho Power's high rates, industry does not find it economical to move into Idaho. If Idaho Power were willing either to buy more power from BPA, which it could do at a low enough price to be able to resell it at a profit but still be competitive with other power companies, or if it were willing to let BPA market its power where it would not be competitive, then the cost of electricity could be lowered enough to offset the high cost of transporting products from Idaho to the East Coast and West Coast markets. But Idaho Power, which cannot or will not expand at the rate necessary for new industries, uses its influence to stop Congress from authorizing BPA to sell its power in southern Idaho, where most of the new plants would be set up because of convenience to rail lines.

F. P. Hendrickson, plant manager for the Monsanto Company at Soda Springs, Idaho, explained it thus in 1964 speech before a Rotary Club: "Our present contracts with Utah Power and Light Company were signed in 1951 and have been in full effect since 1954. Since 1954 we have had almost continuous discussions with both the Utah Power and Light Company and the Idaho Power Company for additional quantities of power in amounts from 10,000 kilowatts to 110,000 kilowatts. We have made every possible suggestion to these two companies to supply our needs individually or together. We have not been able to obtain a satisfactory contract, and in the period of 1954 to 1964 we were forced to expand capacity at our Columbia, Tennessee, plant, rather than at Soda Springs in an amount which would have tripled the Soda Springs capacity."

Monsanto uses phosphates to make marketable ore and fertilizer. Idaho has 85 percent of the country's phosphate supply, yet by 1962 Florida was producing more than 75 percent of the country's output and Tennessee more than 10 percent. "This imbalance," said Hendrickson, "results solely from economics. During the past ten years, phosphorous production increased 29 percent in the West and 83 percent in eastern United States." Had Monsanto been able to get BPA power, it would have ex-

panded its Idaho plant. It could not. Idaho Power would not provide the service. The result: less money, less work, less tax revenue
for Idaho. Cheaper power would also help farmers electrify their
farms, mechanize their production, increase their profits. But
private enterprise is sacred, and few farmers seem willing to be
"un-American."

Idaho Power seems to fear competition from BPA. In point of
fact, however, BPA has helped private power in the Northwest,
not hindered it. Between 1937 (when BPA was born) and 1962,
the net income of the Pacific Power and Light Company soared
940 percent. Portland General Electric, which was losing money in
1937, had a net income greater than Idaho Power in 1962. Western
Montana came into the BPA marketing area in 1950 and quickly
acquired a BPA transmission line running all the way to Butte.
Montana Power was afraid, at first, that this would cut down its
income and that it would not be able to pay the state of Montana
its $6,000,000 in taxes. But from 1950 to 1962, Montana Power's
stock jumped 573 percent, and in 1962, it was paying $16,000,000
in taxes. In every state adjoining Idaho, power has become
cheaper, more people are using it, profits have risen, and more
taxes are being paid into the states' treasuries. In Idaho, on the
other hand, consumption has drastically dropped, relative to its
neighbors. In 1940, for example, Idaho Power customers used
more electricity per home than the customers of any other Northwest power company. In 1962, Idaho Power customers used less
than any other company.

It is quite understandable that the power companies in neighboring states do not want BPA to expand its service to Idaho. If
it did, new industries might go to Idaho rather than to the neighboring states. And if Idaho Power does not expand to meet market
demands, it will have to buy subsidiary power from the power
companies in neighboring states. Furthermore, such Idaho companies as J. R. Simplot, which use the wet-acid process to produce
phosphate fertilizer, also oppose BPA, because with BPA power,
Monsanto would set up competing plants.

It is ironic that today Idaho is the most backward of the western states in power consumption—ironic because Idaho's greatest Senator, William E. Borah, a Republican and stanch free-enter-priser, was well aware half a century ago of the dangers of leaving electric power in the hands of private companies. On September 19, 1918, he rose in the U.S. Senate and said:

> Our new States, far from the centers of population and manufacture, have unlimited water power. Idaho . . . has 5,067,000 horsepower; Montana, 4,031,000; Oregon, 6,613,000; Washington 8,447,000. What a world of wealth and what immeasurable possibilities are foreshadowed in these figures. It is the richest heritage that nature's God ever dedicated to a people. It will continue to serve those States and communities so long as the snows fall in the mountains and the waters flow to the sea. I feel, therefore, I can render no greater service to the people of my State or to that great northwestern empire, rich, marvelously rich in natural resources, than to help to keep this heritage wholly and exclusively for the people as a whole. I can do no greater service, it seems to me, than to help to free it from speculation and from private manipulation and gain. If we under public ownership can sell power for half what it costs under private ownership nothing is more calculated to bring people to settle our lands, to build homes and schools and manufactories, enrich our communities, and enlarge our payrolls. . . . Cheap power will do much in this line. . . . It will bring investment and business and enterprise. . . . There is no domestic question of such vital and lasting concern to us.

Senator Frank Church agrees, and he has been trying to expand BPA power by action in Congress. But the Idaho Power Company disagrees. It does not want to expand too quickly, for it does not want Idaho to get new industries. None of the local wheels do. To them, Idaho is just fine the way it is. "Why should we bring in new industries?" one of the Boise executives shouted at me when I asked him why he supported Idaho Power. "Start new industries and before you know it, you've got unions, and then you've got black men coming in, and then there's no end to it. Drugs, prostitutes, juvenile delinquents. What the hell do you want new industry for?"

I gently suggested the answer: so that there might be more jobs

and more taxes for better schools and a better mental-health program. "Mental health," he scoffed. "Yeah, I know, so you can
save those goddam fairies you've been checking about all over
town. I know. Well, we don't want fairies—or mental health. We
don't want Boise to change. It's grown too much as it is. Next
thing you'll want is legalized gambling."

The executive's reference to legalized gambling was no shot in
the dark. There have long been advocates of legalized gambling
in Idaho. In 1958, Al Derr, a state senator running for governor,
came out for gambling. He won the Democratic nomination, but
lost to Smylie. In 1962, Derr's former campaign manager, Vernon
K. Smith, ran for the same nomination—on the same platform. He
too won the nomination, but lost the election. I asked him in
1965 why he put such emphasis on legalized gambling? "Idaho is
a very poor state," he answered. "We need all sorts of new money,
new industries, new jobs. How can we get it? Legalized gambling
won't bring in that much by itself, but the services industries will.
People will build hotels, motels, casinos, restaurants. There'll be
a construction boom. New jobs for waiters, for bakers, for crou-
piers. Our farmers will have new mouths to feed. More cattle will
be raised, vegetables, policemen. It's the only way to get Idaho on
its feet. Tourism, entertainment—those are multimillion dollar
businesses."

Vernon K. Smith was no liberal. He had bought Borah's old
house and liked to pose as a reformer, but he was a stolid Idahoan
reactionary. In 1964 he publicly came out in favor of Goldwater,
although he was a Democrat. "What Idaho needs is money," he
repeated, "and with money every problem disappears."

But Vernon K. Smith, who could be a great lawyer, was not a
member of the power elite. That elite was not interested in changing Idaho—or Boise. "We like it just as it is, small and friendly,"
said another lawyer, this one a member of the elite. "Isn't it nice
when you can walk down the main street of the state capital and
recognize half the people you see? What good would more business do?" He smiled, then ordered another round of drinks. We
were sitting in the lounge of the Hillcrest Country Club, over-

looking the city of Boise below and the majestic mountains behind it. Everyone there knew everybody else. Everyone was well dressed, even if informally, and everyone had some exciting gossip to talk about, or else an adventure—fishing, boating, hunting. It was the good life, all right. Who would want to change it?

Dr. Moser, for one. In his area, conditions were mighty bleak. He found that industries were unwilling to hire a man over forty, that economic security was nonexistent and that juvenile delinquency was constantly increasing. "The parents are usually vaguely uneasy about these [delinquent] affairs and usually react very violently in blaming the schools, the police, or their children's bad companions rather than themselves," he said. He went on to explain how there were no social workers, no services for vocational guidance, no marriage counseling. "In the entire realm of Mental Health the only services available are for the few persons who are casually and sporadically treated by physicians. At this time in Cascade alone there are six children with major but treatable emotional illnesses who are entirely without treatment." There is a general feeling that these problems "should not occur in this natural paradise," he said sardonically. What's worse, he added, is that "these problems will not be met within the foreseeable future by village, county or state agencies."

But how many of the members of the Hillcrest Country Club ever really saw what went on in these areas? They didn't even know that the same problems existed in Boise—except when a scandal shocked them into panic. But then why encourage such a scandal? Because it serves as a vivid warning. The homosexual scandal of 1955 forced all those nice people whom I met in 1965 at the Hillcrest Country Club to remember that progress only brings problems. Hating problems, they inevitably had to hate progress.

13

MORMONS, NEGROES AND
BIRCHERS

GREATER BOISE, which includes Garden City and the various residential hills surrounding Boise City, has almost 100,000 people. Boise itself has increased very little (only 0.3 percent between 1950 and 1960), but the suburbs have grown quite rapidly, and Boise has periodically incorporated them into its city limits so as to be able to tax their residents. This has not been inequitable, since most of the people living in these outlying areas work and earn money in Boise.

Boise has also increased in importance as a distribution center. Under Governor Smylie, all of Idaho's major cities, which are all located in the south, have been connected by good hard-surface roads, and communication with the north was improved. As a result, rail and especially truck traffic in and out of Boise has gained in importance, and the city has become not only the center of operation for Idaho, which it always was, but also a crucial pivotal nexus for the Northwest. Tourism has gained importance, and luxurious motels have been erected downtown and in surrounding areas. Some, like the Downtowner, are as gaudy—and expensive—as any fancy motel in the country.

This development has not pleased Boise's (and Idaho's) power elite. Some have profited from it, it is true. J. R. Simplot, for example, has diversified its activities to include construction, as well as lumber, farming, ranching, minerals, fertilizer and oil and gas exploration. But for the most part, the old city fathers have tried to keep Boise small and manageable, and they have done their best to make sure that the city remained "tight."

Boise is not a dry city, but the various bars and clubs feature as little exotic entertainment as possible. Every now and then, strip joints have blossomed, but they have usually been caught at some infraction and forced to close or change their entertainment. When I was there in 1965, the "Go-Go" fad had hit Boise, as it had the rest of the nation. But the girls in the cages (or the equivalents) were much more dressed and much less demonstrative than in New York, Boston, Washington or even Philadelphia, not to mention San Francisco, Seattle, Portland or Los Angeles.

In its first article on the homosexual scandal, *Time* talked of the lingering aura of the pioneering spirit in Boise. There was no such thing, nor is there today. Compared to Portland, for example, Boise was the stuffiest, deadest town in the Northwest—and Portland is no superhot spot. Most of Boise's sidewalks were asleep by seven at night, and the few blocks in the center of town where bars were open until late seemed no more hip than Greenwich, Connecticut. There were no legalized peep-show movies, no swinging night clubs. Legalized slot machines, which once flourished in the state, had been removed long before. Boise was no place to let off steam—except by getting drunk.

Of course, like Anytown, U.S.A., illegal operations of all sorts did exist, from gambling to prostitution. Through local friends I discovered a couple of places where, with the right introduction, one could buy anything, from drugs to pornographic books. But the prices, moderate in comparison to, say, Los Angeles, were much too high for the vast majority of Boiseans or Idahoans. A prostitute's fee of $20 is, I gather, not very high these days, but in a state where one out of every five families earns less than $3,000 a year—making it eligible for War on Poverty assistance—few youths could afford such prices.

I am not trying to imply that drugs, illicit sex or organized wildness should be available to every youth. But it is now generally accepted that there is less potential delinquency in towns where the inhabitants can let loose occasionally. The more restrictive the community, the more frustrated are the emotions and the more violent become the explosions. It seems to me quite clear that whenever an attempt is made to regulate behavior that is not antisocial through enforcement of all sorts of laws, not only is resentment created but also rebellion is encouraged. This, I think, was the case in Boise. It is no accident that in 1964 no less than 10.4 percent of all youths seventeen years old had committed some act that had brought them within the purview of the probate courts in Idaho. Although this did not mean that one out of every ten seventeen-year-olds was a juvenile delinquent, it revealed a much higher rate of juvenile agitation than in New York City, where sin and strife supposedly lurk behind every corner.

The repressed hostility against society that I felt in Boise and that seemed to me to stem from Boise's rigid conformity exhibited itself in even the most trivial of circumstances. I remember, for example, standing at a corner in downtown Boise one day waiting for the light to change. There was no traffic coming from any direction, but since I was aware by then that, because of my investigations, I had to behave as a model citizen, I repressed my instinct to cross against the light. There was a nineteen-year-old youth also waiting for the light. He was in an obvious hurry, yet did not dare to cross. I kept pace with him until he got to where he was going—the post office at the corner of the Capitol square—and we had time for quite a long conversation. I asked him why he had been afraid to jaywalk. "They're very strict about jaywalking around here," he answered.

But, said I, there was no traffic—and no visible cops.

"Yeah, I know," he mumbled disgustedly. "But Christ, this city stinks. You can't do anything."

I quickly told him how in New York we also have jaywalking laws and "Don't walk" neon signs but that, unfortunately for the accident rate, not many people pay attention to them.

"Well, this ain't New York," he said, then added in a significant *non sequitur:* "Here you don't do things on principle, not because it's bad. Only the rich can do what they want."

The hate and frustration pent up in that youth were potentially dangerous. If he could find twenty other kids who felt the way he did, they'd form a gang, and that gang might someday pull a robbery or smash somebody's property just for the hell of it. Life has to have some kicks, say the child psychologists. And Dr. Butler, in his analysis of the kids involved in homosexual affairs. found that most did it for just that—kicks. "Did you know that there's a uniformed cop at our dances?" a high-school student told me. In Boise, imposed conformity is great—and, therefore, it seems to me, so is the crime rate.

Such conformity has long been part of Idaho's history, mainly because of the religious beliefs of most of its population. Roughly 10 percent of Idahoans are Catholic, and almost half are Mormon. Most of the Catholics are Basques, descendants of sheepherder immigrants who settled in Idaho at the end of the last century and the beginning of this one. These Basques still maintain many of their old traditions. They dance the *jota,* drink from a *bota,* which is made of hides, and on festive occasions wear (with slight variations) their ancestral costume. The men wear a red *boina* (beret), scarf and sash, white pants and shirt, and white *alpargatas* (cord sandals) crisscrossed by red and green laces, the colors of the Basque flag. The women wear a red skirt, black apron and exterior corsage, white blouse, stockings and red-laced *alpargatas,* and a two-pronged white handkerchief as a bonnet. The Basques are a tough, gregarious, happy people who work hard and consider the family unit sacred. They are an admirable people. In most Basque homes, however, any and all discussion of sex is taboo. Their rigid attitude toward normal human sexual desires—and their scorn for the findings of modern psychology—tend to accentuate frustrations among the young.

But at least the Basques do not forbid liquor, coffee, tea, smoking or gambling. The Mormons forbid all of these "vices," and they are so strict about it that any infraction is interpreted as a loss of religion. There are many explanations of the Mormons' strictness—including, of course, the Mormons' own, which is based on their revelations and their teachings. From a sociological point of view, however, the reason may very well lie in the rigors and the persecutions that the Mormons had to endure, the toughness that they needed to survive.

Mormonism technically began in 1823 in Palmyra, New York, when an angel who called himself Moroni appeared before Joseph Smith, an eighteen-year-old Vermont-born farmboy. The angel revealed to him the existence of sacred records of the Gospel as made known by Christ the Redeemer to the ancient inhabitants of America. In 1827, the angel became convinced that Joseph Smith had passed the test of good behavior and showed him the way to these records, which were in the form of gold tablets and were buried in the woods near Smith's home. The angel also gave Joseph the key to the tablets' marks, or code. Joseph's translation, which is called the Book of Mormon, tells the story of how America was founded by people from Israel between 2000 b.c. and 420 a.d. Basing their religion on this book, Joseph and a few associates in 1830 founded the Church of Jesus Christ of Latter-Day Saints and immediately set out to seek converts.

As the new religious organization grew, persecution began, and since Joseph, who was proclaimed Prophet, Seer and Revelator, sought to establish the land of Zion, the Mormons moved to Kirtland, Ohio, where the first "Stake of Zion" was established. The first Mormon temple was constructed there in 1836, and the organization of the LDS church was defined: Smith was to be president (the presidency included a president and two counselors), backed by twelve apostles with quorums of seventy to assist them. High priests, patriarchs, bishops, and stake presidents were also instituted, but the church remained basically laic in that any member in good standing automatically belonged to the priesthood and could rise in rank simply by his good deeds and the confidence of his fellow priests. But it was not Smith who clearly defined the organization. For Smith was killed in 1844, after more persecutions (and the failure of the Mormons' unchartered bank). He was murdered by a mob while awaiting trial in Carthage, Illinois, for having suppressed a rival newspaper in the Mormons' new community of Nauvoo, Illinois.

A split developed in the church, caused by Smith's new revelations, which had included the doctrine of plural marriages. Those who did not approve and who refused to recognize Smith's successor set up the Reorganized Church of Jesus Christ of Latter-Day Saints and settled mostly in Missouri, with headquarters in Independence. The majority, however, followed the new president, an extremely gifted and tenacious leader—Brigham Young. A shrewd organizer, a vigorous pragmatist and a dedicated proselytizer, Young led the advance guard of his flock—143 men, 3 women and 2 children—across the Great Plains, through hostile Indian territory and over hazardous mountains to the desert valley of the Great Salt Lake, 1,100 miles away. He arrived there, after almost a year and a half of marching, on July 24, 1847. "This is the Place," he said—the Promised Land. And there the Mormons established what is now Salt Lake City and the state of Utah, turning the desert into a rich valley through diligence, hard work and irrigation.

The Mormons' troubles did not end with the blossoming of the desert, however. There were constant Indian attacks (which finally ended because of Young's wise policy that "it is better to feed the Indians than to fight them") and years of friction with the United States government, specifically over the Mormons' polygamous practices. (Brigham Young himself supposedly had twenty-seven wives—some scholars think it was more like fifty.) After the U.S. Supreme Court upheld the validity of the federal law prohibiting plural marriages in 1890, Mormon President Wilford Woodruff issued a manifesto (which Mormons consider only a recommendation without the force of revelation) advising Mormons to obey the law. Not all Mormons have done so, and the government periodically tries to crack down on violators. The last attempt was in 1958, but it was wholly unsuccessful, since even monogamous Mormons refuse to testify against their polygamous neighbors. Besides, many adult Mormons are themselves the offspring of polygamous marriages.

Polygamy is not the only unusual dogma of the Latter-Day Saints. Another, which has yet to be changed, or "adapted," is the belief that Negroes belong to the "marked" or fallen race. One of the plates that Joseph Smith translated claims that while Cain was marked for having killed his brother Abel, Ham, one of Noah's sons, perpetuated the marked race by marrying Egyptus, a Negro. The connection is hard to follow—except for a Mormon. Was Egyptus already "marked" simply because she was Negro? In that case Ham had nothing to do with it, and another explanation is needed as to why the Negro race is marked. Or did Ham perpetuate the mark because he was guilty of miscegenation? In this case, the "marked" would be those who crossbreed races, not all Negroes. Whatever the Mormons' theological reasoning, the effect is that they consider Negroes inferior. A Negro cannot become a priest or hold any position in the church. Nor is he allowed inside a temple, no matter how faithfully he follows the Mormon teachings.

In practical terms, Utah, where the population is more than 70 percent Mormon, has resisted civil-rights legislation. In 1965 it passed an amendment to the fair employment practices act that specifically exempted all church-operated businesses. Such businesses are extensive. The Mormon church, which claims more than 2,500,000 believers, is extremely rich, since members contribute 10 percent of their gross earnings to the church. This tithing amounts to at least $125,000,000 a year, which has been invested in all sorts of enterprises, from real estate to the powerful Utah-Idaho Sugar Company, from newspapers and television stations to ranches in Canada, Florida and California. In fact, so rich has the modern Church of Jesus Christ of Latter-Day Saints become that during the Depression it was capable of taking care of 55,000 Mormons who would otherwise have been on federal relief.

The Mormon church does not recognize the federal government's responsibility toward the citizens it governs and thus does not allow its members to accept welfare aid. Brigham Young University, in Provo, Utah, has almost 20,000 students, and because of its building program it is entitled to federal funds. In 1963, for example, it could have received $4,500,000. But it refused, as it always has, to accept federal handouts. "We take care of our own," say the Mormons, and they do. Each ward (parish) runs small farms and industries, not only to provide canned foods and clothes for its poor but also to provide jobs. In addition, church members are expected to support local Mormon welfare agencies—in addition to their regular 10 percent contribution. Members are also expected to give much of their free time to the church. A typical married man of thirty often works four nights a week, and his wife three, in one of the many LDS projects, from helping the needy to proselytizing. It is an extremely taxing and severe religion. Orders concerning the church are absolute, since they represent divine revelations.

Mormonism is also an aggressive religion, and although it complies with state and federal laws, it does not basically accept the separation of church and state. Since the LDS is fundamentally a lay church, it does not recognize how such separation can apply to itself. Brigham Young once said in 1863: "The time will come when we will give laws to the nations of the earth." And although most Mormons will publicly insist that they have gone beyond that stage, in private they are convinced that someday they will have converted enough people to turn America—and the world—into the Promised Land. Thus they expect every Mormon child to attend Mormon schools, if not during the day, at least on Sundays and evenings, and to continue their religious training in college. After college, Mormon youths are expected to spend two years in missionary work, during which time they cannot be drafted (although Mormons are not conscientious objectors).

All this, especially their attitude toward the federal government—which persecuted them a century or less ago and forced them to abandon their polygamous practices—makes most Mormons extremely conservative. And since they take every aspect of life very seriously, they naturally tend to be intensely active politically. Many are sympathetic to the John Birch Society, including former Secretary of Agriculture Ezra Taft Benson, who was one of the twelve apostles of the LDS church, and his son Reed, who is a staff member of the Birch Society in Washington.

The Mormons are also quite active in local politics, backing the candidates that most fit into their ideology. In Utah, the result is that no politician can be truly successful without being a Mormon.

In Idaho, however, the Mormons are not that powerful. Although the south is at least 40 percent Mormon—and the southeast perhaps as much as 60 percent—the LDS has to fight to get its candidates elected, and they do not succeed all the time. Of course, the LDS never interferes in the political sphere openly. It does so through political-front organizations, such as the Citizens for Better Government or the Idaho Allied Civic Forces. These front organizations are headed by nonpartisans—or rather by both Republicans and Democrats—which gives them the appearance of being genuinely interested in better government and not just conservatism. In fact, however, the LDS tends to support only conservatives, from either party.

In 1956, the LDS tried to use the organizational status of the church to nominate for U.S. Senator two candidates—Dr. Ray J. Davis on the Republican ticket and Claude Burtenshaw on the Democratic. That way the LDS would come out ahead no matter who won the election. The LDS campaign included the following recommendations: [1]

1. Secure the appointment of a stake chairman
2. Urge ward organization
3. Support Ray J. Davis (or Burtenshaw as the case may be) for U.S. Senator
4. Support Hamer Budge for U.S. Congressman, second district
5. Support acceptable county officers
6. Attempt to file precinct committeemen favorable to us
7. Each stake chairman is to collect $150 immediately for the Davis campaign to be sent as collected to President Reed Blatter, 2900 Twenty-sixth Street, Idaho Falls. . . . The need is urgent in order to tie up favorable TV and radio time. . . .
8. As quickly as the ward committee is organized, distribute campaign folders on Mr. Davis. Have committee members make note

[1] Published in the column *"Politically Speaking,"* by John Corlett, in *The Idaho Daily Statesman*, August 8, 1956.

of each person who indicates an interest in the candidate or who is willing to do some work for him. Caution! No attempt should be made to tell people how to vote. Only tell them the facts. In addition to the information in the folder about Mr. Davis, he is a life-long member of the church. He has held many positions and was bishop for over four years.

9. People should make sure they are registered. If they voted in the last election they need not register again.

10. About two weeks before election another visit should be made. Campaign material will be furnished you.

11. On election day, the ward chairman should make arrangements to have a checker at the polls to check off from a previously prepared list the names of those who have voted. Two shifts will likely be necessary and checkers should be persons who know about everyone in the precinct. The law permits each party to have a checker. We don't represent the parties, so this will have to be done outside of the polling place. A car parked in a strategic place probably would answer. In the afternoon the checker should furnish the ward chairman or his representative with a list of those who have not voted. They should be called or called on by a person from a previously organized group to get out the voters.

12. Support of other candidates—which others are being supported, such as county candidates—can be done for them at the same time the visit is made for Dr. Davis.

Hamer Budge, whose support was recommended by the LDS, was already U.S. Representative from Idaho's Second Congressional District. He was very conservative, and Corlett stated in his column that LDS support for him was "designed to rub off his [Budge's] prestige on the 'Citizens' group." Corlett added: "Budge won his way to Congress on his own and without help. And since he is unopposed in the primary there is no particular reason for special action." But in 1960, the Second Congressional District, which includes Pocatello and Bonneville, where growth and development had brought in a strong moderate element, finally threw Budge out. In his place was elected a fighting liberal, Democrat Ralph Harding, who was also a member of the LDS church.

In 1963, however, after Ezra Taft Benson, Ike's Secretary of Agriculture, praised the John Birch Society, Harding courageously delivered on the House floor an impassioned attack on Benson—who was, let us remember, an apostle of their church. Shortly thereafter, Benson was dispatched by his superiors in the church to a European LDS mission, but the campaign against Harding in Idaho became intense. In 1964 he was defeated for reelection. State Senator Perry Swisher, from Pocatello, attributed the defeat to a "death-wish"—that is, to the tactical mistake of having pounced on Benson. In the *Idaho Observer*, editor Sam Day commented that

> the theory [of the death-wish] is interesting, but one doesn't need a psychoanalyst's couch to explain Harding's defeat. He lost because he was too liberal. Not too liberal for the nation, but too liberal for Idaho's Second Congressional District. He was too liberal in the sense that he was too committed to programs of domestic welfare; urban relief and redevelopment, medical care for the aged, full civil rights for minority groups. Close identification with such programs would have been an asset in most districts, but in Idaho it enabled his opponents to identify him with big government and big spending, objects of a provincial distrust.

Mormon attitudes toward Negroes also affect civil rights in Idaho. In theory, Idaho has excellent civil-rights legislation. In practice, however, discrimination is extensive. Negroes, no matter how well educated, can expect only menial jobs. In 1965 there was only one Negro lawyer in the state, no Negro policemen. Only a few Negroes (out of 1,500) had escaped the ghettos, whether in Boise or Pocatello. That year, Father James P. Trotter, former president of the Pocatello Civil Rights Committee, put it this way: "In Selma, Negroes can't vote. In Pocatello, they can't live outside the 'ghetto.' " A United Presbyterian Church field study reported in 1965: [2]

---

[2] "Report on Field Trip and Feasibility Study of Pocatello, Idaho, April 21–24, 1965" (United Presbyterian Church, U.S.A.). Mimeographed. Names of operatives withheld, since they are secretly continuing their surveys throughout Idaho.

[In Pocatello] the housing for Negro families in the east side of town is extremely inadequate. Some families have made attempts to paint and refurbish, but the general neighborhood is cheaply constructed in the first place.

Most of the streets in town are in bad repair. In the Negro section they are deplorable, full of potholes and deep ruts. Small mountains of trash have been dumped in many of the side yards. There are few trees, gardens or sidewalks. There is a general air of neglect and hopelessness. A few Negro middle-class people have escaped from the old ghetto and occupy more attractive and modern housing in a new ghetto not far from the Presbyterian Church. In fact, the old ghetto is within three or four blocks of the Presbyterian Church. The Presbyterian Church is obviously "inner city," but there is little evidence that it ministers to minority groups in the area. . . .

All of the persons whom we interviewed in the Negro community spoke of the housing problem and the fact that it is extremely difficult if not impossible for Negroes to acquire property outside the ghetto. White persons whom we interviewed affirmed that there was no restriction as such, it was simply that the Negroes didn't have the money to buy the property that was available. Mr. and Mrs. Conley [the Baptist minister and his wife] told us that this was not true. There are some Negroes who could well afford to acquire property which was not available to them. . . .

In Almeda, which is now incorporated in Pocatello city, the land is still controlled by the Mormons, and it has about 90 per cent Mormon occupancy. This whole section of the community is closed to Negro occupancy. There seems little likelihood of changing this situation. . . .

In my own survey of the 350-odd Negroes living in the Boise ghetto by the train tracks, I found that the older generation strongly opposed rocking the boat. Most worked for the railroad, for Simplot or as janitors around town. The women were employed mostly as day maids, with no social benefits whatsoever. Since the maids were paid in cash, their employers did not even contribute to the U.S. Social Security Administration.

The younger residents of the ghetto, however, were mostly waiting to leave. Some of the boys had menial jobs, but the girls complained that they couldn't even become waitresses. The rate of dropouts was high: Out of twenty-six youths who were willing to talk to me, twenty had never finished high school, either in Boise or elsewhere, and twenty-two told me they were going to "blow this joint" for some decent city—Seattle being the favorite choice. The youths were bitter toward the community at large as well as toward their own elders, who, as one youngster told me, "just shit in their pants, man, every time we say we're going to put the heat on. They tell us, things are great, and start talking about the way things are in the South. Man, I tell you, they'll shine shoes with their tongues as long as nobody comes around in white sheets." I asked them to what they attributed Boise's *de facto* discrimination. "Christ, man," replied one tall Negro, who said he was unemployed. "Did you know we're inferior to you? We stink, man!" And one girl quickly added: "Besides, we've been cursed by the Lord, or didn't you know?" When they stopped giggling, I asked if they attributed this to the Mormons. "They're all the same. They all think the same way, whether they admit it or not!"

But there was no doubt that they had heard these remarks from the Mormons, whose anti-Negro prejudices are deep-rooted. David Underhill, the Harvard graduate who in 1965 was working for the *Southern Courier*, told me about one experience he had had a decade earlier.

"I don't know how things are now in Boise," he said, "but back then, Negroes had to cut their own hair and sit in the balconies in the movies. I was head of the Youth Group in the First Presbyterian Church and I wanted to get together with the equivalent group at the African-American Episcopal Church, but pressure was too strong. Every year, for graduation, the graduating class at the Boise High School voted on who would address them. Inevitably, because of the distribution, the vote ended up with one Catholic, one Protestant, and one Mormon. But there was an agreement that if any one of the three chosen could not attend, whoever had gotten vote number four would fill in. When it was my graduating class, I tried to get Reverend Brown, of the African-American Church, invited. His name had not been put on the list submitted by the Boise Ministerial Association. I protested and got his name on it. There were lots of protests, but I thought we could win. A good friend of mine, a Mormon girl, told me: 'You are always trying to ruin things, now you'll ruin my graduation.' But I was president of the student body and governor of Boy's State, organized by the American Legion, and I guess I had some pull. Anyway, we fought on and we got Reverend Brown on the list and he came out fourth. Then it turned out that the Catholic priest who had been elected as one of the first three could not make it. Well, another priest was invited to take his place. We protested, but we failed. Reverend Brown was not invited to address the graduating class."

Right-wing influence has also traditionally supported the police strongly. In 1965, I asked Police Chief Jack Barney whether he had received such support. He said that he didn't know where it originated, but, yes, he had. He handed me a pamphlet titled "Support Your Local Police," which he thought was prepared by the John Birch Society. It condemned such shows as the CBS documentary "The Biography of a Bookie Joint," which, it said, "made all working officers appear to be graft corrupted" whereas all the "facts" in the show were "fiction." The pamphlet also claimed that "it has been conclusively established that the Communist Party is deeply involved in racial agitation as well as instigation and manipulation of riots," and it went on to imply that any charge of "police brutality" or "cruelty" is Communist propaganda. It then insisted that the majority of traffic accidents "are caused by traffic rule violations," which is as untrue as its previous statements,[3] and concluded with an appeal to "Oppose the Continuance or Establishment of Unethical [Police] Review Boards." Perhaps the cutest recommendation was this: "When you see or hear questionable criticism of your local police by news media, or by a commentator, do something about it. Find the real facts if you can. Usually, the fellow officers of those being criticized will give you the unvarnished truth."

I found that especially amusing, since at the very moment I

[3] See Ralph Nader: *Unsafe at Any Speed* (Grossman, 1965).

read the pamphlet in Police Chief Barney's large office, in back of City Hall, I was clutching under my arm a thick book entitled *A Survey of the Police Department, Boise City, Idaho,* which had been prepared and written, at the request of Boise's mayor, by the Field Service Division, International Association of Chiefs of Police, April 1965. The survey insisted that Boise's police department had many problems. One exception was the youth-morals squad, which, by 1965, having learned from the 1955 scandal, was doing precisely the opposite of what the Birchers and most Mormons would want it to, as we shall see later. Otherwise, the investigating cops found the investigated cops incredibly inept. The crime rate had soared, the detective bureau was inefficient, the recruiting standards for rookies were too low, the paperwork and bureaucratic services were impossibly confused, and the organization was top-heavy. Said the survey: "On the average there is one supervisor or administrator for each 3.3 police officers or, including civilians, 3.9." The result is that "certain thefts have been ignored and, in fact, information concerning the thefts has not been recorded. . . . The chief of police has not instituted proper staff control over the receipt and recording of complaints of crimes and other violations."

The inability of the Boise police to investigate crimes was shown through the following statistics based on the year 1963:

Offense class	Offenses known	Cleared by arrest	Persons charged
Forcible rape	2	2	2
Aggravated assault	45	44	31
Burglary	225	59	53
Larceny	1,632	140	147
Auto theft	100	32	25

In the cases of rape and aggravated assault, where there are always witnesses, the police record was not bad. In the case of burglary, where there are sometimes witnesses, the record was not so good. And in the cases of larceny and auto theft, where studious investigation and follow-ups by the police are usually needed, the record was horrible.

Other tables presented by the investigating cops showed that in 1963 two individuals who had violated the weapons law (illegal possession) were convicted, that three out of four prostitutes and one narcotics violator apprehended were found guilty. But of fifty-six individuals arrested for embezzlement or fraud and eleven arrested for forgery, not one was convicted. The investigating staff for the International Association of Chiefs of Police concluded that "a definite break with traditional practices is in order, thus permitting investigative personnel to concentrate on the more important phases of their potential to the end that an increase in the qualitative results of their efforts may be realized." Which was a polite, diplomatic way of saying that Boise's investigative staff just didn't know how to handle its business.

The survey did give one extenuating factor for the poor performance of Boise's police: They were underpaid. But John Mirich, who teaches police science at Treasure Valley Community College in Ontario, had another explanation. In 1965 he said that the police simply need better training. "The typical police officer must know how to handle the typical citizen . . . 95 or 96 percent of law enforcement is not physical. We don't wrestle with people any more. The problem is psychological."

To the John Birch Society, this is pure tommyrot. Any psychological interference or imposed psychological conditioning on cops is tantamount to Communist subversion. In February 1965, John Rousselot, national public-relations director of the John Birch Society, came to Idaho as a guest of the Treasure Valley Freedom Forum, a strongly Mormon right-wing organization. Rousselot's topic was "United Nations—Instrument of the International Communist Conspiracy." And he meant every word of it. When he ended, he was asked questions. Is the UN to blame for a breakdown in U.S. morals? Partly, he said, but "also the Communists, the Socialists and the believers in centralized government." Then somebody asked, How about the churches? "Too much of the stuff has been coming from the pulpit," he said. "I know of a minister who has been advocating that homosexuals be accepted by society as a means of relieving social tensions."

Obviously a Communist minister! And perhaps—why not—Rousselot even meant to imply that all homosexuals are Communists.

In 1955 and 1956, an awful lot of Boiseans, already convinced that Negroes are inferior, that cops are great and that their own way of looking at the world would someday become the law of nations, also thought that homosexuals were Communists.

14

THE SECOND DAY OF RECKONING

IN VIEW of all the pressures confronting Judge Koelsch and Judge Young, who had to sentence the homosexuals, it is quite amazing that in 1956 they suddenly seemed to have become more lenient. Or perhaps it was that Boise's two psychiatrists, Dale Cornell and John Butler, were finally making headway in the courts. Whatever the reason, Boiseans were surprised to learn, on January 14, 1956, that Judge Koelsch had sentenced one of the homosexuals to six years' probation. He was the first—besides Brokaw, who had been a stool pigeon—not to get a jail term.

The homosexual who was given probation testified during his hearing that he had been led to believe by Prosecutor Blaine Evans and Sheriff Doc House that he would get medical attention if he cooperated. But he had little to say about other homosexuals, much about himself. He admitted having had homosexual experiences for ten years—the first in the Navy, the last the previous May—and he said that he had been under treatment by Dr. Cornell since December 1. "Fundamentally," said Cornell when he testified, his patient was "a heterosexual," and his mother's death when he was a boy could have "upset the applecart." There was also no proof that the defendant had ever been involved with minors.

In sentencing him to probation, Judge Koelsch pointed out that the defendant was not "the aggressive type." But he placed many conditions upon his probation, including that "the defendant shall seek and accept treatment from Dr. Dale Cornell of Boise, Idaho, until such time as Dr. Dale Cornell informs the defendant's probation officer that the defendant is no longer in need of medical or psychiatric treatment. In the event that for any reason Dr. Cornell is unable to continue to treat the defendant, the defendant will seek and accept treatment from a psychiatrist approved by the District Court of the Third Judicial District of the State of Idaho, in and for the County of Ada."

The next case to come up for sentencing was that of the pianist, who also had not been involved with minors. The facts of the case were rather typical, and Judge Young studied them well, not only to learn about the individual involved but also to broaden his knowledge of homosexuality in general. Also, the pianist's case seemed especially important, since it had a bearing on another homosexual case—that of Gordon Larsen. The same accomplice, Eldon Halverson, was involved.

The pianist was born in Boise in 1922. Fred Davis, the district probation and parole agent, inserted the following description, with spelling mistakes, into the record:

> The subject relates that he was raised in a home that was dominated by his own Parents and his Grand Parents and being the only Grand son he grew up to be very much of a Sissy, the way his Mother and Grand Mother wished. Moreover it is said that he was an 8 months old baby at Birth and then he had scarlet fever at the age of 3 years he had measles a Mastoid Operation at the age of 4, Tonsels removed at the age of 4, glasses at the age of 8, besides having a broken leg when 7. He was a very sickly child and this caused him to be very much under the domination of the Women folk of the home.
> When he did get to play with neighborhood kids he recalls being ignored by the boys even when in the early grades of school.
> Education:
> Relates he sucured Average Grades in school graduated from Boise High School in 1939. Majoring in Science. Graduated BJC in 1941 in Music.
> Military:

Rejected from Military Service due to Eye Sight.

Marital: Never Married

Past Offenses:

   None:

   F B I report . . . . reveals . . . Inv Pervert.

This is related as being a routine check up by the Officials.

There were no charges pressed.

Present Offense:

   The having of relationship with a male by name of Eldon Halverson on the 15th day of May 1955.

Employment:

   * * * is an accomplished Musician has followed that as a vocation
since finishing the Boise Junior College, worked as such after leaving
Boise going to Washington D C where he worked in Night clubs etc.
On returning to Boise worked for one of the T V Companies. * * *
owns his own Piano also an Organ which are in the Home of his
Parents at * * *

Summary:

   * * * was born to a good family but one where the Mother appears
to be dominating factor. She was interested in Music and it is said
that her son had to spend meny hours at the Piano practicing and
playing and she saw fit that there was nothing else that distracted him
from the Piano.

He was a sickly child having all the diseases known and then some.
at the time his parents and Grand Parents lived in the same house
and he was pretty mcu under the influence of two women his mother
and Grand Mother. He relates that as a child in school he was
ignored by other boys and was referred to as a Sissy even thru High
school.

He related that he thot there was something wrong with his thinking
but was ignorant of what was right as he and his father did not discuss
life. In fact he did not go with his Father to any of the Sporting
functions that usually a father and son enjy together.

Because of this the subject relates that he grew to where he was not
interested in Women or girls but became attracted to Men.

Since his Arrest and the assistance he has had from Various Doctors
the subject relates that he an altogether outlook on life much to the
better. . . .

(I am still fascinated by Boiseans' sense of syntax and spelling. "Thot" for "thought" may be shorthand, and anyway, many people can't spell. But why should "Grand Mother" and "Piano" always be capitalized, mother and father sometimes, but girls never? And "High" capitalized but "school" not? Mind you, this is a probation officer!)

The pianist's record also included testimony, in the form of letters, from two psychiatrists: Richard B. Jarvis of Seattle and John Butler. Jarvis had submitted two letters, both addressed to Judge Young, one dated December 24, 1955, the other January 12, 1956. The first read, in part:

> * * * was examined in the office on 21 December and 22 December 1955. On 23 December I admitted him to hospital in this building where I performed an examination under narcosis induced by intravenous sodium amytal.
>
> * * * was uniformly strightforward [sic] and cooperative during all examinations. His story was logical, coherent and consistent. I feel quite confident that he was truthful.
>
> He admits to a long series of homosexual contacts over the past thirteen years. These have been oral-genital contacts with willing adult males. He denies, and I think truthfully, any interest in perverse activities involving younger people, the inflicting of pain or use of force. In other words, I find no evidence of a tendency to the more malignant symptoms of sexual deviation.
>
> * * * has himself been distressed by his inclinations, which he recognizes as being contrary to the public welfare and personally immature. He has hesitated to seek medical help, fearing that he might be cast out as a pariah or that he might find that there was no hope for him. He states that he has an earnest desire to alter his personality, to become heterosexual and to marry. The manner in which he states this thesis and defends it under probing leads me to feel that this is indeed his conscious desire and is not dictated by expediency. The pattern of his history indicates that this is also a genuine feeling within his unconscious, in short, that he is one of those fortunate individuals who is not aligned against himself.
>
> He is remarkably free from other psychopathologic symptoms, has an active and well-integrated conscience and a strong feeling of re-

sponsibility to society. I would not expect him ever to become engaged in criminality except the present situation which is the expression of a type of neurosis. It is possible, of course, to lie under barbiturate narcosis, but I found his answers remarkably consistent with the material he had produced in the waking state. . . .

The second letter simply affirmed Dr. Jarvis' "willingness to accept * * * for treatment if the Court should find that probation or suspension of sentence is justified." And it went on to explain what that treatment would entail and that there was no way of knowing how long it would take or, in fact, whether it would succeed.

Dr. Butler's letter, dated February 23, 1956, confirmed the findings of Dr. Jarvis, added that since the patient's return to Boise from Seattle he had been seeing a lay analyst in Boise almost daily, and concluded:

> . . . at the time of my interview with * * *, he gave evidence of having a tremendously deep grasp and understanding of the forces that had operated upon his personality development. He related several factors which reflected considerable clinical improvement of his own behavior. He has practically stopped the practice of masturbation. He is now for the first time beginning to be attracted to certain personality components of women. He realizes that a complete reformation of his personality is improbable; but does know that if he searches out certain personality qualities, and later physical qualities in women, he may be able to find a marital partner.
>
> In view of the present orientation of * * *, I believe the problem of his rehabilitation is not a problem, but already an accomplished fact. . . .

In other words, the pianist was a perfect example of the type of homosexual that Dr. Bieber and his associates considered changeable. Judge Young took all these factors into advisement and on March 9, 1956, sentenced the pianist to five years' probation, conditional on continued psychiatric treatment. "You can straighten yourself out in this matter," said Judge Young.

What had happened to the concept of punishment? Why, suddenly, had both judges decided to listen carefully to the recommendations of trained personnel? Judge Young did say that he had decided on probation "primarily" because no minors were involved, but other homosexuals who had not been involved with minors and who had been recommended for probation by psychiatrists had already been sentenced to the penitentiary. Besides, once it is admitted that the sentence can vary according to the character of the criminal and/or the circumstances surrounding the crime—instead of the crime itself—then the argument that punishment is imposed on the guilty in order to show justice to the innocent is no longer valid. If I, the innocent, am to be convinced that stealing does not pay, I will want to be sure that all thieves caught are punished. Otherwise, if I am suddenly told that thieves who are one-armed or who hold guns upside down or who are poor can escape punishment, then I might very well try to arrange favorable conditions to justify stealing. Under the deterrent theory, there can be no room for exceptions since all human beings consider themselves exceptions at one time or another.

Of course, few judges apply the deterrent theory so strictly that they do not take into account such extenuating circumstances as age, character and so on. But when they do, they listen to expert advice. They do not assume that because they are judges in a court of law they are also psychologists and sociologists. It would have been perfectly logical for Boise's judges to send all homosexuals to prison on the deterrent theory or to jail only those who had involved minors. But once the judges began to find extenuating circumstances to vary their sentences in both groups —the homosexuals who had involved only consenting adults and those who had preyed on minors—they flouted their own stated logic. A judge has no right, it seems to me, to ignore psychiatric evidence in some cases on the grounds that "not to punish a criminal would be unfair to the innocent" and then use psychiatric evidence in other similar cases to justify probation on the grounds that the crime was committed under special circumstances. Not even judges can have their cake and eat it too.

The case of the pianist has a happy ending. On May 22, 1958,

Fred B. Davis, the Idaho parole agent who did not write a grammatically correct statement in 1955, wrote a letter to Judge Young in which he stated that the pianist had fulfilled all the conditions of his probation, had moved to California with permission, had obtained a job and had continued treatment. He further stated that the Adult Department of Probation of San Francisco had recommended his final discharge. Not only was Mr. Davis' letter correctly written, but its recommendations were sustained. The pianist became a totally free man.

On March 23, 1956, another homosexual who had not been involved with minors was also probated by Judge Koelsch, with the warning that the punishment (probation) would be harsh anyway since "you'll be the object of ridicule and scorn." A week later, Koelsch probated another man, this one on the grounds that the crime had occurred three years earlier. In this case the crime had been with a minor, but Koelsch pointed out that there was no evidence of any crimes since the one in question. Thus the criteria became more and more confusing, and perhaps because of that, on March 30, 1956, Gordon Larsen, whose "crime" had been committed with a consenting adult—Eldon Halverson—decided to plead not guilty. His lawyer was Vernon K. Smith.

In the next few months, the people of Boise tended to forget the homosexual scandal, or at least not to talk about it. Dr. Jack Steneck was hired by the state Health Department to set up a mental-health clinic (under Dr. Butler), which was obviously a step taken by State Health Director L. J. Peterson to bring preventive mental health to Idaho. But few Boiseans cared about preventive measures. Also, the next few months featured other excitements. Former Senator Glen Taylor ran against Frank Church for the Democratic nomination for Senator, and lost by only 200 votes. Then came the election itself, in which Church defeated Welker. Prosecutor Blaine Evans decided he had had enough of prosecuting homosexuals and was obviously well known enough to aim for higher office, and so he ran for the state senate and won. Finally, there was the Baker murder trial. All these goings-on were enough to eclipse, for a while at least, the three most important homosexual cases still pending: Moore and Wilson on appeal to the State Supreme Court, and Larsen.

Tex, as the Baker youth was called by his friends, got the benefit of a great defense—at the hands not of Carl Burke, who had first represented Theresa Baker, but of Sylvan A. Jeppesen, who later became U.S. attorney. The testimony presented by Jeppesen described Tex's father as a violent, brutal man who terrorized his family and had been involuntarily committed to the mental hospital at Blackfoot. After his release, the father had attacked his wife and Tex's sister with his fists and, according to the sister's testimony, "forced mother to eat a cigarette and then chew up a piece of soap." Jeppesen then called on Probate Judge Ariel Crowley of Idaho City, where the Baker family was living at the time, and the judge confirmed that the mother had bruises all over her face when she appeared before him to charge her husband with battery. Jeppesen also successfully blocked any reference to Baker's juvenile record. Once, after a deputy sheriff testified that he had seen Mrs. Baker's bruises, Prosecutor Evans asked, "Do you know the boy?" Jeppesen leaped to his feet, accused the prosecutor of trying to introduce Tex Baker's past into the trial and threatened to demand a mistrial if it were. Judge Young sustained him.

With the "insane character" of the father established, Jeppesen's insistence that Tex had killed his father in self-defense began to gain ground. The lawyer showed how the youth's bragging that he would kill his father could very easily have been that he would kill his father *if* he attacked his mother. And Tex's own testimony was confusing enough to be believable. He explained that he fired more than once because the first time "I thought I hit the plate instead of my father, so I fired again." When the prosecution pointed out that Tex had been told his father was still living and had walked back and fired twice more, Jeppesen claimed that by then the boy was "too hysterical and frightened" to know what he did and why. The prosecution demanded a verdict of first-degree murder (but did not ask for the death penalty). Jeppesen, who had been appointed by the court, demanded acquittal on the grounds of self-defense.

After more than eight hours of deliberation, interrupted so the jurors could re-hear a tape recording of Baker's testimony, the verdict was voluntary manslaughter. Only then was Blaine Evans allowed to introduce Baker's previous delinquency record, in his motion to forbid probation, and Judge Young agreed. He sentenced Tex Baker to the maximum allowed by law—ten years. With good conduct, the boy could be freed after a little more than three years. No wonder that Jeppesen said that he thought his client had received "an eminently fair trial" and that he did not plan to appeal. The only question that remained was whether Baker's conviction would affect the outcome of Moore's appeal.

Moore's defense attorney, John A. Carver, Jr., hoped that it would, and he submitted a brief explaining why it should. He also challenged Koelsch's points in sentencing Moore. Carver pointed out that "the naked statement that protection to society is involved begs the question. We have to protect society from disease, too, but we have to take into account whether the disease is arrested, communicable, or the like. In this case, the uncontradicted testimony was that the tendency was under control, and could be kept under control. In other words, there was neither a finding nor a basis for a finding that society needs protection from this appellant"—Moore. Carver also challenged the rationale of deterrence. "The all-male society of a prison, however well run, is not a deterrent environment," he said. "In some cases, contrary to deterrence, prison may represent exactly the kind of society most desired by the violator." And Carver questioned the principle of punishment as well. "It is exactly as if we were to make tuberculosis a crime. Straight punishment is on a par with the Salem witchcraft in moral justification."

Idaho's attorney general, Graydon W. Smith, countered bluntly. "If a parasitic homosexual can prey upon society, including even our teen-age boys, for thirteen years and then, when brought to the bar of justice, be immune to our Idaho law, why not all criminals?" The brunt of his argument, however, was strictly on the letter of the law. He said:

> The law of Idaho is very plain and has been observed and applied by the District Court from which this appeal is taken. So far as the personal opinions of those who have written books on the subject of mental illness and its results are concerned, it is of no importance whether they approve of Idaho law in such matters as this or not. Those who do not should address their complaints to Idaho's legislative body. Until they do and until and unless such a body sees fit to change Idaho law, we submit that there is nothing that either the judicial department or the executive department can do about it. . . .
>
> Accordingly, at this point we think it suffices to say only that while all normally-minded adults will enthusiastically welcome the day, if it ever comes, when someone or some group has discovered the real cause of such crimes as here concerned, together with the means of eliminating that cause, that certainly has not happened yet. In the meantime, society must depend wholly upon our laws and their proper enforcement. That has been the bulwark of social well-being since the dawn of history.

Except for that last highfalutin sentence Attorney General Smith's argument was perfectly sound. But both Judge Koelsch and Judge Young had already shown that they were willing not to follow the letter of the law. They had given probation terms to various kinds of homosexuals, involved with either consenting adults or minors, and they had invoked all sorts of rationales for doing so. Thus, though the respondent's brief was to the point, it would have been hypocritical for Koelsch or Young to agree with it. But the appeal was not to Judge Koelsch or Young. It was to the Idaho Supreme Court, composed of a panel of judges.

Supreme Court Chief Justice C. J. Taylor briefly reviewed the case, then stated:

> The primary consideration is, and presumptively will always be, the good order and protection of society. All other factors are, and must be, subservient to that end. Important as are the humanitarian considerations affecting the accused, his family and other relatives, and the importance to society of rehabilitation itself, such considerations

cannot be allowed to control or defeat punishment, where other factors are ignored or subordinated to the detriment of society.

His conclusion: "The judgment and orders appealed from are affirmed." The other justices concurred, as they did in the case of Wilson, whose appeal was also unanimously rejected by the Idaho Supreme Court. Moore and Wilson went to jail.

Carver was stunned—and disappointed. Not because he had lost a case, but because he thought that a great and grievous error had been committed. "He was so shook up," his partner, Don McClenahan, told me in 1965, "that he even considered giving up law. It was a great blow to him. He could never understand how the people, the judges, everyone, could be so blind, so unwilling to face reality and the problems that come with it, no matter how nasty they may be."

And so it was no surprise to learn, on December 13, 1956, that John A. Carver, Jr., would soon leave Boise to return to Washington—not as a personnel clerk, but as Senator Frank Church's special assistant. His personal defeat—which in his eyes, and mine, was Idaho's defeat—would benefit the whole country, as he was to go on to become the capable Under Secretary of the Interior.

But for Idaho, the sustainment of Moore's and Wilson's convictions and sentences made a mockery of all the attempts by sensible, educated, dedicated men to open a new chapter in Idaho's mental-health program. L. J. Peterson, who spearheaded that program, was well aware of what the defeat meant. On the day after Carver's announcement that he would go to Washington, it was said that Peterson was going to resign. Commented State Senator Perry Swisher: "His real crime is that he's been running the public-health department as if it were a state agency instead of a plaything."

15

"THE COMMUNIST PLOT"

A STRONG, sound mental health program has always been difficult
to establish in Idaho, as it has everywhere in the United States.
And yet, mental illnesses have plagued this country right from
its beginning.

The first hospital in America was built by Quakers in 1773
and was called the Pennsylvania Hospital. Significantly, of the
first two patients admitted to that hospital, one was described as
a "lunatic." It can be said, then, that 50 percent of hospital patients in 1773 were psychiatric. Neither time, progress, nor such
wealth that America became the richest country in the world
changed those early statistics. In 1963, the American Hospital
Association reported that 51 percent of all hospital beds were
occupied by psychiatric patients, and the American Medical Association today considers mental illness the most pressing health
problem in America.

At first, Idaho Territory sent its mentally ill elsewhere. Then,
in 1886, Idaho inaugurated its first "insane Asylum" in the tiny
southeastern village of Blackfoot. A little less than twenty years
later, it launched another insane asylum, this one in the northern
village of Orofino. Those are still the only insane asylums—now
called mental hospitals—in the state.

As the years passed, the "hospitals," whose main function was
to serve as a permanent refuge for people considered dangerous
or unable to function, were taken over by charities, headed by the
Charitable Institutions Commission. Only in 1955 did they be-

come part of the unified health program administered by the Idaho State Board of Health. And this came about only after a long campaign, which was spurred by the National Mental Health Act of 1946. This act was intended to provide incentives for the creation of mental health services, mainly to cope with the huge number of military psychiatric casualties of World War II. The State Board of Health became responsible for the two mental hospitals, the Nampa school for the mentally retarded, the State Tuberculosis Hospital, the Department of Health (which included the mental health centers), and the Air Pollution Control Commission. At the time of this writing, the Board of Health still does not have jurisdiction over the Idaho Youth Training Center at St. Anthony, which is Idaho's reform school and is administered by the Board of Education.

The first major, comprehensive and rational attempt to improve Idaho's mental-health program was made in 1951 by Dr. Dale Cornell. He was then employed by the State Mental Health Authority and was working for his M.A. in psychiatry. His thesis was a plan to revamp and reorganize the state's mental-health services, including the creation of a unified Division of Mental Health under the Board of Health (which was eventually done), the establishment of mental-health clinics in the three population centers (which were launched in 1958, 1959 and 1961), and the organization of an interdisciplinary state staff to coordinate health activities, which became a reality in 1965 when it produced a detailed, documented Plan for Community Mental Health Services.

Meanwhile, mainly through the dedication of Irene Wilcox, a social worker, the Idaho Conference of Social Welfare took place in 1960 and recommended the creation of the Children's Code Commission. In 1961, Governor Smylie requested the legislature to create such a commission with "the comprehensive responsibility of looking into all areas of child health, welfare and education and of making a quantitative and qualitative analysis of laws and services related to children." The legislature complied (H.B. No. 316), the commission was created, and in October 1962 it produced a complete report. There was no doubt that both

the enactment of the bill to create the commission and the funds
allocated for its operations were approved by the state legislature
at least partly because of the 1955–1956 homosexual scandal.

The Children's Code Commission also was an indirect result of
Dr. Butler's constant harping on the necessity of Idahoans to
wake up to their problems. The brilliant Dr. Butler was never
popular in Boise, and eventually life was made so intolerable for
him that he left—long before he could see the fruits of his labor.
But there can be no doubt that his frank, often blunt, and continuous campaign to bring mental health to Idaho convinced
many key people to think about it seriously. Sam Day, who is
now the editor of the crusading *Idaho Observer* but was in 1956
a staffer for the Associated Press, remembers how an interview
he had with Butler back then infuriated the *Statesman*'s editorial
boss, Jim Brown. "He didn't like the idea that some communities
might be more advanced than others," Day told me. Yet that was
precisely the prong Butler was using to spark needed reforms in
Idaho.

It worked. The Idaho Children's Code Commission report was
thorough, its statistics highly revealing, and its recommendations
sound. The statistics showed that Idaho's children were much
more delinquent than the children of other states, that the laws
dealing with them were outdated, that law-enforcement practices
concerning them were absurd, and that these three points were
interdependent. Some of the statistics were:

1. That Idaho had 347 trainable mentally retarded children
who were not enrolled in any school. They came under the public
school system, but the Board of Education did nothing about
them.

2. That 3.16 percent of Idaho's child population between the
ages of ten and seventeen were delinquent, as compared to 1.8
percent in the United States at large.

3. That between fiscal years 1956–1957 and 1960–1961, delinquency referrals to probate courts (the juvenile courts) increased 59 percent, which, when adjusted to the population
increase, was still a net boost of 37.5 percent.

4. That 70 percent of the delinquency cases known to the state's forty-four courts came from the ten counties with the most population. (This fact was obvious, and was another reason why the Boise power elite encouraged the homosexual scandal to cause panic in the city: The city fathers hoped that such a scandal would help *not to curtail delinquency but to curtail growth,* which presented or could present Boise's corporations with unwanted competition.)

5. That only six of the probate judges out of the thirty-seven who answered the commission's questions were law school graduates, that the judges' average salary was $4,321, and that only fourteen employed full-time or part-time probation officers.

6. That where there were probation officers, their work loads averaged more than three times the maximum national standard, yet that the full-time probation officers' salaries were as low as $3,000, "with no correlation between salary and training and experience."

7. That more children were jailed than were placed in foster homes or given probation. And:

> The children in the cells were, for the most part, unsupervised, out of sight and hearing of the adults in charge. A cry for help would not be heard. Suicide could be easily accomplished within these cells. Older, more sophisticated and larger juveniles could mistreat the smaller and younger ones without being seen or heard by adults in charge of the jails. The children observed during these visits [by commission members] were always idle. They had nothing to do. Some children were placed in solitary confinement and were not permitted even reading material except for the Bible.

8. That although many of the children jailed were sixteen and seventeen years old (323 out of 686), there were 233 aged fourteen and fifteen, 67 aged twelve and thirteen, and 7 aged eleven or less (56 did not state their ages).

9. That although 427 of the 686 children jailed had committed offenses that would have been violations of the law had they been committed by adults, 203 children were also in jail for offenses not

punishable by adult laws. Furthermore, 6 children were jailed for no offense whatsoever, and 50 for offenses that were not stated.

The commission concluded:

> Children should not be held in jail. It is apt to be a personally damaging if not degrading experience. That any child was held in jail is most unfortunate. That approximately 781 [the 686 counted by the commission plus 95 recorded but uninterviewed] were held in jail in Idaho should be a matter of great concern to the citizens of the state. The very action of placing children in jail to control delinquency may foster the development of future adult criminals.

The commission then recommended a series of major and minor proposals so as to fix responsibility for children on appropriate agencies, to reorganize the judicial structure, to set standards, to increase salaries and minimum requirements, to compel parents to answer for their children's behavior and, most important, to set up centers "for early diagnosis and treatment of emotionally disturbed, retarded, and other problem children so as to attempt to cure these children's problems so that they can become healthy citizens in the community and not become wards of the state." If enacted, the commission's complete program would have cost $470,798 in the fiscal year 1963–1964, which, it pointed out, is equivalent to the cost of keeping fourteen children in the Nampa State School for the mentally retarded for a year, or forty-five children in the State Penitentiary for a year, or eleven children in the State Hospital South at Blackfoot for a year. Very few of the commission's recommendations have been enacted, however.

Meanwhile, in September 1962, the Board of Health convened a three-day planning conference on mental illness and health, which was attended by one hundred leading citizens from all over Idaho. The conference recommended intensified activity to promote mental-health legislation and institutions and the coordination of all agencies and all departments within the state to make the program more effective. That year, Congress provided $4,200,000 to support state comprehensive health planning activities from July 1, 1963, to June 30, 1964. In February 1963, President Kennedy committed the federal government to a wider mental-health program:

> For too long the shabby treatment of the many millions of mentally disabled in custodial institutions and many millions more now in communities needing help has been justified on the grounds of inadequate funds, further studies and future promises. We can procrastinate no more.

But in Idaho, precisely on such justification, procrastination continued. The state did prepare a proposal describing the planning activities designed to meet the mental-health needs of all Idahoans, did thus qualify for federal help, and did create the Comprehensive Mental Health Planning group. The group's "Plan for Planning" was accepted by the U.S. Public Health Service in June 1963, and the funds for the first year of planning operations ($65,000) were granted to Idaho.

At that point, right-wingers, Birchers, many Mormons and other opponents of mental health launched their counterattack. The gist of it was simple: Mental health is a Communist plot. Idahoans began to receive all sorts of pamphlets denouncing the pending legislation. Perhaps the best prepared of these attacks was sent through the mail by "The Network of Patriotic Letter Writers, P.O. Box 2003D, Pasadena, California." Entitled "Evils of Mental Health Program," it purported to be "excerpts from a lecture by Allyn J. McDowell, M.D. before ARIZONIANS FOR MENTAL FREEDOM, P.O. Box 7269, Phoenix 11, Arizona." It read, in part (on yellow paper):

> The commitment procedures of the Mental Health legislation endanger the freedom and abrogate the Constitutional rights of every citizen.
>
> The Fifth Amendment of the U.S. Constitution guarantees that no citizen shall be deprived of life, liberty, or property, without due process of law. The Sixth Amendment defines "due process" as including a public and speedy trial in the same district in which the alleged offense was committed, the right to confront your accuser, to call in your own witnesses and to have counsel. Nowhere does the Constitu-

tion say that these rights depend on your ability to prove your "mental health" to the satisfaction of some government-appointed psychiatrist.

The Draft Act, sponsored by the Mental Healthers, originated in the U.S. Department of Health Service, was passed by Congress and is in effect in a number of Federal Districts and institutions. Local mental health groups constantly lobby for its adoption by all state legislatures despite its having been declared unconstitutional by the Supreme Court of Missouri. It completely negates all Sixth Amendment rights by substituting a private hearing, by providing that the patient may not even have to be present at his own hearing, and that the court is not bound by the ordinary rules of evidence. Judge Joseph Call of the Los Angeles Superior Court, who has 25 years' experience (almost double the combined experience of all the U.S. Supreme Court Justices at the time of their appointment) also has declared the Draft Act to be unconstitutional. . . .

Provisions of the Draft Act in California make it possible for a citizen to be arbitrarily picked up, confined in a mental institution for up to six days, during which time he can be treated in any manner decreed by the person in charge of the institution. Mental Health enthusiasts protest that no one in charge of a mental institution would do anything not in the best interests of the patient. But I keep remembering Dr. Robert Soble, supervising psychiatrist of a large mental hospital in New York, dispensed with the civil rights of patients for years until he was convicted of being a Soviet spy right out of Beria's ring. I don't want my civil rights or any treatment arbitrarily decided by one person like that! . . .

President Kennedy's multi-million dollar network of clinics to be set up in every city and town under bills currently in Congress, will be authorized, under the vague definition of "mental health," to scrutinize and correct your thoughts and beliefs, with or without your consent. These clinics, subsidized and controlled with Federal money, will be staffed with government employees with the mission of preventing you from having "mentally ill" thoughts. I think you must admit that even Hitler never had it so good. You ought to be inspired to think that it is only going to cost you a few hundred million more per year.

The tie-in of these clinics with the Mental Health programs in the schools is another cause for concern. Through the National Education

Association's position on the Joint Commission on Mental Health, the doctrines of UNESCO and world government appear in our classrooms, despite laws which prohibit teaching world government. This is in the guise of Social Health in the Health Readers. Teachers are warned of the challenging problem of the 10% of their pupils who will become mentally ill unless prevented by the Mental Health program; the Mental Health corrective therapy turns out to be the same old left-wing UNESCO-World Government propaganda. In California, the Department of Mental Hygiene actually collaborates with the Department of Education in writing tests. We find many tests have nothing to do with scholastic improvement, but to pry into political and religious beliefs. . . .

COMMUNIST INFLUENCE IN THE AMERICAN MENTAL HEALTH MOVEMENT

One of the top officials in the world organization from which Mental Health legislation emanates is Dr. G. Brock Chisholm. While I do not contend that he is a member of the Communist Party, his philosophy calls for, freely and in sophisticated terms, the main key points of Communism, namely: an amoral society, ridicule of the family, of religion and of patriotism, ruthless worldwide police force and redistribution of wealth. Mental Health enthusiasts decry as preposterous the many documented charges of Communists being active in the movement; in fact, they don't want to discuss such "irresponsible" criticisms. But there are plenty of such connections. . . .

The Mental Health program embraces Freudian psycho-analysis. Patients are indoctrinated with the Freudian philosophy of personal irresponsibility, based on the idea that man is a weak, irresolute, irresponsible creature, who is not at fault when he errs, since society is the culprit. Richard La Pierre, Sociology Professor at Stanford University, in his book "The Freudian Ethic," points out that acceptance of this doctrine of determinism and irresponsibility is what has led us into embracing the fallacies of progressive education, Socialism, the welfare state and the condonement of crime. It might also explain why the Mental Health movement is heavily dominated by left-wingers.

Directors of the two big companies that publish psychological tests include members of the Board of the World Federation of Mental Health. Questions from these tests illustrate the subtle means em ployed by psychiatrists and sociologists who disseminate internationalist propaganda and undermine and destroy patriotism and Christian faith in God. Samples—"How much money would you want to spit on the crucifix, eat a pound of human flesh, or desecrate a church service?" "Which is worse, spitting on the Bible or spitting on the American flag?" These give the student a choice between God and country, but do not permit him to have both.

The U.S. Public Health Service is also part of the movement, so you will find local Health Department officials pushing the programs. The Joint Commission on Mental Health is a sort of quasi-official grouping which includes various psychiatric associations, and more importantly for students, the National Education Association. The NEA can funnel in "psychological tests" which indoctrinate students with such propaganda as "Man has no soul or spirit; he is just a superior animal with nothing but a physical body." (Karl Marx) "Values are all relative; there are no absolute standards of right and wrong." (Dr. G. Brock Chisholm) "Religion is merely a crutch for insecure people to rely on." (Freud) I fail to see how this adds up to produce mentally healthy adults. . . .

Actually, this pamphlet, and the original speech, which included a series of examples for all major points made, is very clever. It uses the old technique of association to imply that the whole mental-health program is a Communist maneuver, which, I would assume, is what most people got out of reading it. People are told that A works for X, X puts out product P, P is distributed by company C, and that since A is a Communist, then P and C must equally be Communist. People are encouraged to infer that everything about mental health, the UN (UNESCO being the UN's Educational, Social, and Cultural Commission), and planned education is Communistic. In fact, an innocent might conclude from this speech that the whole federal government is Communist.

Nevertheless, the selectivity, the half-truths, the innuendoes and the outright lies in the above text make their point. And they do it carefully. No one who might sue is directly accused of being a Communist, and when the writings or teachings of an individual or organization are described as Communist, "Communist" is defined by the speaker. It goes like this: Anybody who says that values are relative is a Communist—by my definition. By that logic, all cultural anthropologists who have discovered that there are primitive tribes who encourage theft, others who kill deformed children, others who worship rocks and birds—in fact, have discovered that values *are* relative—must necessarily be Communist. But that kind of logic is very dangerous. During the McCarthy era, and also in 1965 during the Vietnam debates, many government officials claimed that anyone who compared the U.S. government to Hitlerism must obviously be a Communist. Well now, the speaker quoted in the above pamphlet did just that—therefore *he* is a Communist.

As for the sample questions that the speaker quoted, I agree that they are rather tasteless. I would be curious to see the whole test from which they came and to know who prepared that test. But they certainly do not "give the student a choice between God and country, but do not permit him to have both." The questions are obviously designed to test the student's primary attachment: Is he more influenced by patriotism or by his church? Such questions are perfectly meaningful to sociologists and psychologists who want to know how students derive their values. So, too, for the previous question. Although it is hard to take such a test seriously because of its crude nature, nothing in it implies a Communist plot. The tester simply wants to know at what point the testee would discard his values because of his greed. Only a simpleton would answer such a question, and perhaps it was a simpleton who thought it up. But in no way can that question be interpreted as "internationalist propaganda" with intent to "undermine and destroy patriotism and Christian faith in God."

Speaking of patriotism, it is interesting to note that all rabble rousers are the first to use it to hide their hate mongering. Mormons who wield the banner of patriotism to condemn government interference in education, health, welfare, etc., should remember that the persecutions suffered by their grandparents were also justified on the grounds of patriotism, when Mormonism and plural marriages were considered un-American and contrary to the values of society.

In any case, such anti-mental-health propaganda as the above pamphlet mailed into Idaho in 1963 had its effect: Resistance to state mental-health legislation was great. Nevertheless, with the support of Governor Smylie, two important bills did pass the thirty-eighth legislature: the Community Mental Health Center Act, which created local mental-health centers, and the Exceptional Child Act, which defined "handicapped children" to include all types of exceptionality and provided for joint school district employment of special personnel for their training, to be partially supported by state funds. Both bills were signed by the governor. But appropriating money for implementing these bills was something else again. Jack Steneck and John D. Cambareri, the two co-directors of the Comprehensive Mental Health Planning group, tried their best. In a letter (dated February 23, 1965) to State Senator Rodney S. Hansen, Chairman of the Legislature's Joint Appropriations and Finance Committee, they pointed out the following:

> . . . In Idaho, we have three community mental health centers supported heavily by the Federal grant-in-aid money: (1) Ada County Mental Health Center, opened February 1958; (2) Southeastern District Mental Health Center, opened September 1959; and (3) Latah–Nez Percé Mental Health Center, opened September 1961.
>
> The three existing mental health centers offer services to only six counties (Ada, Bannock, Bingham, Butte, Nez Percé and Latah). The remaining 38 counties have no community supported mental health services.
>
> It is estimated that during this biennium (1963–65) total expenditures for community mental health services in the three existing centers will be approximately $231,000.
>
> $126,000—or 55%—will be spent by the six counties supporting these services.
>
> $96,000—or 41%—of the operating expenses will be paid for by the Federal grant-in-aid mentioned above.
>
> $8,500—or 4%—will be paid for from state general funds.

Since the Federal grant-in-aid will not be increased (it has remained constant for the past four years), it is obvious that the proportion of state general funds must be increased beyond its present 4% level if these vital community services are to be extended to those other 38 counties which presently do not have these services but which are eager to initiate and support them.

Among the counties which have not only expressed interest in providing these services but which have actually budgeted money for them are the following:

1. *City-County Public Health Department* (Idaho Falls and Bonneville County): The County Commissioners have appropriated for calendar year 1965 the amount of $6,500 and have agreed to appropriate a like amount for 1966. . . .

2. *Valley County:* This county during the past two calendar years (1963 and 1964) budgeted $12,000 per year for mental health services. They desire to hire resident psychologist and social worker and become affiliated with the Ada County Mental Health Center for psychiatric services, consultation and administration. During these two year periods, there was no money available from the state general fund to match the Valley County money. Therefore, this valuable service never materialized. . . . [This is the county that Dr. Moser investigated and found that the inhabitants have no chance to better themselves unless they move out.]

3. *Moscow School District:* This school district desires to employ a social worker, affiliated with the Latah–Nez Percé Mental Health Center, but working full-time in their own school system. They have allocated a sum of $6,500 per year. . . .

4. *Latah, Nez Percé, Idaho and Clearwater Counties:* The existing Latah–Nez Percé Mental Health Center desires to expand mental health services both geographically and in quality by adding the services of a full-time psychologist, a full-time clinical social worker, and a quarter-time psychiatrist . . . [costing] during the forthcoming biennium, a total of $38,000.

5. *The Southeastern District Mental Health Center* (Bannock, Bingham and Butte Counties): Currently, this center has access to only a one-fifth-time psychologist. They wish to employ a full-time psychologist . . . [and] to increase their expenditures by $12,500.

6. *The Panhandle District Health Department:* Citizens in this area are in the process of getting the various county commissioners to

appropriate funds for a demonstration mental health center providing the services of a full-time clinical social worker and . . . will, during the forthcoming biennium, budget a total of $18,500.

The six illustrations above show the following additional "local" (county, city, school, etc.) anticipated expenditures for expanding mental health services during the forthcoming biennium: . . . [1 through 6, total] $119,000.

On the assumption that the above services will be developed in these areas in conformance with provisions of the Community Mental Health Act, the State of Idaho will be expected to participate on a matching basis—or $119,000 of general fund money.

[The other established centers will contribute $126,000, which totals $245,000 of which] $95,000 Available from Federal grants-in-aid [leaving only $150,000 to come from the state general fund].

The "statewide mental health planners" are aware of the fiscal problems faced by your committee. However, they are convinced of the necessity of developing these vital mental health services within their communities during the coming biennium and have instructed us to communicate with your committee directly and ask for an appropriation in the amount of $150,000.

Not very much, $150,000! The fancy Downtowner motel cost $1,000,000. Boise Cascade's 1962 profits were more than $5,000,-000. The Morrison-Knudsen Company's backlog alone amounted to some $415,000,000, and its president, Jack Bonny, asked why the company kept its headquarters in Boise when it is incorporated in Delaware, answered that it costs less to operate an office in Boise. Yet no one seemed capable of raising a mere $150,000 needed to provide Idaho's counties the barest minimal mental-health facilities possible—despite the fact that the counties themselves were willing to pay almost $100,000 *more than that* out of their own pockets. The bill to implement the Community Mental Health Center Act was defeated, and today there are still only three mental-health centers in the state.

"We weren't very surprised, though of course we were furious," said Cambareri when I talked to him and Steneck in 1965. "We have great legislation on the books in this state, but we can never get the money to put that legislation into practice." But the gentle, crew-cut, roly-poly psychologist was not giving in. "We'll keep fighting," he said. Steneck, a tall, more ascetic-looking chap, explained that Idaho's constitution was "conservative" in its basis. "It specifically specifies that public budgets must balance."

Couldn't money be raised through bonds at least? I asked. "No," said Cambareri, "bonded indebtedness is also prohibited by law." He added: "So little money is available for social projects of any kind, or education, or public salaries, that we keep going around in circles. For example, there are no training facilities for mental-health personnel in the state, so we have to bring out-of-staters who know they can get more money for doing the same job elsewhere yet don't have a particular attachment to Idaho. We don't even have a medical school in this state, or residency programs in psychiatry or approved graduate programs in clinical psychology, social work or nursing. In 1964, the University of Idaho graduated six students trained in psychology. Not one is working in Idaho. In that book [he pointed to Idaho's Plan for Community Mental Health Services, a complete document on health in the state] you'll see the results."

I did indeed. In 1962, there were 1.9 psychiatrists per 100,000 population in Idaho. Among the states, the median was 4.3. This ranked Idaho fiftieth (out of the fifty states and the District of Columbia). Here are some other statistics:

PROFESSIONAL MANHOURS IN OUT-PATIENT PSYCHIATRIC CLINICS PER WEEK
PER 100,000 POPULATION

	1955	1959	1962	1962 Rank
Idaho	61.9	15	35	Rank 46
United States Median	73	92	113	

. . . In this case perhaps the United States Median of 113 hours per week per 100,000 population does not demonstrate the dramatic impact of the need. Let us contrast our 35 hours per week with the 467.3 hours available in the District of Columbia, the 339.8 hours available in New York and the 293 hours available in Massachusetts. Even if we were to accept the questionable assumption that those areas have more emotional problems per 100,000 population, it is even more questionable that they have 13 times as many *problems*. What they really have are more services available to people who need them.

ANNUAL PER CAPITA MAINTENANCE EXPENDITURES FOR PUBLIC
MENTAL HOSPITALS

	1956	*1958*	*1960*	*1962*	*1962 Rank*
Idaho	2.39	2.73	3.00	3.09	Rank 42
U.S. Median	2.97	3.59	4.26	4.46	

. . . only in nine states is the annual cost per citizen less than it is in Idaho. It means that you and I, each, pay $3.09 in taxes *per year* for State Hospital maintenance, which means that it costs each person in the state less than one per cent per day to maintain the hospitals.

. . . in regard to per capita expenditures for Community Mental Health centers . . . New York State, for example, spends $2.11 per capita while we spend 31 cents. . . . In only seven other states is the *proportion* of public health funds, expended for mental health, less than in Idaho. For every dollar spent for "health" in Idaho, only 15 cents is spent for mental hospitals and community mental health. In the *average* state about 25 cents out of each dollar is spent for mental health. This compares to the almost 42 cents per dollar spent by New Hampshire; almost 41 cents per dollar spent by North Dakota and Rhode Island.

And so on . . .

That thirty-eighth Idaho legislature session, which killed the appropriations to implement the mental-health act, also killed another bill that bears on health. This was a move to transfer the administrative responsibility for the Youth Training Center (St. Anthony's) from the Department of Education to the Department of Health. The difference is much more important than a simple question of administration—involved are fundamental attitudes toward the mental health and rehabilitation of Idaho's delinquents.

Some 200 kids are now at the Youth Training Center, Idaho's reformatory, living in long, brick dormitories rising on flat farmlands a mile west of St. Anthony. The kids get up at 6 A.M., wash, dress, straighten the covers on their Army-style cots, walk in stockinged feet down a spit-and-polished corridor to where they have left their boots, put them on, file two abreast into the dining room, then, after breakfast, reassemble with their "company managers" before heading off to the barn or laundry or shops or, for some, classrooms. At 5 P.M., when the whistle blows, they reverse the procedure, and after dinner they can play Ping-Pong, read magazines or watch TV until nine or ten, depending on the night of the week. Doors are locked and discipline is severe, and one out of every four discharged inmates returns for at least one more hitch.

They are there, the center says, because "neglect, environment or misfortune" have caused them to go "without proper homes" and they "have fallen into error." Though this would imply that it was not the children's fault, the center does not believe in mental health. Said St. Anthony's superintendent, Winston Grant Taylor, in 1962: "There are a number of primary principles to be considered in the evaluation of laws which are presently in effect as regards the youthful offender against society. The underlying principles of the criminal law, that is, to protect the innocent, to punish the guilty and to deter others, cannot in the final analysis be lost in the semantics that surrounds the approach to the child who violated the rules which society has established. Treatment concepts must be considered without abandonment of the punishment concept. Efforts must be made to resist total orientation towards sociological, psychological or psychiatric programs. . . . "

Thus spoke the representative for the Board of Education. No wonder that the Board of Health wanted to take over the center (and had Governor Smylie's backing). As one psychologist reacted: "I have never before heard quite so punitive a position by anyone working with juveniles. The logic escapes me, too. We should not 'treat'; we should 'punish'; we are in the business of 'education'; therefore, it would seem to me, educating and punishing are synonymous."

Despite his 1962 statement, Superintendent Taylor has, over the years, listened to modern sociologists, psychologists and psychiatrists enough to get rid of whips and paddles, and he has modernized and streamlined the center as a whole. But classes are skimpy, there is no library, students do not have homework, and emotionally disturbed "delinquents" are not satisfactorily separated or distinguished from others. In fact, St. Anthony, with its basic emphasis on punishment, *is* a training center—for future criminals.

Thanks to Dr. Erwin C. Sage, its superintendent since 1961, the Nampa State School for the mentally retarded is in pretty good shape. In 1964 it gained a new modern training center and Dr. Sage brought in a capable staff to run it. But it can handle only 800, or at the most 1,000 out of Idaho's 21,000 mentally retarded. Huge new appropriations are thus here too much needed. And the two mental hospitals, as the statistics on psychiatric personnel indicate, are in a hopeless mess. Understaffed, old-fashioned, inadequately equipped, they merely serve as warnings to the people of Idaho: Don't become mentally disturbed if you can't afford to be sent elsewhere.

16

THE TRIAL—ROUND ONE

GORDON LARSEN HAD BEEN ARRESTED on December 11, 1955, for a homosexual act allegedly committed with Eldon Halverson on October 3, 1955. He was not brought to trial until almost a year later, on November 19, 1956—partly because of defense maneuvers, partly because the prosecution obviously did not want a trial, hoping instead that Larsen would plead guilty.

But Larsen claimed that he was innocent. Born in Idaho and the oldest of three sons, Larsen had been a salesman for the Boise Fruit & Produce Company when the alleged act took place. When he was first picked up for questioning, however, he was head of the men's section of the Mode Department Store in Boise. He had been married and divorced and was about to marry again. He had been drafted as a private in 1943, had served with the Army Corps of Engineers in the Philippines and Okinawa during World War II and had been honorably discharged after the war as a staff sergeant. He had used his GI Bill of Rights to go to college for two years, then had gone to Boise.

Immediately after his arrest, he lost his job and was evicted from his apartment. He was first given twenty-four hours to get out, but thanks to the intervention of his defense attorney, Vernon K. Smith, he got a reprieve long enough to find another place. He had to sell his furniture at a great loss—and, of course, he lost his girl. While he waited for his trial, he moved to Spokane, managed to find one job, was fired when he had to report to Boise for a hearing, went back, found another job and another girl. By the time his trial came up, he was again planning to marry.

Meanwhile, Vernon K. Smith kept trying to find out whether his client would be tried at all. He has stated in a sworn affidavit that as late as 10 P.M. on November 15, 1956, he had a telephone conversation with the prosecutor, Blaine Evans, and was told that no decision had yet been made. Evans suggested that they meet at 9 A.M. the next day at his office, but, Smith has sworn, Evans never showed up. Later that day, informed at last, Smith made various motions to the court to be able to see the documents of the case. Specifically, he wanted the court to subpoena the tape that was made during Larsen's interrogation (or so said Larsen) at the house of Bill Goodman, or at least "that the defendant and his counsel be permitted to inspect the same prior to the time of trial which is now set at 10:00 o'clock A.M. on the 19th day of November, 1956." Smith's motion was denied.

And so, on November 19, the trial began. Smith first challenged the jurors who had been selected in a drawing without the presence of the Ada County sheriff or his deputy. Since not all of the jurors had been chosen during that drawing, Judge Koelsch, who was to preside at Larsen's trial, sustained Smith's challenge only in part. A new roster of jurors was selected, and the prosecuting attorney put his main witness, Eldon Halverson, on the stand. In the following abbreviated court record, my own comments appear in *italics*.

Whereupon,

ELDON HALVERSON,

called as a witness on the part of the State, first having been duly sworn, testified as follows:

DIRECT EXAMINATION

By Mr. Evans:

Q. Would you give us your name, please?

A. Eldon Halverson.

Q. And where do you reside?

A. In Wisconsin.

Q. In Wisconsin?

A. Yes.

Q. Calling your attention to October 3, 1955, where were you residing on that date?

A. In Payette.

Q. Idaho?

A. Yes.

Q. Are you a native Idahoan, Mr. Halverson?

A. Yes. I lived here nine years.

Q. And you spent a good deal of time in Boise and this vicinity?

A. Yes. I have relatives here.

Q. What is your occupation?

A. Then?

Q. Yes.

A. I worked for the bee keeper.

Q. And when were you born, Mr. Halverson?

A. April 17, 1934.

This answer was important because it clearly established that Halverson was over twenty-one when the alleged act took place, despite what Prosecutor Evans later said.

Q. Now, calling your attention to October 3, 1955, did you have occasion to come to Boise, Idaho, on that date?

A. Yes.

Q. And where had you been immediately preceding that?

A. In Salt Lake City.

Q. And when did you come back to Boise then?

A. Early Monday morning.

Q. October 3, 1955, was Monday, was it?

A. Yes.

Q. Are you acquainted with the defendant in this action, Gordon Larsen?

A. Yes.

Q. Had you known him prior to October 3, 1955?

A. No.

Q. Did you know who he was?

A. I had seen him, yes.

Q. And you knew him by sight, did you not?

A. Yes.

Q. Now, calling your attention to October 3, 1955, did you have occasion on that date to see the defendant?

A. Yes.

Q. And where were you when you first saw him?

A. In the Greyhound bus depot.

Q. And is that located in Boise, Idaho?

A. Yes.

Q. And where were you in the bus depot?

A. In the men's room.

Q. And you saw the defendant in the men's room?

A. Yes.

Q. Did you and the defendant have any conversation at that time?

A. No.

Q. And then what happened?

A. Why, I walked a block north. I had my car across from Hendren's, and I was just getting into my car and he drove up in his car.

Q. What happened at that time?

A. Well, I don't remember what was said, but we agreed to meet out at Julia Davis Park.

Q. When were you to meet out there?

A. At noon. . . .

Q. And what happened when you arrived there?

A. Mr. Larsen came.

Q. And did you have a conversation with him at that time?

A. I think he just said to follow him up to his apartment. . . .

Q. Did you have your own car?

A. Yes.

Q. And did he have his own car?

A. Yes.

Q. And you each drove separately to his apartment?

A. Yes. . . .

Q. And so did you then go to his apartment?

A. Yes.

Q. And where was his apartment located?

A. In the Highland Village.

Q. Was it Hills Village?

A. Hills Village, I mean. . . .

Q. Did you both park your cars when you arrived there?

A. Yes.

Q. And then what happened?

A. We went upstairs to his apartment.

Q. You both entered his apartment?

A. Yes.

Q. Now, when you went into his apartment what happened, Mr. Halverson?

A. Well, we went into the bedroom. . . .

Q. Did you have a conversation before you went into the bedroom?

A. I don't remember.

Q. When you went into the bedroom what happened?

A. Well, we each dropped our clothes.

Q. Dropped your pants?

A. Pants, yes.

Q. And then what did you do?

A. He took my penis in his mouth.

Q. He put your penis in his mouth?

A. Yes.

Q. And then what did he do?

A. Well, I don't remember. I said that I—

Q. Would you state whether or not he sucked on your penis?

A. Yes.

Q. He did?

A. Yes. . . .

Q. And then what happened?

A. Well, I said I wanted to leave.

Q. Was he still sucking on your penis at the time you said that?

A. No.

Q. Then what happened? Did you leave?

A. Not right away.

Q. Did you have a conversation with him?

A. Yes.

Q. What did he say to you?

A. Well, the only thing I can recall was he asked if I had ever kissed a man and I said "No."

Q. And what else happened while you were there on the bed?

A. Well, he wanted me to take his penis in my mouth, and I said I didn't want to and finally I did but I didn't suck on it.

Q. So then what happened after that? Did you leave?

A. Yes.

Q. Where did you go?

A. I went home.

Q. Where were you living at that time?

A. Payette.

Q. Did you have an orgasm, Mr. Halverson?

A. No.

Q. Why did you break this relationship off? What happened to cause you to break that off?

A. Well, I just had a change of mind or something.

Q. Did you tell the defendant to stop doing this to you?

A. I don't remember the exact words, but I just said I had to leave.

Q. And then you stopped the relationship?

A. Yes.

Q. I am asking this merely for the purpose of the record: Both you and the defendant are male persons, are you not?

A. Yes.

Mr. Evans: I think that is all.

CROSS-EXAMINATION

By Mr. Smith:

Q. Mr. Halverson, I believe we have met in court before, haven't we?

A. Yes.

Q. At a preliminary hearing?

A. Yes. . . .

Q. So you grant me, Sir, that I know your voice?

A. That's right.

Q. Now, last night at a quarter to 11:00 o'clock, did you just get into town?

A. No.

Q. Last night at a quarter to 11:00 o'clock a voice called me on the telephone, whose voice I identified as yours, and told me that [it] was Eldon Halverson. Was that your voice?

MR. EVANS: We are going to object as outside the scope of the direct examination. There is no foundation laid. It is incompetent, irrelevant and immaterial.

THE COURT: Is this preliminary to something, Mr. Smith?

MR. SMITH: Yes, your Honor.

THE COURT: Objection overruled.

Q. It was you who called me last night?

A. Yes.

Q. And I believe the conversation went like this: "Is this Mr. Smith?" and I said, "Yes. Who is this?" and you said, "I need some legal advice." Is that correct?

A. Yes.

Q. To which I said, "Who is this?"

A. Yes. . . .

Q. To which you said, "This is Eldon Halverson and I need some legal advice as to whether I have to testify tomorrow"?

A. Yes.

Q. To which I told you, "Mr. Halverson, I represent Gordon Larsen and can not talk to you"?

MR. EVANS: If the Court please, we want to object to this as an extraneous matter and irrelevant to the issues in this case.

THE COURT: Objection is sustained now.

Q. In other words, I will ask one more question:

THE COURT: Yes.

Q. I told you if you needed legal advice as to whether or not you would have to testify, you should go to see an attorney of your own choosing?

MR. EVANS: We are going to make the same objection. This matter is irrelevant to the trial of this case.

THE COURT: I am going to exclude the Jury for a few minutes and see what, if anything, counsel is trying to arrive at, what you are driving towards, if anything, Mr. Smith. Gentlemen of the Jury, I will ask you to retire to the jury room, and I will hear from counsel.

AT THIS TIME The jury retired to the jury room.

THE COURT: This can be treated in the nature of an offer of proof. State generally what this is going to lead to, Mr. Smith.

MR. SMITH: In the 15 years I have been practicing law, your Honor, this is the first time that a witness for the State in a criminal proceeding has called me at night wanting legal advice, wanting to know whether or not he had to testify. I refused to talk to him. I probably wish I had talked to him now. I don't know what he had in his mind. It may well be that—I don't know what he wanted to tell me. I want to find out what he wanted to tell me about this case.

THE COURT: This is too collateral. I had in mind you were going to show that he had made some suggestion to you or an offer to you of some kind, something of that sort.

MR. SMITH: Maybe he has something that he wanted to say.

THE COURT: But unless you are prepared to prove that, I am going to have to sustain the objection. This is simply an excursion, and that apparently is all that it is.

MR. SMITH: Very well.

THE COURT: Call in the jury.

AT THIS TIME the Bailiff returned the jury to the jury box.

THE COURT: Be seated. Continue your cross-examination.

By Mr. Smith:

Q. I believe you said, Mr. Halverson, that up there in the apartment you wanted to leave—is that correct?

A. Yes.

Q. I believe you meant and I believe you once stated the whole thing repulsed you—is that correct?

A. Yes.

Q. It repulsed you.

(Three dockets of Justice of the Peace were marked respectively as "Defendant's Exhibit A for identification," "Defendant's Exhibit B for identification," and "Defendant's Exhibit C for identification.")

Q. From your comment that it repulsed you, do I understand that you mean to imply from that that you are not a homosexual?

A. Yes.

Q. That you are or are not?

A. I am not.

Q. You are not. I believe you stated that you had just returned from Salt Lake City on a trip?

A. Yes.

Q. You were in the company of one Charles Brokaw on that trip to Salt Lake City, were you not?

MR. EVANS: We are going to object to this as being irrelevant, outside of the issues in this case.

MR. SMITH: He says he is not a homosexual.

MR. EVANS: That's right, so he isn't.

THE COURT: He can answer that yes or no.

Q. You were in the company of one Charles Brokaw on this trip?

A. Yes.

Q. And that was a two or three day trip, was it not, to Salt Lake?

A. Yes.

Q. And Charles Brokaw is an admitted, confessed homosexual, stands accused, tried and convicted in this Court—is that correct?

MR. EVANS: We are going to object to this as incompetent, irrelevant and immaterial, an attempt to bring in a side issue.

THE COURT: Sustained.

Q. Now, I am going to hand you what has been marked as Defendant's Exhibit "A," being a certified docket of the Justice of the Peace J. M. Lampert, entitled State of Idaho vs. * * * ?

Smith was using another tactic to try to establish that Halverson was a homosexual. The exhibits "A," "B" and "C" were court records involving other homosexuals and Halverson.

MR. EVANS: We are going to object to that. It has not been identified yet.

MR. SMITH: Let me finish my question. I have got to identify this docket before I can offer it.

MR. EVANS: We would like the witness to identify it.

MR. SMITH: It is certified. Now, in order to identify this docket—

MR. EVANS: If it please the Court, if it is certified, we would like to examine it before it is offered.

THE COURT: Yes.

MR. EVANS: Are you offering this?

MR. SMITH: No. I am going to ask a question.

Q. Now, I will ask you, Mr. Halverson, if you are not one and the same person—

MR. EVANS: Now, I am going to object to this, your Honor. This document is not in evidence and hasn't been identified and hasn't been offered.

THE COURT: Yes.

MR. SMITH: I want to ask my question before—

MR. EVANS: This is obviously an attempt to prejudice the jury, and we ask that it then be admitted, if he wants to offer it, then let us make our objection, and if it comes into evidence, that is something else.

MR. SMITH: Well, if this person is not one and the same person, then the docket is immaterial.

THE COURT: I don't know what this states, what this shows.

MR. SMITH: Well, let me ask him the question.

Q. Are you one and the same—

MR. EVANS: Then we want to renew our objection. We wish to see the exhibit.

THE COURT: (Examining Ex. "A") I will sustain the objection.

MR. SMITH: This witness, your Honor, has testified that he is not a homosexual and that he left the house up there because it repulsed him, and he claims that this defendant had pursued him. I wish to show that in the case, that in four cases—

MR. EVANS: If this is an offer of proof, we would like to have the Jury excluded.

THE COURT: Yes. Proceed.

MR. SMITH: Do you wish to examine this?

MR. EVANS: Are you offering this now?

MR. SMITH: No. I am going to ask him—

THE COURT: No, Mr. Smith. You will have to get something in the record before you can inquire about it.

MR. SMITH: Very well. I will offer Defendant's Exhibits "A," "B" and "C."

THE COURT: Have you seen these, Mr. Evans?

MR. EVANS: No, we haven't, your Honor.

MR. SMITH: It is further the position of the defendant—

THE COURT: Just a moment, Mr. Smith.

MR. EVANS: We will object to Defendant's Exhibits "A," "B" and "C" on the grounds that they are incompetent, irrelevant and immaterial; there is no foundation for them. Primarily we will object on the grounds that they are incompetent, irrelevant and immaterial. They are certainly not relevant to the issues in this case.

THE COURT: Objection is sustained.

Q. Now, I will ask you, I will hand you Defendant's Exhibit "A" and ask you to read that first paragraph.

MR. EVANS: If it please the Court, these have not been introduced in evidence. We are objecting to that.

MR. SMITH: I am going to ask him to read it.

THE COURT: He can read it to himself.

Q. No, I am going to ask you: Are you, Eldon Halverson, one and the same person as the Eldon Halverson referred to in Defendant's Exhibit "A"?

MR. EVANS: We are going to object to this on the same grounds, incompetent, irrelevant and immaterial.

THE COURT: Same ruling.

Q. Now, I am going to hand you Defendant's Exhibit "B," and I will ask you to examine the first paragraph. Will you take it and look at it, please?

MR. EVANS: If it please the Court, well—

Q. And I am going to ask you now whether or not you are one and the same person as the Eldon Halverson referred to in Defendant's Exhibit "B"?

MR. EVANS: To which we make the same objection, incompetent, irrelevant and immaterial.

THE COURT: Same ruling, and I assume you are going to do the same with Exhibit "C," and I will make the same ruling there again.

MR. SMITH: Very well. Now I will make an offer of proof.

THE COURT: All right. Gentlemen of the Jury, I will ask you again to retire to the jury room until we are ready to proceed, and observe the admonition I gave you preceding the recess.

WHEREUPON the Jury left the courtroom.

I have eliminated the names of the homosexuals here since all three, A, B and C, were convicted but put on probation (one was the pianist) and were therefore capable of establishing new lives without the stamp of ex-con, and perhaps without their convictions disclosed.

MR. SMITH: Comes now the defendant, who would offer to prove by the witness Eldon Halverson that this witness Eldon Halverson is one and the same person referred to in Defendant's Exhibit "A" for identification as Eldon Halverson, being a certified copy of the docket entry in the case entitled State of Idaho vs. * * *, wherein * * * was accused of having committed the infamous crime against nature with this witness. We would further offer to prove by this witness Eldon Halverson, if he were permitted to testify, that he is one and the same person as the Eldon Halverson designated and named in Defendant's Exhibit "B," being a certified copy of the docket entry of J. M. Lampert, Justice of the Peace, in which case * * * was accused of having committed the infamous crime against nature with this witness. We would further offer to prove by the witness Eldon Halverson, if he were permitted to testify, that he is one and the same person as the Eldon Halverson referred to in Defendant's Exhibit "C," being a certified copy of the docket entry in the case entitled State of Idaho vs. * * *, in which case * * * was accused of having committed the infamous crime against nature with this witness.

The purpose of our offer of proof in these matters, your Honor, was threefold: First, this defendant has taken the stand and testified in such a manner as to lead this jury to believe that Gordon Larsen engaged him and encouraged him to come to his house; secondly, in his testimony he testified in such a way as to lead this jury to believe that he is an innocent young man who was repulsed by this act, when in fact this offer would tend to prove and show that he is a frequent engager in homosexual acts; and, thirdly, that the plea of not guilty in this case puts every issue, every fact in issue, including the credibility of every witness, and the extensive immoral conduct of this particular witness is a fact which should and ought to be taken into consideration by the jury when it comes to the time for that jury to consider the credibility of his testimony, and that is the purpose of our offer, your Honor.

THE COURT: I don't propose to make any extended comment, and I don't mean to cover all the matters that you have stated, but, fundamentally, this is an attempt to weaken the credibility, to impeach the witness, by showing specific immoral acts not connected with the particular offense on trial. It has been held time and time again that such evidence is inadmissible. The manner of impeachment is fixed by statute, and all we have to do is to look at the annotations following the statute to see how extensive the cases are and to what extent they go and what they permit and what they do not permit. The objection was made. I take it a like objection would be made to the offer of proof.

MR. EVANS: It is, your Honor, for the purpose of the record.

THE COURT: The offer is refused, and the objection sustained. Mr. Bailiff, return the jury.

WHEREUPON the Jury was returned to the jury box.

Smith had failed again. But he did not give up.

By Mr. Smith:

Q. Now, Mr. Halverson, have you ever discussed the facts of this case with anybody else prior to this time?

A. How do you mean by facts of this case?

Q. Well, Mr. Halverson, have you ever told the story that you have just told here to any individual before, particularly referring to any police officer or the prosecuting attorney's office? Did you?

A. Yes.

Q. Who did you first tell this story to, Mr. Halverson?

A. Bill [Goodman].

I have changed the investigator's name (as I mentioned earlier) to protect his business, despite the fact that this trial does not show him in a favorable light.

Q. Bill [Goodman]; and who is Bill [Goodman]?

A. A private investigator.

Q. He was the private investigator who had been employed or was in charge of this extensive investigation that was going on?

MR. EVANS: Now, we are going to object to that on the ground there is no foundation; it is incompetent, irrelevant and immaterial, and it is collateral to the main issue of the trial here.

THE COURT: Sustained.

Q. Well, Bill [Goodman] was an investigator anyway?

A. Yes.

Q. Now, how did you ever happen to get together and talk to Bill [Goodman] about this?

MR. EVANS: We will object to that on the ground it is incompetent, irrelevant and immaterial, doesn't tend to prove or disprove any of the issues in this case, your Honor.

THE COURT: Objection is sustained.

Q. Well, when did you talk to Mr. Bill [Goodman]?

A. It was during the early part of December.

Q. The early part of December. You were brought to him, weren't you, by a police officer?

A. No.

Q. How did you get in touch with him?

MR. EVANS: We are going to make the same objection. This is a collateral matter. It is not relevant to the issues of this case.

THE COURT: Objection overruled. He can testify to that.

A. Charles Brokaw made a 'phone call to me about noon and said I should come over to Boise and talk to Bill [Goodman].

Q. And what were you to talk about, or what did you talk about?

MR. EVANS: I am going to object to this, your Honor. It has nothing to do with the trial of this case; it is incompetent, irrelevant and immaterial, outside of the scope of the direct examination certainly.

THE COURT: Overruled.

MR. EVANS: Well, I will object on the ground it is hearsay.

MR. SMITH: He knows what he talked about.

THE COURT: This is cross-examination by the defendant's counsel. Objection overruled. He may answer.

Q. Well, might I help you? You were called over to discuss your personal involvement in homosexual activity in and around Ada County —is that correct?

MR. EVANS: Now, I want to object to this entire line of testimony. It is apparent Mr. Smith is trying to drag in some side issue which is incompetent, irrelevant and immaterial and has nothing to do with the issues of the case.

MR. SMITH: I am trying to show his own personal status at the time that he made this statement against this man.

THE COURT: The objection is overruled.

MR. SMITH: Yes.

Q. You were under investigation yourself, were you not?

A. I don't know.

Q. Well, they got you in to see how many different people you had been having homosexual relations with?

A. I came in voluntarily.

Q. Yes. You came in voluntarily, but that is what you came over for and that is what you talked about?

A. Yes.

Q. Yes; and you involved yourself with * * *, * * * and—

MR. EVANS: We are going to object to this, your Honor. It is incompetent, irrelevant—

MR. SMITH: Let me finish my question.

Q. And * * *, did you not?

MR. EVANS: Wait a minute. This has nothing to do with the case. I know what his answer is going to be, but I don't think it is proper we should get off into the side issue of the homosexual investigation.

THE COURT: Objection is overruled. This goes into certain phases which are proper on cross-examination. Go ahead.

Q. You did involve yourself in homosexual activities with these three named individuals, did you not?

A. Yes.

Q. Yes. At that time then you occupied the position of one who has admitted having homosexual acts and were at that time subject to the possibility of criminal accusation and criminal complaint, were you not?

MR. EVANS: We are going to renew our objections to this, your Honor.

THE COURT: Overruled.

A. Yes.

Q. Yes; but you have never to this day been accused of your own homosexual acts, have you?

A. No.

Q. No. This man, [Goodman], he was not a part of the prosecuting attorney's office, was he?

A. I don't know.

Q. He was not. He was not a part of the Boise City police, was he?

A. No.

Q. He was a private investigator that had been hired to conduct this wholesale investigation. Now, you were promised by him, were you not, that if you would cooperate with him and involve other people, including this man, that you would not be prosecuted?

A. No.

Q. You were not?

A. No.

Q. And yet an admitted homosexual, you have never to this day been accused—

A. No.

MR. EVANS: Come, come now, Mr. Smith; really this is going far, far afield, your Honor. He said that he was not promised anything. We want to object to Mr. Smith's arguing with the witness and making an argument to the jury here.

THE COURT: Sustained.

Q. The facts are that you have not yet been accused of any crime —you have not been charged for your homosexual acts with Mr. * * *, nor Mr. * * *, nor Mr. * * *, nor Mr. Larsen, have you?

A. No.

Q. No; and you came back here from Kansas City, didn't you?

A. No.

Q. Well, where did you come from?

A. From Wisconsin.

Q. Voluntarily?

A. Under a subpoena.

Q. Well, you got on the train by yourself?

A. Yes.

Q. And you came by yourself?

MR. EVANS: I object to that. He testified he came back under subpoena. He didn't come back voluntarily.

THE COURT: Sustained.

Q. And you did not come back in the custody of any police officer, did you?

A. No.

Q. You came back to fulfill your bargain that you would even testify against this man with the assurance and belief that still you would not be prosecuted?

A. No.

Q. Now, you were in attendance on the 11th day of December, 1955, in a private home out here in the Hyde Park Addition where Gordon Larsen was brought in the afternoon for an extensive interrogation and inquisition, were you not?

A. Yes.

Smith was referring to Bill Goodman's private home, where he conducted his investigation.

Q. And in the course of that grueling inquisition you were brought in to be displayed to Gordon Larsen, were you not?

A. Yes.

Q. You came over freely in your own automobile, did you not?

A. Yes.

Q. And when you were brought in this Bill [Goodman] showed you to Gordon Larsen?

A. Yes.

Q. And there you were asked to tell this story, about the same story you have told today?

A. That's right.

Q. That's right; and when you were finished, in the presence of Gordon Larsen—now, this was all before the arrest—you were asked in the presence of Gordon Larsen, "Halverson, will you testify to those facts under oath?" Did that occur?

MR. EVANS: We are going to object to this question. I don't see where it is relevant to the issue here; it is incompetent, irrelevant and immaterial.

THE COURT: Overruled.

Q. Did you so testify or state?

A. I don't remember those actual words.

Q. But it was, that was the effect of it, that you were asked whether you would testify against him under oath, and you said "yes" or something to that effect?

A. I think, to be correct, it is "Could you testify?"

Q. Well, all right. We will split the frog hair and that is what it will be then. Now then, following that Bill [Goodman] handed you three one dollar bills and said, "Now, Halverson, Eldon, you may go," and turned to the defendant Gordon Larsen and says, "See, Gordon, he is cooperating and we give him money and let him go home"?

MR. EVANS: Object to all this as incompetent, irrelevant and immaterial, your Honor.

Q. Is that right?

THE COURT: Objection overruled. He may answer.

MR. EVANS: I would like to have the question broken down at least, your Honor.

THE COURT: All right. Split it up.

MR. SMITH: Very well, Sir.

Q. Just as you were about to leave this Bill [Goodman] person handed three one dollar bills to you to buy gas with, didn't he?

A. I don't remember.

Q. You don't know whether it was two or three.

A. I don't remember.

Q. Well, do you remember he gave you money to buy gas with?

A. Yes, I remember he did once.

Q. Yes. He gave you money to buy gas with, and then he turned to the defendant Gordon Larsen and he says, "See, Gordon, this man is cooperating and we are letting him go. Why don't you cooperate with us?"

MR. EVANS: Object to that. This is the purest sort of hearsay. It assumes facts not in evidence, and I don't see where it is relevant.

THE COURT: He may answer.

A. Well, it happens at the time I wasn't working and I was broke, so I had no way to get home and I told him when he called me and he wanted to talk to me and wanted me to come over, and I said I just didn't have any money to get over there, I was broke and hadn't been working. . . .

Q. Did it occur that he told you that you could go?

A. Yes, he said I could go.

Q. And then commented to Gordon Larsen to the effect that "See, he is cooperating"?

A. I remember nothing like that. I don't remember that.

Q. Now, this Greyhound bus depot that you claim you met Gordon Larsen at, that is in Boise?

A. Yes.

Q. Mr. Halverson, you met Gordon Larsen on the corner by Hendren's, did you not?

A. Yes.

Q. Yes. You didn't meet him at the Greyhound bus depot, did you?

A. I saw him there.

Q. You saw him. You didn't talk to him in there, did you?

A. No.

Q. Well, now, you went to the Greyhound bus depot yourself?

A. Yes, I was in there.

Q. The Greyhound bus depot, where you say that you first saw him, had at that time a sort of a general reputation of being a place where homosexual persons sought out other homosexual persons, did it not?

A. I don't know.

Q. You didn't know that?

A. I didn't know.

Q. Now, you have no business with Gordon Larsen, did you?

A. No.

Q. As I understood your testimony, you only knew who he was. You didn't even know him?

A. Yes.

Q. Then I take it from that, Mr. Halverson, that regardless of whether you went to the monkey cage, or where you went, you were out searching for a homosexual activity that day—is that correct?

A. No.

Q. You were not?

A. I was not.

Q. You was not. Do you say that Gordon Larsen told you to meet him in a monkey cage?

A. At Julia Davis Park, yes.

Q. At the monkey cage?

A. Yes.

Q. And you went down there?

A. Yes.

Q. You didn't know the man?

A. No.

Q. You had no business with him?

A. No.

Q. There was no legitimate reason in the world why you would go down to meet him, was there?

A. No.

Q. You were looking for a homosexual experience, weren't you?

A. Not in the Greyhound bus depot.

Q. Well, down at the monkey cage, if that is where you went, you were in the hopes, were you not, that you might inveigle this man to engage in a homosexual experience with you, weren't you?

A. I had already met him up at Hendren's . . .

Q. Were you in the hopes of trying to engage with him if you could in a homosexual experience?

A. Well, it was just taken for granted.

Q. That if you could get him to do it, that is what you were after?

A. It wasn't my thinking.

Q. It wasn't your thinking?

A. That isn't what I had in mind.

Q. Will you please explain to me what legitimate thing you could possibly have had in mind?

MR. EVANS: I am going to object. He has answered the question.

THE COURT: Overruled. He may answer.

A. (The witness made no answer.)

Q. I am willing to go ahead. All right. Now, the facts of the matter are, Mr. Halverson, that you were standing on the corner at Hendren's and Gordon Larsen walked up and you said "Hello" to him, didn't you?

A. I wasn't standing on the corner. I was getting into my car.

Q. Where was your car?

A. Across the street from Hendren's.

Q. Is that where you said "Hello" to him?

A. I don't remember saying "Hello" to him.

Q. You don't remember saying "Hello" to him. Did you talk at all there?

A. He just drove up in his car, and I don't remember exactly what was said.

Q. You mean—what did he say?

A. One thing was that he had something to do and he would be tied up for about an hour.

Q. I believe your story was that he said "Meet you at the Park"?

A. Yes.

Q. And you had not spoken to him before that?

A. No.

Q. You saw him in the bus depot and you didn't say a word to him?

A. No.

Q. You didn't know him, and you say all at once he drove up to the side of you and said, "Hi! Meet me at the Park"—is that correct?

A. I don't remember the words.

Q. Well, is that about all that happened?

A. Yes.

Q. Yes. Nothing more. He just says, "Meet me at the Park," so you met him at the Park?

A. Yes.

Q. And what happened down at the Park when he came up to you? Did you talk down there?

A. He just asked me to follow him up to his apartment.

Q. He didn't talk about anything else?

A. We may have, but—

Q. You don't remember; in other words, all you can remember he drove up and parked and again says, "Hi! Follow me home"?

A. I don't know what all was said. We talked.

Q. So anyway it is your story that he approached you and asked you to meet him down at the monkey cage and then he asked you to go to his apartment?

A. Yes.

Q. That is your story?

A. Yes.

Q. And without any discussions, without your having any legitimate or lawful business of any kind with him, without discussing what you were going to do, you just simply went along with his suggestions, as you put it?

A. Yes.

Q. The facts of the matter, Mr. Halverson, are these, aren't they, that you followed Mr. Larsen home after you had asked where he was going and he said he was going home for lunch, that you followed him up to his apartment and when you got up there you approached him on a homosexual act, and he told you to get out—those are the facts, aren't they?

A. No.

MR. SMITH: I have no further questions of this witness, your Honor.

Smith had made his points. He established that Halverson was a homosexual, that he had been paid (very little, it is true) to testify, and that either both Halverson and Larsen were homosexuals or else only Halverson was. Smith had effectively discredited the prosecution's witness—but Blaine Evans was not through yet.

REDIRECT EXAMINATION

By Mr. Evans:

Q. Mr. Halverson, you came here under subpoena from the State of Wisconsin, did you not?

A. Yes.

Q. And you had prior to that refused to return to testify—isn't that correct?

A. Yes.

Q. In fact, we had to postpone the trial once—is that right?

A. Yes.

Q. Now, you say you told this fellow Bill [Goodman], or whatever his name is, about * * *, * * * and * * *—is that right?

Evans was bluffing here—he knew Goodman very well.

A. Yes.

Q. And they were homosexuals?

A. Yes.

Q. And you also told [Goodman] about the defendant Gordon Larsen?

A. Yes.

Q. And he was known to you to be a homosexual?

MR. SMITH: Well, now, just a moment. I object to that as calling for hearsay.

MR. EVANS: Well, I'm trying to find out what he told [Goodman]. You opened it up.

THE COURT: Objection is overruled.

Q. Yes. Go ahead and answer.

A. Yes.

Q. That's right. Now, of the four people that you told Mr. [Goodman] about * * *, * * *, * * * and the defendant Larson, three of them have been convicted of committing the infamous crime against nature?

A. Yes.

MR. SMITH: Object to that as incompetent, irrelevant and immaterial.

THE COURT: Objection is sustained. Strike the answer and, gentlement of the jury, when I say anything is to be stricken from the record that means for you to disregard it, put it out of your mind.

Q. So when you saw the defendant Gordon Larsen on the streets of Boise on October 3rd and he approached you, you knew at that time that he was a homosexual?

A. Yes.

MR. SMITH: Well, I object to that question as being highly leading and highly suggestive and calls for opinions and conclusions of the witness.

THE COURT: Objection is overruled. The answer may stand.

Q. You did?

A. Yes.

MR. EVANS: That is all.

Having lost his attempt to keep out of the trial the fact that Halverson was not only a homosexual but also a stool pigeon against other homosexuals, Prosecutor Blaine Evans then decided to use that information for himself. He successfully established that if Halverson, a homosexual, was out to seduce Larsen as Smith tried to imply, then Halverson did so only because he knew that Larsen was a homosexual—that others had told him about Larsen. The result was that now, instead of Halverson in the role of a poor innocent youth seduced by Larsen, there were two homosexuals. This made them accomplices. But the testimony of one accomplice against another is not enough to convict. There must be corroborating evidence. Even if the jury believed Halver-

son, which was doubtful at this point, his testimony was useless unless some kind of circumstantial evidence, different and not derived from Halverson's testimony, was presented. Thus there can be little doubt that Smith had won the first round of his bout against Evans.

17

THE TRIAL—ROUND TWO

Eldon Halverson's testimony against Gordon Larsen could still be salvaged—and believed. What was needed was corroborating evidence. Predictably, therefore, Blaine Evans and his deputy, Eugene Thomas, tried to introduce such evidence—a confession obtained without threat, duress or promise—and Vernon K. Smith did his best to stop it, or at least to discredit it. Round Two began with the prosecution calling Earnest G. Quinton to the stand.

DIRECT EXAMINATION

By Mr. Thomas:

Q. Will you state your name, please?

A. Earnest G. Quinton.

Q. Where do you reside, Mr. Quinton?

A. 1503 Vermont Avenue.

Q. What is your occupation?

A. Police officer.

Q. And that is the Boise City police is it?

A. Yes.

Q. Were you so employed in December of 1955?

A. Yes, I was.

Q. Referring particularly to December 11, 1955, were you so employed?

A. Yes.

Q. And were you at that time on a special assignment, Sir?

A. Yes, I was.

Q. And what was that assignment generally?

A. To conduct investigations on homosexuality.

Q. Right. Did you on the 11th day of December, 1955, have occasion to see the defendant Gordon Larsen, the man seated to Mr. Smith's right?

A. Yes, I did.

Q. And where did you first see the defendant on that day?

A. In his apartment in Hills Village.

Q. Would you tell the jury, please, where Hills Village is?

A. It is up in the northern part of Boise. You go up North 8th and turn to your right on Brumbach and go up to the lower part of the hills.

Q. Sergeant Quinton, do you know whether that is in Ada County, Idaho?

A. Yes, it is.

Q. Now, what time of day, if you know, was it that you first saw the defendant, Gordon Larsen, on the 11th of December?

A. I think it was approximately 20 minutes about—I think it was about 3:30, maybe 20 minutes of 4:00.

Q. You say "about." Are you fairly certain it would be in that time range?

A. Yes, I know it would be in that time.

Q. What did you do when you first saw the defendant on that day?

A. Well, I went in his house and talked to him.

Q. That would be his apartment?

A. Yes, his apartment.

Q. I see; and how long did you talk to him there?

A. Oh, approximately 5, maybe 6, minutes.

Q. And who was present at that time?

A. There was no one there but Mr. Larsen and myself.

Q. What, if you recall, was the substance of that conversation?

A. I asked him if he would accompany me to my office and talk.

Q. I see. Then did he agree to come?

A. Yes, he did.

Q. Did you place this man under arrest?

A. No, I did not.

Q. Would you tell the jury, please, Sergeant Quinton, what you did after that conversation?

A. Why, Mr. Larsen wanted to—he wasn't dressed, he was in his bathrobe, and he wanted to dress, and he asked me if I would mind waiting while he dressed, and I said, "No, I wouldn't," and he dressed and we went out and got in the car and drove to our office.

Q. And where is that, Sir?

A. 1019 North 16th.

Q. Is that still your office?

A. No, it isn't.

Q. What type of office was that?

A. It was a private home with an office-attached.

Q. That was on the front porch?

A. Yes. It might be called the front porch.

Q. And is that the office of the investigation staff on this homosexual matter?

A. Yes.

Q. What time of day, if you know and remember, did you arrive there, at the [Goodman] residence, I take it?

A. Yes.

Q. With this defendant?

A. Approximately 4 o'clock.

Q. Approximately 4 o'clock?

A. Yes.

Q. And, Sergeant Quinton, what did you do upon arriving? Did you take the defendant into your office?

A. Yes, I did. I took him inside.

Q. Who was present there?

A. The chief of police, Jim Brandon, and I am pretty sure that the sheriff, Doc House, was there, and Bill [Goodman].

Q. Yes, sir. That was approximately 4 p.m., December 11th?

A. Yes.

Q. And what, if anything, occurred thereafter, if you know?

MR. SMITH: No, let me ask a question in aid of an objection.

THE COURT: Yes.

By Mr. Smith:

Q. Mr. Quinton, at that time that you brought Mr. Larsen into the office of this Bill [Goodman] residence, there was a tape recording there which recorded all questions and all answers in the entire proceedings that occurred from the time that you arrived up to the time that you left, was there not?

MR. THOMAS: I object to that. There is a proper time for this to be gone into.

THE COURT: Sustained.

Having been rebuffed before the trial when he tried to obtain the tape recordings allegedly made during the interrogation, Smith was trying to get it now through testimony.

MR. SMITH: Well, I will make an offer of proof so I will have a foundation for my next objection.

THE COURT: All right.

MR. SMITH: I offer the proof to be—

MR. THOMAS: Now, your Honor, may I ask that he approach the bench or that the jury be excused?

THE COURT: All right. Gentlemen of the jury, I will have to ask you again to leave the courtroom and go in the jury room and be summoned back when we are ready to continue.

AT THIS TIME the jury retired to the jury room.

MR. SMITH: I am awfully sorry for this interruption, but I have to practice law the only way I know how, your Honor.

THE COURT: Go ahead.

MR. SMITH: Comes now the defendant, who would offer to prove by the witness—Mr. Quinton is your name, isn't it, Sir?

A. Yes.

MR. SMITH: If he were permitted to testify, that there was in this residence of Bill [Goodman] a tape recording and that all proceedings had, including questions asked and answers given by the defendant, were recorded on the tape recording. My purpose of the offer would be—I understand the question was, what occurred there, what were the proceedings, and the purpose of my offer is that I would object to that question on the ground that the tape recording would be the best evidence as to what those proceedings were, what was said. I understand they are probably laying the foundation for a statement.

THE COURT: Are you leading up to some admission or confession, Mr. Thomas?

MR. THOMAS: Your Honor, we are leading—what we are doing, your Honor, is trying to lay the entire day before the jury from the time this defendant first came in contact with the authorities. We take the position that this does not lead to a confession at this point, at a later point.

THE COURT: All right. You can make your objection, if you have one, to the offer.

MR. THOMAS: Your Honor, I object and request the Court to deny the offer upon the ground that even if the facts asserted were true it would not show good cause for objection to the question or the line of questions we will pursue.

THE COURT: Objection is sustained and the offer is refused. Mr. Bailiff, return the jury.

The tape, of course, was crucial. If it could be produced and if it showed that Goodman had used threat, duress or promise of reward in obtaining a confession, Smith would there and then have won his case.

AT THIS TIME the jury returned to the jury box.

THE COURT: Be seated.

By Mr. Thomas:

Q. Mr. Quinton, I just asked you what, if anything, do you recall transpired after you arrived at the residence on South [North] 16th Street with this defendant, Gordon Larsen?

A. Yes. When I went inside with Mr. Larsen he was introduced to all that was there, and Mr. [Goodman] asked him some questions when he first came in.

Q. I see; and what, if anything, did Captain Brandon say at that time, if you recall?

A. He informed Mr. Larsen that he didn't have to be here, he wasn't under arrest, and although anything that he did say could be used against him at a later date.

Q. Did he say anything about a right to counsel?

A. Yes. He said that he could call an attorney and didn't have to say anything at all until the attorney got there.

Thomas was trying his best to establish that Goodman and all the law-enforcement officers had acted legally, so that the confession would be unchallengeable.

Q. For what period of time, if you know and remember, was this defendant Gordon Larsen present at that residence in that office at that time?

A. He was there from approximately 4 o'clock to right about 6:30.

Q. Was he at any time under arrest while in that office?

A. No, he was not.

Q. Was anything said with respect to arrest during the time he was there that you know of?

A. No, not that I know of.

Q. Was he told that he was not and could leave?

A. He was.

Q. By whom?

A. Bill [Goodman], I believe, told him two or three times that he could leave if he wanted to, that he wasn't under arrest.

Q. What was the subject of discussion at that time?

A. Homosexuality.

Q. Was there a discussion with reference to this particular gentleman, Eldon Halverson, who had just testified in this case?

A. Yes, there was.

Q. And Eldon Halverson was there, was he not, for a short time?

A. Yes, for a short time.

Q. And did the defendant at that time deny the affair with Halverson?

A. Yes, he did.

Q. I see. Sergeant Quinton, you say that was from about 4 until about 6:30?

A. Yes.

Q. Now, at any time during that discussion and interview did this defendant ever admit going into that Boise Hills Village area?

A. Yes, I believe that he did admit knowing Halverson and admitted going up there.

Q. He denied any homosexual affair?

A. That's right.

Q. I see. What, if anything, if you know, took place after the 2½ hours there on South [North] 16th?

A. Mr. Larsen and myself went down to the Ada County sheriff's, the Ada County office building, here in this building.

Q. To the prosecuting attorney's office?

A. The prosecuting attorney's office, yes.

Q. You came back to my office?

A. Yes.

Q. And I was there?

A. Yes, you were.

Q. Do you recall approximately what time of evening it was when you arrived at that office, in my office?

A. I would say it would be about a quarter to 7.

Q. And who was present at that time, Sergeant Quinton?

A. Just yourself and myself at the time I first brought him in.

Q. And the defendant?

A. And the defendant Gordon Larsen, yes.

Q. And what, if anything, was the defendant told at that time with reference to his rights?

A. He was advised at that time that he had rights to have counsel and that he didn't have to say anything.

Q. Was he advised that what he said could be used against him?

A. Yes, he was.

Q. And by whom was that advice given?

A. By you.

Q. And could you describe to the jury, Mr. Quinton, the room that we were in at that time?

A. Well, it is a small room with a large desk. There is just room comfortably to seat possibly four people around the desk in big chairs like the one I am sitting in here, and that's about all there is to the room.

Q. Do you happen to know whether that is my usual office where I carry on my work?

A. Yes, it is.

Q. And, Sergeant Quinton, what, if you recall and can relate to this jury, was the substance of our conversation with this defendant Gordon Larsen at the time we talked in the prosecuting attorney's office that night?

A. Well, it was about the trip up to Hills Village with Halverson.

Q. That was with respect to a trip in October of 1955, with Halverson and Larsen?

A. Oh, yes, yes.

Q. I see. At the time we were talking to this defendant Gordon Larsen there, Sergeant, would you describe to this jury if you can recall, what his general demeanor and condition was?

A. Mr. Larsen was well dressed and probably nervous without much doubt, but very clean and cooperative to talk to. He talked and didn't get loud or anything; he just talked normally.

Q. Was he made any promises at that time?

A. No, he wasn't.

Q. Was he under arrest?

A. No, he wasn't.

Q. Was there any physical conduct on the part of any official there that would have any bearing to intimidate this man?

A. No.

Q. What, if anything, then did the defendant at that time say with respect to this October 3rd trip to Hills Village which he and Halverson had?

A. It has been a long time since that happened; it seems like a long time to me, and it is hard to remember exactly.

Q. Do you remember in substance, Sergeant?

A. Yes. I remember him talking about being up in the Village in his apartment with Halverson and setting on the bed with him and they played with each other, the way I understood it.

Q. Those are not the exact words, as I understand your testimony.

A. No, they are not the exact words.

Q. Are you testifying as to the substance of what he said?

A. Well, that is as close as I can remember to what he said.

Q. Are you certain or are you uncertain?

A. No. I am certain that he said that, but I don't remember just what led up to it.

Q. And about what time of that night was it, if you recall, Sergeant Quinton, that you left the prosecutor's office?

A. I left there at approximately 8 o'clock.

Q. And at the time you left and as you left, was there anyone else in my office?

A. Yes. Well, at the moment I left the room I don't believe there was, but as I left I believe Captain Brandon came in.

Q. Came into my office?

A. Yes.

Q. So as you left he came in—is that right?

A. Yes.

Q. And did you talk to the defendant Gordon Larsen further that evening?

A. No, I didn't.

Q. Did you do any further investigative work on this particular charge?

A. No.

Q. Let's be certain of one thing, Sergeant, before we turn you to Mr. Smith. Did the defendant at that time testify that he had been in his apartment with Halverson on the 3rd? Did he state that?

A. Yes, he stated that he had.

Q. And you have referred to some sexual relationship there. What, if anything, did he say that relationship consisted of?

A. Mutual masturbation.

Q. And where did he say it took place?

A. In his bedroom, I am pretty sure it was; I don't remember exactly, but I am sure it was in his bedroom.

MR. THOMAS: All right. Your witness.

Sergeant Quinton's testimony was very believable; he admitted not remembering things, which strengthened what he did remember.

CROSS EXAMINATION

By Mr. Smith:

Q. Mutual masturbation, I believe your words are?

A. Yes.

Q. Now, I realize, Mr. Quinton, like you said, this has been a long time. I do have notes. This Sunday afternoon that you went to see Gordon Larsen was December 11th, up to his apartment?

A. Yes.

Q. I believe you drove up there in the company of another policeman, did you?

A. Yes, I did.

Q. And he was in his bathrobe, you said?

A. You mean Mr. Larsen?

Q. Yes. He was in his bathrobe?

A. Yes.

Q. Now, the time that you came up there was around 2:20, was it not?

A. Not that I remember it. According to all my recollections I never even was called to my office until 3 o'clock.

Q. Do you have a memorandum on that of some kind?

A. Yes. I took some notes.

Q. Did you make an official diary of that day, of your activity as to where you went and what you did?

A. I had some, yes. It wasn't exactly official. It was just for my own benefit.

Q. Is there one down to the police department that showed your diary, so to speak, for the day, what time you went here and what time you went there?

MR. THOMAS: I will object to this line of cross-examination unless a foundation is laid showing that this witness will benefit by refreshing his recollection by looking at a diary.

THE COURT: The objection will be sustained.

Q. Well, it has been a long time. If you had the opportunity to look at your daily diary of that day or your report, you could refresh your recollection more exactly as to the time, could you, Sir?

A. No.

Q. You could not?

A. Because that is the time I wrote down.

Q. You feel your recollection now a year and a half later, a year later, is more exact than your record?

A. No, I don't feel that it is.

Q. Now then, in any event the defendant was taken down to this private home?

A. Yes.

Q. And you have always been in the traffic department, haven't you?

A. I have been, yes, in traffic.

Q. As long as I have known you haven't you been assigned to traffic with the exception of this investigation?

A. Yes.

Q. This is the first time you have ever worked on anything outside of traffic, is it not?

A. Well, no, not this case, no.

Q. Now, before you came up here today did you sit down and talk with Mr. Thomas as to what your testimony would be?

A. I talked with Mr. Thomas, yes.

Q. This morning?

A. Yes.

Q. Or yesterday?

A. Yesterday. I don't believe I even seen him this morning.

Q. And in the course of your discussion with him he said, "Now, Mr. Quinton, I will ask you whether or not the defendant was told that he didn't have to stay if he didn't want to"—did you discuss that?

A. I remember that distinctly. That was told to him several times during his stay up there.

Q. Well, you ordinarily don't do that, do you, Mr. Quinton?

A. We wanted the defendant to know that he was not under arrest, that he could go if he wanted to.

Q. All right. Now, when you discussed with Mr. Thomas yesterday or whenever it was you discussed what your testimony would be, did he discuss with you, "Now, Mr. Quinton, I am going to also ask you as to whether or not the defendant was told if he didn't want to say anything he didn't have to," and your answer would be "He was so advised"? Was that discussed?

A. No sir. He didn't tell me what my answer would be.

Q. Well, did you discuss it yesterday?

A. We discussed it, yes.

Q. You discussed it. To your present recollection that would be one of the questions?

A. I think he asked my answer to that, yes, but he never told me what to say.

Q. Now, you never do that in your other investigations, do you, Mr. Quinton?

A. Not in traffic, no.

Q. Nor in other investigations you have operated on?

A. No.

Q. As a matter of fact, the Boise police department doesn't follow that as a policy, does it?

MR. THOMAS: Objection, your Honor.

THE COURT: Sustained.

Q. In any event Mr. Larsen stayed there until about 6:30, was it?

A. Yes, sir.

Q. Now, you were not in the room all the time, were you?

A. No, I believe I was out of the room for awhile.

Q. Well, as a matter of fact, after the thing had droned along for quite awhile Mr. [Goodman], this Bill [Goodman], suggested that you and Doc House and Jim Brandon all leave the room and leave him and Gordon alone—isn't that correct?

A. I don't remember the exact words, but I do know that we left the defendant alone with Mr. [Goodman].

Q. So he remained alone then the rest of the period of time up there, along with Mr. [Goodman]?

A. I don't remember exactly how much took place after we went in, after I went back in that room.

Q. Well, this is one of—was there 16 or 17? How many people did you investigate altogether?

MR. THOMAS: Object, your Honor, as to how many people were

investigated. It is improper cross-examination and irrelevant in this case.

THE COURT: Overruled.

Q. How many different people did you take up there?

A. How many different people?

Q. And question or grill or grid or whatever it was? . . .

A. You understand that that would include all kinds of people, all different classes of people.

Q. How many did you interview altogether?

A. I can give you an estimate. I would certainly not—I couldn't tell it was complete—I would say a couple of hundred people.

Q. That included witnesses and suspects and everything, that 200?

A. Yes.

Q. Now, I think there were some—what was it? 18 other suspects that were finally accused?

MR. THOMAS: I object, your Honor. This is immaterial.

THE COURT: I am going to sustain this objection.

Q. Well, there is nothing, is there, Mr. Quinton, that made this particular interrogation stand out in your mind so that you would absolutely and distinctly remember that this admonition was given: "You don't have to talk if you don't want to; you can go home if you want to; if you want attorneys you can have one?"

A. Is there any reason why it should stand out? Is that what you mean?

Q. This was no different than any of the others, was it?

A. No. We told them all that.

Q. You told them all that?

A. Yes.

Q. Then what you are actually testifying from here, really and truly, is not from actual recollection but you thought it was your policy to follow that in each case, and you think you followed it then?

A. No, sir. I know we followed it then.

Q. Now, you did leave the room and left Gordon with Mr. [Goodman]?

A. Yes.

Q. For a considerable time?

A. Yes.

Q. How long was he with him alone—an hour, half hour, three-quarters of an hour, an hour and a half?

A. Half an hour or so. I don't know. I don't really know.

Q. And what occurred in there while this Bill [Goodman] had this young man by himself, you don't know?

A. No, I don't.

Q. What, if any, promises were made, what if—nothing, you don't have any idea?

A. No. I wouldn't know. I wasn't in there, and I couldn't tell you.

Q. Incidentally, was there a tape recording made of that interview?

A. I don't know whether there was or not.

Q. Then you went down to Gene Thomas' office?

A. Yes, sir.

Q. This young man continuously denied any implication with this man when he was up to the house?

A. Yes, he did.

Q. As a matter of fact, they brought this Eldon Halverson in there and this Eldon Halverson made this statement about the same way he made it here, and Gordon Larsen says, "You're a damn liar," didn't he?

A. That's true.

Q. He called Eldon Halverson a damn liar right there?

A. That's right.

Q. Yes; and I think Bill [Goodman] then told him to sit down and shut up, to Gordon Larsen?

A. I don't recollect that.

Q. You don't remember that?

A. No, I don't.

Q. Now then, when you got down to Gene Thomas' office, or the prosecuting attorney's office I should refer to it, it was around 6:30?

A. I think we left the office up there about 6:30. It was probably closer to a quarter to 7 when we got down there.

Q. And I believe you said that in the course of the interview there that it is your recollection that there was some discussion of "playing" and that was interpreted as being mutual masturbation?

A. That was what Mr. Larsen told us it was.

Q. Now, I apologize for having to have to use the words that I am about to use, but in the course of that interrogation, both up there at 16th Street and in the prosecuting attorney's office, the word "blow-job" was frequently used, was it not, by everybody?

A. I don't really recollect whether that term was used. I know that it was tried to—if I had anything to do with it, I tried to avoid the word.

Q. Yes, but it was used by everybody, Bill [Goodman] and everybody talked about it?

A. I couldn't testify that it was.

Q. You don't testify it was and you won't testify that it wasn't?

A. No, I won't.

Q. Now then, to get down real specific, the very last thing that Gordon said when he left Mr. Gene Thomas' office was that this was not an attempted "blow-job"—you heard that, didn't you?

A. No sir, because I didn't hear any confession from Mr. Larsen.

Q. Did you see it written down any place that this was not an attempted "blow-job"?

A. I read the confession, but I don't remember exactly what it had in it.

MR. SMITH: This is an amazing statement. I move that that answer be stricken as an opinion and conclusion of this witness and not responsive to the question.

THE COURT: Yes. Strike the answer just now given by this witness which, gentlemen of the jury, as I said before, means to disregard it.

Smith had managed to cast some doubt on Quinton, but mostly his attack was on Goodman, who had remained alone with Larsen. Smith also succeeded in suggesting the stress that the law-enforcement officials were putting on the homosexuals. That Quinton and Thomas had talked about this very question the day before also helped Smith.

REDIRECT EXAMINATION

By Mr. Thomas:

Q. Sergeant Quinton, what time of day was it that you picked up this defendant at his apartment in Boise Hills Village?

A. What time of day?

Q. Yes. What time did you pick him up there and bring him in?

A. Approximately a quarter to 4.

Q. Now, defense counsel talked about your notes. Do they reflect that same time?

A. Yes, they do.

MR. SMITH: I object to that. The notes would be the best evidence.

THE COURT: Sustained.

Q. Sergeant Qninton, you have stated on cross-examination that you have read some papers purporting to be a confession?

MR. SMITH: I object to that question on the ground that the testimony was stricken.

THE COURT: Sustained.

MR. THOMAS: Very well. That is all. Thank you, Sergeant.

RE-CROSS-EXAMINATION

By Mr. Smith:

Q. Since counsel has mentioned it, could you produce those, that daily diary of yours that would show the time?

MR. THOMAS: I object to that on the grounds previously set forth.

THE COURT: Same ruling. . . .

Q. . . . was there a piece of paper on Mr. Thomas' desk at the time you left his office on the 11th?

A. Yes, there was a whole yellow pad.

Q. And there was some writing on it?

A. Yes, there was writing on it.

Q. And you looked at it?

A. No, I did not, not at that time.

Q. You never looked at it?

A. No, I never seen anything on his desk that night.

MR. SMITH: I see. Very well. That is all.

MR. THOMAS: No further questions.

This last bit of questioning could have seemed very useful if Smith had gone on to show, or to contend, that Larsen's "confession" had already been written by Thomas before Quinton left the office—that is, before Larsen did confess—since Quinton claimed he had left at 8 P.M. and Larsen was still insisting on his innocence then, according to Quinton. But Brandon's testimony put an end to that possibility.

DIRECT EXAMINATION

By Mr. Thomas:

Q. Will you state your name, please?

A. James Brandon.

Q. Where do you reside, Sir?

A. Boise, Idaho.

Q. What is your occupation, Mr. Brandon?

A. Police officer, Boise City police department.

Q. Are you at this time Captain?

A. I am.

Q. Captain Brandon, are you not in charge of the juvenile division of the Boise City police?

A. I am.

Q. Captain, were you with the Boise police during December of 1955?

A. Yes, sir.

Q. At that time you were chief of police, were you not, Sir?

A. Yes, sir.

Q. And referring to December 11, 1955, were you on duty as chief of police in your official capacity?

A. I was.

Q. And did you at that time have occasion to see this defendant Gordon Larsen?

A. I did.

Q. Had you ever seen him before?

A. I may have seen him around Boise but I was not personally acquainted with him.

Q. Your recollection is that was the first time that you ever saw him?

A. That is the first time I ever saw him to know who he was.

Q. Captain Brandon, referring to the 11th of December, 1955, when do you recall was the, what was the time of day that you first saw him?

A. It was 3:45 p.m., in the afternoon.

Q. Thank you, Sir. Where was that, please?

A. It was at 1019 North 16th Street.

Q. Captain Brandon, that is the residence of one William [Goodman], or was at that time?

A. Yes, sir.

Q. And it was being used as an office, was it?

A. It was.

Q. And for what purpose? What type of office was it?

A. Well, it was a large room in the front part of the building on the ground floor that he had converted into an office, and it had two large desks and the necessary other furniture such as chairs, and so forth, and that office was the headquarters of the investigations of the homosexual activities in Boise, Ada County, Idaho, at that time.

Q. I see. At the time you first saw this defendant Gordon Larsen there on that day, who else was present, if you recall?

A. Sheriff House, William [Goodman], Officer Earnest Quinton and myself, and the defendant Gordon Larsen.

Q. I see. In whose company did the defendant Gordon Larsen first appear at that residence?

A. He appeared in the company of Officer Earnest Quinton.

Q. What, if you can recall and if you know, took place on his arrival there at the [Goodman] residence?

A. When he came into the room, why Mr. [Goodman] first introduced himself to him and then he introduced Sheriff House and myself to the defendant Gordon Larsen; otherwise, he made everybody known to each other there.

Q. Would you describe to the jury, if you recall it, the general demeanor and appearance of this defendant at that time?

A. Well, he was well dressed; he was very neat appearing, nothing unusual. He seemed normal in every respect.

Q. What, if anything, happened next immediately following the introductions that you referred to?

A. Everybody got seated, and Mr. [Goodman] then informed him as to what his status was as to being the man that was in charge of the investigation of this homosexual activity and that he had been retained by the County and City officials and he stated his status, and then I informed the defendant of his rights.

Q. How did you do that, Sir?

A. I informed him that he had a right to an attorney at all stages of the proceedings; he didn't have to talk if he did not desire to do so; that if he did, anything that he stated could be used against him at a later time in court.

Q. Captain Brandon, are you quite certain in advising him of his rights you used substantially that language?

A. Yes. That's usually the language that is used when we advise all people of their rights.

Q. How long have you been in police work, Sir?

A. Thirty years.

Q. I take it you have advised a lot of people of their rights?

A. Yes, sir.

Q. Captain Brandon, what was the substance of the conversation that followed, if one did?

A. The conversation that followed was carried on entirely by Mr. [Goodman] and the defendant. I never talked to the defendant any more, nor did anyone else. Mr. [Goodman] interrogated the defendant in regard to the information that he desired to obtain from him with reference to his activities and such as that.

Q. I see; and what precisely, if you recall, was said in this conversation with respect to this defendant and the State's witness Halverson in this case?

A. [Goodman] continued quite a long line of interrogation regarding his knowledge or acquaintance with the witness Eldon Halverson along the lines that he knew him or that he had been with him and such as that, and the defendant denied any knowledge or knowing him.

Q. I see; and did the defendant during that interview face Eldon Halverson?

A. Yes, he did. After he had been interrogated for some period of time, Halverson was sent for and he came into the room in the presence of the defendant at that time.

Q. And what, if anything, if you recall it, did the witness Halverson say to the defendant Larsen at that time?

A. Halverson identified Larsen as the man that he had known and he, Halverson, the witness in this case, stated that he had met the defendant and identified him as the man that he had met and went to an apartment in Hills Village with.

Q. I see; and what, if anything, did Halverson say had happened at that apartment?

MR. SMITH: Let me ask a question in the aid of an objection, your Honor.

THE COURT: Yes.

By Mr. Smith:

Q. Mr. Brandon, there was a tape recording taken of this interview, was there not?

A. Not to my knowledge.

Q. As a matter of fact, wasn't there a tape recording taken of every one of these interviews to preserve any admissions that the man might make, if he did?

A. You are saying every one of the interviews?

Q. Yes.

A. Not to my knowledge.

Q. You say that there was no tape recording taken?

A. I say not to my knowledge at every one of them.

Q. Was there a tape recording taken of this one?

A. Not to my knowledge.

Q. There may have been?

A. Possibly.

Q. The tape recording would show everything that you are telling if it is available?

MR. THOMAS: Your Honor, I will have to object to that line of question; it is improper.

THE COURT: Yes. The objection is sustained.

By Mr. Thomas:

Q. What, if anything, was said by the witness Halverson, as you recall it, to and in the presence of the defendant Larsen here respecting the activity there at the apartment?

A. Eldon Halverson made the statement that at this apartment in the bedroom he had had a homosexual act with the defendant. He stated that in the presence of the defendant and the other people.

Q. And the defendant denied that, did he not?

A. He did.

Q. And about how long was the witness Halverson present there?

A. Well, I would estimate that he was there approximately not over 20 minutes.

Q. I see. Now, what, if you know and recall, did the defendant Larsen say with respect to even recognizing Halverson?

A. At first he denied that he knew the man, and then after Halverson had completed his statement there the defendant stood up and says, "That's a damn lie."

Q. Did the defendant Larsen continue to claim that he did not know and had never seen Halverson?

A. Well, after Halverson left, on later questioning by Mr. [Goodman] the defendant Larsen finally admitted that he had been up to the apartment with the witness Eldon Halverson.

Q. I take it, he continued to deny the homosexual act there?

A. He did.

Q. Now Captain Brandon, what time did this interview end at the North 16th Street residence?

A. It ended at 5:57 p.m.

Q. 5:57; and you were there at the time it ended, were you?

A. I was.

Q. And did the defendant Gordon Larsen leave that residence at that time?

A. Shortly thereafter he did.

Q. You say "shortly thereafter." Will you tell the jury about how long you think that would be, how much time would be involved in that, within how many minutes?

A. Oh, I would say probably within the next, between five and ten minutes, the defendant went to the prosecuting attorney's office in the company of Officer Earnest Quinton.

Q. Did you actually go with them to the prosecuting attorney's office?

A. No, sir, I did not.

Q. Yes. Now, Captain Brandon, did you have occasion to see the defendant Gordon Larsen at a later hour on that same day?

A. I did.

Q. And when was that?

A. 9 o'clock. I came to the Ada County prosecuting attorney's office in this courthouse, and the defendant was in your office.

Q. And who was present at the time you arrived?

A. Officer Earnest Quinton, yourself, and I when I arrived.

Q. And the defendant Gordon Larsen?

A. And the defendant Gordon Larsen.

Q. Captain Brandon, what was going on at that office at the time you arrived?

A. Well, he was being interrogated.

Q. By whom, Sir?

A. By you.

Q. What was the subject of that discussion?

A. Well, when I first arrived, I didn't go in the office right then. I went up and looked in and you were talking to him.

Q. Yes, sir.

A. And very shortly thereafter Officer Quinton went out and you asked me to come in and I went in and sat down, and you continued interrogation of the defendant.

Q. What was the subject of that discussion at the time you came in?

A. It had to do with the activity in the bedroom of this apartment in Hills Village concerning the defendant Larsen and the witness Eldon Halverson.

Q. Yes, sir; and what, if anything, did the defendant Gordon Larsen say at the time you came in there with respect to that activity?

A. He made an oral admission that he and Halverson while on the bed in the apartment had a homosexual act.

Q. I see. During the time you were there in that office and during this interrogation, did anyone else come to that office and walk into it?

A. Yes, they did.

Q. Who was that, Sir?

A. Mr. Blaine Evans.

Q. Mr. Blaine Evans; and was there any discussion and conversation between Mr. Evans and the defendant?

A. Mr. Evans just stepped inside the office, and he asked the defendant Larsen, he said, "How did you come to get mixed up in this business?" or "Started in this business?" or words to that effect.

Q. What did the defendant Larsen answer to that?

A. "While I was in the service."

Q. Captain Brandon, you have referred to statements made by the defendant Larsen. Would you tell the jury in precise language what he said had happened on that day?

A. The defendant stated that he and Halverson was playing around on the bed and that they had each placed each other's penis in their mouth.

Q. Captain Brandon, what happened next following the admission by the defendant of this fact?

A. Well, there was a yellow pad of paper on your desk, and you began to write up some type of wording there which later was read.

This would tend to contradict Quinton's previous testimony that there was some writing already on the yellow pad.

Q. Captain Brandon, I would like you to tell the jury, if you will, please, describe to them the demeanor and appearance of the defendant Gordon Larsen during all of the times you have referred to in my office.

A. Well, he was normal. There was nothing unusual about him at that time. His appearance was good. I will say that he seemed slightly nervous, but he was in full command of his facilities at all times. He knew what he was talking about. He would think before he would answer.

Q. How did his appearance compare with his appearance at 3:45 that afternoon when you first saw him?

A. I would say it was practically the same.

Q. Captain Brandon, was he made any promises at that time?

A. Not to my knowledge he wasn't, not in my presence.

Q. During the time you were there was he under any apparent duress?

A. No, sir.

MR. THOMAS: May I have this marked?

(A statement on yellow paper was marked as "State's Exhibit No. 1 for identification.")

Q. Now, Captain Brandon, you say you arrived there about 8 p.m.?

A. Yes, sir.

Q. About how long were you there altogether during this interrogation?

A. I was there until the interrogation ended.

Q. About when?

A. Approximately about 30 minutes.

Q. Now, you have testified that the defendant admitted certain facts. About how long after you arrived did he make these statements that you have testified to?

A. I would say approximately in about 15 minutes.

Q. Yes, sir. What happened next after he had made these statements that you have testified to?

A. Well, you begin writing notes on the pad, and then you made the statement, "Let's get this down in writing."

Q. Yes, sir.

A. And you then wrote out a heading of a statement and read that back to the defendant.

Q. Yes, sir.

A. And that was the statements again stating his rights, he had been advised of his rights to counsel, and whatever he might sign in the statement could be used against him at a later time, and that he did not have to make a statement, I believe, unless he desired to do so.

Q. Captain Brandon, what, if anything, was done or happened following that?

A. Well, then the subjects of the oral admission were written down by you; in fact, you asked him a few questions about that again and then wrote the subjects of that on the paper.

Q. The story was gone over the second time?

A. Yes, sir.

Q. And I was making notes or writing something at that time, was I?

A. Yes, sir.

Q. And then, Captain Brandon, what happened after that?

A. The sheet of paper that was being written on was placed on the desk and the defendant Larsen read the statement.

Q. I see. Was it read aloud?

A. He himself did not read it aloud.

Q. Yes, sir; and then what happened after that?

A. You asked him if he wanted to sign it, and he said, "Not until we make a correction."

Q. What did he say that was?

A. That was adding of another sentence onto the statement, which he wanted added, to the effect that, as he referred to as, "playing around," and that he himself did not make any attempt, was the language as I recall it, to perform a "blow-job" on Eldon Halverson.

Q. I see.

A. And that was written on the statement and he again read it.

Q. And then was that statement read aloud by me?

A. It was.

Q. And where was the defendant Gordon Larsen at the time of this reading?

A. He was setting right there by the head of the table at your desk.

Q. Was he apparently reading it and following it along?

A. Yes, sir.

Q. Captain Brandon, was the language in the statement substantially in accordance with the defendant's own language as he described the incident?

A. Yes, because you had asked him questions along during the writing of the statement, and the writing as you read it back you wrote clearly what he stated there.

Q. Now, Captain Brandon, following this reading did the defendant then sign the statement?

A. He did, and he also initialed the statement at the top and bottom.

Q. Was the statement witnessed then at that time?

A. It was.

Q. And did you witness it?

A. I did.

Q. And I did, too, didn't I?

A. Yes, sir.

Q. And, Captain Brandon, do you know the time of day or time of evening that that signature was affixed to the statement?

A. It was 8:30 p.m.

Q. One-half hour after he arrived—is that right?

A. Yes.

Thomas must have meant, in that last question, "after you arrived."

Q. Handing you what has been marked for identification as State's Exhibit No. 1, Captain Brandon, would you look at that, please? (Witness examines Ex. 1.) Will you tell the jury, please, what that is?

A. This is the statement that was written by Mr. Thomas on the date of December 11, 1955, in his office, and it was signed by Gordon Larsen, and it was witnessed by myself and Mr. Thomas, and the statement contains the—

MR. SMITH: Well, the statement speaks for itself.

THE COURT: Yes.

Q. Captain Brandon, that is the statement about which you have testified, is it not?

A. It is.

Q. And would you tell the jury whether or not it is in the identical form in which you last saw it that evening?

A. It is except for the identification stamp.

Q. And these holes in the top weren't there, were they?

A. No sir.

MR. THOMAS: Your Honor, we will offer State's Exhibit 1. . . . It begins with the initials "G.L." and then reads:

"This statement was given voluntarily at Room 103 Ada County on the evening of December 12, 1955, in the presence of Eugene C. Thomas, James Brandon and Bill [Goodman]. It is made voluntarily, without promise or duress, and with the advice that it might be used against me and that I have a constitutional right to counsel. It is given voluntarily. About noon on or about October 3, 1955, at my apartment in Boise Hills Village in Boise, Idaho I had a homosexual experience with Eldon Halverson wherein I recall taking his penis into my mouth and he took my penis into his. Neither of us had an orgasm. My name is Gordon Larsen, and I reside at Boise Hills Village in Boise, Idaho. The time is 8:30 p.m. This incident involved 'playing around' and was not an attempt on my part to 'blow' Halverson." Period.

Initial "G.L." Signed "Gordon R. Larsen." "Witnessed:

James E. Brandon 12–11–55

Eugene C. Thomas 12–11–55,"

then a zigzag line down at the bottom.

Goodman, who showed up in time for the signing, did not witness the confession, because he did not want to be liable for a court order demanding his appearance, since he did not want to testify.

Q. Captain Brandon, handing you State's Exhibit 1, you will observe the date referred to in the preamble there is December 12th?

A. Yes, sir.

Q. That is not the same date as you are witnessing?

A. No, sir. We called that to your attention at the time that I witnessed the signing of this document and inserted the date 12–11 myself and signed it.

Q. Do you know what day of the week that was?

A. It was on Sunday.

Q. Yes, sir. So the inconsistency in date stems from confusion on my part—is that right?

A. Apparently.

Q. Captain Brandon, what happened next that evening of December 11, 1955, after 8:30 p.m.?

A. Well, after the statement there was signed we informed the defendant Larsen that a complaint would be filed, so then I took the defendant to the police station and as a matter of record we photographed him and fingerprinted him, and I returned him to your office.

Q. Yes, sir; and then what happened?

A. Mr. Evans was typing the complaint, and you called Judge Lampert at his home to make arrangements for an appearance before Judge Lampert, Justice of the Peace, and he was advised that we would be there at approximately 9 p.m. After the complaint was completed by Mr. Evans, you, the defendant Larsen and myself drove to Mr. Lampert's residence, which is located on Rogers Heights in the north end of town, and appeared before Judge J. M. Lampert at his home.

Q. About what time, if you recall, did we arrive there?

A. It would be very shortly after 9:00, or right at 9:00, around five minutes to a quarter after 9:00 o'clock.

Q. And would you describe to the jury what took place there at Judge Lampert's residence?

A. Well, going into Judge Lampert's home we entered what I take to be a large dining room, and he had a small table on the south side of the room, which he sat down at, and you gave him the copy of the, or the complaint and warrant, and Mr., the defendant Larsen and I were present, standing right immediately near the table, and Judge Lampert signed the documents and handed me the warrant, and I read the warrant to the defendant, the warrant of arrest, and returned it to the Judge; then Judge Lampert read the complaint to the defendant. After reading the complaint he advised him that he was entitled to a preliminary hearing. I don't think the defendant was, fully understood what a preliminary hearing might be, and the Judge gave him an explanation of what it was, what a preliminary hearing consisted of, and then the defendant sat down beside this small table, and the defendant turned to you and asked you what he should do, and I recall very distinctly you advised him as prosecutor it was not your duty to advise him and that he probably should consult an attorney. Judge Lampert handed the defendant the complaint and he sat there and read it for quite, oh, a period of probably a few minutes, and he asked you, Mr. Thomas, who had written the complaint, and you notified, told him that Mr. Evans had, and he stated that he did not like the last part of that complaint. Then you asked him specifically what he referred to, and he said the last line. He had the complaint on the table, and I was standing rather closely to him at that time, and he read it over, and, as I recall, you pointed to the last line of the complaint and you said, "This?" and he said, "Yes," and you asked him if he objected to the word "sucking," and he said "Yes." You asked him if the rest of the complaint was true, and he said "Yes."

Q. Can you tell the jury what portion of the last line he pointed to or do you know?

MR. SMITH: Now, just a moment. Where is the complaint?

THE COURT: I believe it would be with the official file here.

MR. SMITH: Let's get it into the record.

MR. THOMAS: Do you want to stipulate that it be marked State's Exhibit 2 and be admitted, Mr. Smith?

MR. SMITH: Yes, I want it before this jury.

. . . (The criminal complaint referred to was deemed marked

"State's Exhibit No. 2 for identification" and deemed admitted in evidence.)

Q. Captain Brandon, referring to State's Exhibit 2 for identification, the complaint, is that the complaint you were referring to?

A. Yes.

Q. And referring to the typed-in, what we call the "charging" portion, would you tell the jury which language of the complaint, which portion of it the defendant objected to at that time?

A. Shall I read it?

Q. Yes, if you know which part it is.

A. "A male human being, then and there sucking the same."

Q. And that is the portion from the comma to the period on the last line there of that charging part, is it not?

A. It is from the first comma—there are two commas there—it is from the first comma to the last period.

Q. What, if anything, did he say with respect to the other portion of the complaint?

A. He said that was true.

Q. Captain Brandon, referring now to the interview in my office, was Mr. [Goodman] present at any time during the taking of that statement?

A. Yes, he was. Right at the very end of the, I should say the writing of this paper, he came into your office there, into your office.

MR. THOMAS: That is all.

Thomas' examination of Brandon served one fundamentally important function: It showed that Larsen was very clear-headed about what was going on and thus fortified the impression that the confession was legitimately obtained. Smith would have to cast doubts on Brandon to offset that impression.

CROSS-EXAMINATION

By Mr. Smith:

Q. Mr. Brandon, up there at Judge Lampert's home, did I understand you to say that Gordon Larsen didn't like the last part of the complaint? Is that what your testimony was, that when the complaint was read to him he said that he didn't like the last part?

A. He didn't say that until he had read it himself.

Q. Yes; and what did he say about that last part of the complaint?

A. As I recall, he said that he didn't like that last part.

Q. He said that he didn't like it. Are you positive those were his words?

A. He either said, "I didn't like it," or "I object," one of the two.

Q. He objected to the last part of the complaint?

A. He possibly objected.

Q. Yes. As a matter of fact, you were a witness at the preliminary hearing and at that time you so testified that the defendant said that he objected to the last part of the complaint?

A. It is very likely I did.

Q. That's correct; and the last part of the complaint said, "The said Gordon Larsen's mouth"—the whole complaint reads this way:

"That the said defendant, Gordon Larsen, a male person in Ada County, Idaho, on or about the 3rd Day of October, 1955, did then and there wilfully, unlawfully and feloniously commit the infamous crime against nature,"

now, the last part:

"By then and there wilfully, unlawfully and feloniously taking into his, the said Gordon Larsen's mouth, the penis of one Eldon Halverson, a male human being, and then and there sucking the same,"

and he objected to the last part of the complaint?

A. Yes.

Q. Yes, sir. Now, in Gene Thomas' office, Mr. Brandon, while you were all in there at the end of this long day of examining of Mr. Larsen you finally got down, Mr. Thomas got down to writing up something; this sheet Plaintiff's Exhibit 1, or State's Exhibit 1, is in Mr. Thomas' hand-writing, isn't it?

A. Yes, sir.

Q. Mr. Thomas wrote the whole thing?

A. Yes, sir.

Q. Composed it himself and then handed it over to the defendant to sign, didn't he?

A. Yes, sir.

Q. And the defendant refused to sign it, didn't he?

A. He did at first.

Q. Yes. The defendant says, "Mr. Thomas, we both agreed and we agreed continuously that this was not a 'blow-job' "? That is what he said, wasn't it?

A. I don't recall that he said those exact words. He wanted it changed there.

Q. Yes; and Mr. Thomas took it back and said, "All right," and then Mr. Thomas added something more to it and handed it back?

A. He did.

Q. And what he added, "This was not an attempt on my part to 'blow' Halverson," is the way he put it?

A. That's right.

Q. And the defendant was not willing to admit even at that last minute, after all of those numerous hours—

MR. THOMAS: Your Honor, I will have to object. Counsel's preambles to his questions are argument to the jury.

THE COURT: Objection sustained.

Q. Until that statement had been amended?

A. That's right.

Q. Now, you say that this interrogation started at 3:45?

A. Yes, sir.

Q. In any event it was in the afternoon. According to your testimony it lasted, the whole thing lasted from 3:45 until 9:30, is when he was finally up to Judge Lampert's court?

A. Yes, sir.

Q. During all that time Gordon Larsen was not given any opportunity to have dinner?

A. I left.

Q. Yes, you left.

A. And I don't know what opportunity was given then.

Q. He had run out of cigarettes early in the afternoon.

A. He might have.

Q. Yes. When you first took him to that house there was you and Doc House and Bill [Goodman] there, wasn't there, the three of you and the defendant?

A. Yes, sir.

Q. And you sat around there, oh, for a couple of hours before you finally left the room?

A. Yes, sir.

Q. Was that about how long you were there?

A. Approximately, yes.

Q. Yes; and this was a private home up here in the Hyde Park area that had a fireplace burning?

A. Yes, sir.

Q. And you brought these suspects and witnesses in and set them down at a table on which there was a mirror and glass of water? . . .

A. There was a glass of water, but I don't recall any mirror.

Q. Very well, and then you started into an accusation of Gordon Larsen that he was a homosexual, the four of you did?

A. I never said one word to Larson [sic] after I advised him of his rights.

Q. You didn't say one word. Well, I believe that is true; I think that is true. Mr. [Goodman] conducted this inquisition, did he not?

A. He did.

Q. Yes. You and Doc House sat around and answered questions as [Goodman] would ask you questions?

A. Mr. [Goodman] never asked me any questions.

Q. Well, let me help refresh your recollection. At one point Mr. [Goodman] was accusing Gordon Larsen of being a liar. He turned to you and says, "Mr. Brandon, what do you think? Is he a liar?" and you said, "Yes," and he turned to Doc House and says, "What do you think? Is he a liar?" and he said, "Yes." Do you remember that?

A. No sir.

Q. You don't remember?

MR. THOMAS: I ask the counsel be admonished to ask questions here and not to make speeches.

THE COURT: On cross-examination he may ask proper questions, and these are. Overruled.

Q. During that entire afternoon there at this Hyde Park residence there were you four policemen and Gordon Larsen. He continued time and time and time again to tell you folks that this Halverson is not telling the truth, didn't he?

A. While Halverson was there he made that statement, yes, sir.

Q. He continued time and time to assert his innocence of this?

A. Yes, sir.

Q. And finally Mr. Bill [Goodman] suggested that you and Mr. Doc House and Mr. Quinton leave the room so that he could have him alone?

A. He did.

Q. And so then Mr. [Goodman] had him alone for about the next hour?

A. Oh, I don't think it was an hour.

Q. Well, how long was it, Mr. Brandon?

A. We went out and sat on the porch, and I don't think it was over 30 minutes.

Q. You think that he had him alone for 30 minutes?

A. I think he did, yes. . . .

Q. At this particular hearing did somebody have a tape recorder there?

A. Yes, there was a tape recorder there.

Q. There was a tape recorder. Then when you said on examination awhile ago when I asked you "Was there a tape recorder?" and you said "No," you were not telling the truth?

A. You asked me if a recording was taken.

Q. Was there a tape recorder there being used then?

A. There was one there, but to my knowledge I don't know whether it was being used or not. . . .

Q. . . . You say there was a tape recorder there at Mr. [Goodman's] place of business?

A. Yes, there was.

Q. And there was a stack of tapes there, was there not?

A. Yes. I saw some tapes there.

Q. And it was there to be used, was it not?

MR. THOMAS: I will object, your Honor, to the question as improper.

THE COURT: Sustained.

Q. And you don't know whether a tape recording was taken of Gordon Larsen's interview?

A. No, sir, I do not.

This seems rather improbable. Goodman told me that he made tapes of every session, and offered to let me listen to them after he read my manuscript. He also told me that he had given some of the tapes to Brandon, but refused to specify which. Brandon may not have known whether there was a tape, but I am sure that there was.

Q. Now, Mr. Brandon, you say you used to be the chief of police. You are not any more?

A. No, sir.

Q. You were relieved from that office, were you not?

A. Yes, sir.

Q. As a matter of fact, at the time that this homosexual investigation was going on, Mr. Brandon, you were somewhat under fire yourself?

MR. THOMAS: Your Honor, I will object—

MR. SMITH: Let me finish my question.

MR. THOMAS: I request that counsel be admonished not to continue that question. He is trying to change the subject from the guilt of this defendant.

MR. SMITH: Again your Honor—

THE COURT: Objection sustained.

MR. SMITH: It shows the status of this witness at the time this investigation was made.

THE COURT: I have ruled.

MR. SMITH: Very well.

Smith was desperately trying to discredit Brandon—here, by reminding the jurors that he had been fired as police chief.

Q. Now, in this prosecution you have an interest, do you not, Mr. Brandon?

A. I don't quite understand what you mean.

Q. In other words, your department accused this defendant in this whole investigation of which you were a part, and you are testifying here in support of that accusation that was made?

A. I am testifying for the State, yes.

Q. So you are interested in sustaining your original accusation, aren't you?

MR. THOMAS: I object to that as vague and uncertain. Let counsel say what he means by "interested."

THE COURT: Rephrase the question. The objection to the present question is sustained.

MR. SMITH: Yes.

Q. Mr. Brandon, this group of which you were a part, who were investigating this homosexual activity in Boise, culminated in accusation of Gordon Larsen of the infamous crime against nature?

A. Yes, sir.

Q. That grew out of that group of which you were a part?

A. Yes, sir.

Q. And you are interested in seeing to it that your original accusation is sustained if you possibly can sustain it?

MR. THOMAS: Your Honor, I still object to the vague and uncertain language used here. If he wants to know if the witness is biased, let him ask that question.

THE COURT: Sustained.

Q. Now, on December 11th when you had Mr. Gordon Larsen up there at the [Goodman] residence, there had been set up here in Ada County this new health unit which was supposed to give psychiatric treatment to those people, had there not?

MR. THOMAS: Object to that as incompetent, irrelevant, improper cross.

THE COURT: I don't know where this is leading. I will have to overrule the objection for the time being and you may continue, Mr. Smith.

A. I believe there was at that time.

Q. Yes; and in the course of the interrogation of Mr. Larsen he was frequently told by Mr. Bill [Goodman] that "We don't believe you; we believe that you are a homosexual and all we want to do is to send you to that school." It was mentioned time and time again, wasn't it?

A. No, I don't recall that type of question.

Q. Was the school mentioned?

A. At the very outset of the time that Mr. Larsen came there, Mr. [Goodman] advised him of his status in connection with the investigation—

Q. Let me ask you to answer my question. The question was, Mr. Brandon, was the school mentioned?

MR. THOMAS: The witness is answering the question if counsel will be patient.

MR. SMITH: The question calls for a yes or no answer.

THE COURT: You can answer that yes or no, can't you, Mr. Brandon?

A. Yes.

Q. It was mentioned by Mr. [Goodman] many times, was it not, to Mr. Larsen?

A. No, not many times. Right at the first it was mentioned.

Q. Now, you were also present when this Eldon Halverson was brought in, were you not?

A. Yes, sir.

Q. You were here yesterday when he testified concerning receiving money from Mr. [Goodman]?

A. Yes, sir.

Q. That is a fact, is it not?

A. Yes, sir.

Q. Mr. [Goodman] gave this Eldon Halverson $3.00 or some money and told him he could leave?

A. Yes, sir.

Q. After he had accused Mr. Larsen?

A. I believe it was $3.00 he gave him.

Q. You believe it was $3.00; and you also heard Mr. [Goodman] call to Mr. Larsen's attention, "See, Mr. Halverson is cooperating and we are letting him go"—you heard that, too, didn't you?

A. No, I didn't hear that statement.

Q. You didn't hear that statement?

A. That wasn't mentioned in my presence.

Q. In any event Mr. Halverson did walk out of that room?

A. He did.

Q. After having admitted or claimed that he, in the presence of you as chief of police, Doc House, deputy sheriff, and Mr. [Goodman], chief investigator, after having claimed that he had committed a homosexual act?

MR. THOMAS: Your Honor, objection as irrelevant and improper cross.

THE COURT: Overruled.

A. He did.

Q. He walked out of that room; and to this date, Mr. Brandon, Mr. Eldon Halverson has never been charged with any crime?

A. Not to my knowledge.

Q. Yes. Mr. Brandon, after having heard the admission to you by Mr. Halverson concerning Mr. Larsen, if you believed Mr. Halverson you would file a complaint against him, wouldn't you?

MR. THOMAS: Objection, your Honor; it is irrelevant, it is incompetent and not proper cross-examination.

THE COURT: He may answer.

A. The prosecuting attorney had charge of filing the complaints.

Q. And you were the chief of police who is charged with the duty of enforcing the law?

A. Yes, sir.

Q. You don't believe Mr. Halverson, do you?

A. I don't quite understand your question. I don't believe him what? Explain it a little further.

Q. You don't believe Mr. Halverson when he claims that he had a homosexual act with this man or you would have charged him?

A. Yes, I believed him.

Q. You believed him. You prefer to believe him and disregard your duty?

MR. THOMAS: Objection, your Honor, improper cross.

THE COURT: Objection sustained.

MR. SMITH: No further cross-examination of this witness.

Although Smith had effectively reminded the jurors that Brandon was a man with a heated past, he did not, in my opinion, shake his creditability enough to help. The points that struck me upon reading the court record—such as the fifteen-minute confession and the fact that Brandon did not know whether the tape recorder was recording—did not seem to bother the jurors. The most striking damage to the prosecution should have been the fact that Goodman had not been served with a subpoena because he was dodging the process server sent by Smith. Why would he not testify? Goodman told me the answer, and I have stated it earlier in the book, but the jurors should also have asked themselves that question. Then, by deduction, they might have concluded that Goodman was ducking because he did not want to perjure himself, because he did offer Larsen a deal, perhaps because he threatened him too. Smith brought these points out in his examination of Brandon. He did it indirectly, and often against sustained objections, but not strongly enough. And he did not discredit Brandon and Quinton sufficiently to swing Round Two to his side. That is why he had to put Larsen on the stand and hope for a knockout in Round Three.

18

THE TRIAL–ROUND THREE
AND KNOCKOUT!

Defense Attorney Vernon K. Smith knew very well what he was getting into by putting Gordon Larsen on the stand. But he had no choice, and if the jurors would simply not disbelieve his client, then the corroborating evidence against him would not be enough to warrant conviction. So after making his point against Goodman, he called Larsen.

MR. SMITH: The subpoena is outstanding for Mr. Bill [Goodman]. Is Mr. Bill [Goodman] in the courtroom? (No response.) I understood that it had not been served, but I wanted to check. Call the defendant Gordon Larsen.

Whereupon,

GORDON LARSEN,

The defendant, appearing as a witness in his own behalf, first having been duly sworn, testified as follows:

DIRECT EXAMINATION

By Mr. Smith:

Q. Will you please state your name?

A. Gordon Larsen.

Q. And how old a man are you?

A. Thirty-two.

Q. Are you a married man or a single man?

A. Single.

Q. Have you been married?

A. Yes, sir.

Q. Where are you living now, Gordon?

A. In Spokane, Washington.

Q. How long have you been living in Spokane?

A. Since last January.

Q. Did anything occur in this community last January or December that occasioned your moving from Boise?

A. Yes, sir.

Q. As of the fall of 1955 here in Boise, where were you working?

A. At the Mode Department Store.

Q. What were you doing there, Gordon?

A. I was head of the men's department.

Q. What department is that? What kind of work is that?

A. Well, it is buying and managing the men's wear department of a department store.

Q. That's the Mode Department Store here in Boise?

A. Yes.

Q. How long had you been on that job? How long had you been there?

A. Well, I had just gotten the job. It was brand new. I just took the job in October, I believe.

Q. In October you had taken the job. Prior to that where had you been working?

A. I was a salesman for the Boise Fruit and Produce.

Q. And is that a business establishment here in Boise?

A. Yes.

Q. And you say a salesman. What was the nature of your work?

A. Well, I went around and called on grocery stores and restaurants and took their orders for produce.

Q. I take it the Boise Fruit and Produce sells vegetables and that type of stuff?

A. Yes.

Q. And frozen foods, too, I guess?

A. No.

Q. Just fresh vegetables; and you called on the restaurant trade—is that what you did?

A. Yes.

Q. Were the restaurants in the bus depots and hotels on your list?

A. Yes.

Q. Particularly what hotels?

A. Well, the Boise and the Owyhee, and those were the only two hotels that have large dining rooms.

Q. Were there restaurants—in the Trailway bus depot?

A. Yes. Well, I called on Watson's Cafe adjacent to the bus depot.

Q. And what about the other bus depot—is there a restaurant there?

A. Yes.

Q. Were they on your list?

A. No. No, sir.

Q. They were not?

A. They were not.

Q. I see. Now, do you recall the 11th day of December, 1955?

A. Yes, very vividly.

Q. Do you recall meeting a man by the name of, that you now know as Sergeant Quinton?

A. Yes.

Q. Where did you meet him?

A. He came to my door at the apartment and showed me his badge.

Q. Where were you living then?

A. In Boise Hills Village.

Q. And what, if any, request did he make?

A. He said, "I would like to have you come down town; an officer wants to talk to you. Come with me."

Q. What is that?

A. He said, "Come with me. There is an officer down town who would like to ask you a few questions."

Q. An officer down town wanted to talk to you?

A. Yes.

Goodman was not an officer.

Q. Did you go with him?

A. Yes.

Q. Did he tell you what he wanted?

A. No, he didn't. I asked him at that time and he says, "Well, you will find out in a few minutes."

Q. "You will find out." Then what did you do?

A. I went with him, went out and got in the car. There was another fellow driving it and presumably a police car.

Q. Any conversation on the way down?

A. No.

Q. None at all. Now, when you got down there—where did you go?

A. I believe it is on the corner of 16th and Sherman. It's an old house.

Q. In Boise?

A. Yes.

Q. Now, when you went in, I want you to describe the general, the inside of this house.

A. Well, as I tell you, it was an old house and you went into a small hallway and turned to the left and went into what I suppose was a part of the living room, and it had a fireplace burning and two desks back to back and there was one light on the desk, and they had the Venetian blinds closed tight, and there were a few chairs around the room, and that is about all I can remember of the room.

Q. Yes. Now, were you asked to sit down some place?

A. Yes. They asked me to sit down at the desk across from Mr. [Goodman].

Q. Mr. [Goodman]. There were two desks back to back and he was sitting over there and you were sitting here (pointing)?

A. Yes.

Q. What was on the table?

A. Well, on the desk facing me there was a glass of water and a mirror.

Q. Which way did this mirror face?

Smith wanted to imply that the mirror represented an act of intimidation.

A. It faced me.

Q. It faced you. Now I want you to relate to this jury in your own words, the best that you can recall, what happened during that period of time that you were out there at that house on 16th Street.

A. Well, I don't know who made the introductions. Somebody introduced Mr. [Goodman] and Doc House and Chief Brandon and this cop who came after me—I didn't remember his name at the time, but it is now Quinton—and they told me to sit down, that they wanted to have a talk with me about the homosexual investigation in Boise, so they started talking and they said, "We know you can give us some help," and I said, "Well, what kind of help can I give you?" and they says, "Well, we know you are a homo," and I said, "Well, what makes you think so?" and then [Goodman] said, "Well, I have been studying homosexuality all my life and I know one when I see it." He said, "I could tell when you were walking in the door that you were a homo by the way you walk," and I said, "Well, just because a person walks a certain way, does that make him a homo?" and he said, "Well, it does in my books, because I have been studying homosexuality and I know all about it." So they said they wanted, told me about the investigation going on here in Boise, about cleaning up the homosexual situation and trying to protect our children and everything, so that they knew that I had something to offer and that if I did I would be cooperative. So I told them I was in complete agreement with anybody who molested children and they had a perfect right to conduct an investigation if there was children involved, and so they kept, I kept saying that "I don't have anything to offer; I would be glad to help you out if I could, but there is nothing that I have that could help you out," and they says, "Well, we know you can and we know that you are," so in so many words they were just accusing me and calling me names, and I mean they didn't mince any matters as far as the terminology they used when they were talking to me, and they called me a queer and, as I say, a homo and all this stuff, and so this went on and on and on, and I told them I would be glad to help them if I could but there was nothing that I knew or, of my knowledge, that would help them out any." So then they said, "O.K. We'll show you." So they told this cop, they said, "O.K. Go out and get him." So he went out and got this Halverson—I didn't know who it was at the time or his name—and brought him in and stood him in the doorway, and they said to Halverson, "Is this the man?" and Halverson said, "Yes," and they said to Halverson, "Well, now you tell us what happened when you went up to his apartment," and Halverson said, "Well, he asked me up to his apartment and he blew me and I blew him," and I stood up and I said, "You're a damn liar," and they told me to shut up and sit down.

Q. Who told you to shut up and sit down?

A. [Goodman].

Q. All right.

A. And so then they said to Halverson, "Would you swear to that in court?" and he said he would, and they asked him his name, and he said he was twenty-one, and then [Goodman] threw him three one dollar bills and says, "O.K., buddy, here is some gas money; go on home," and he left.

Q. Now, what comment—go ahead.

A. And [Goodman] said to me, he says, "See, Gordon," he says, "That's what happens to a guy who cooperates. Now, it could happen to you if you would just cooperate," and I said, "Well, there's nothing to cooperate about; I didn't do anything; I haven't done anything; I can't give you guys any information," and say "O.K., if you want to make it hard on yourself."

Q. Let's go back; and what accusations, if any, were made about whether or not you were telling the truth?

A. Well, at one time there—I mean this all happened over a period of a couple of hours—and when they kept telling me that I was a homo and that I knew something that they wanted to know and I wouldn't tell them, they kept calling me—well, first he said, "Well, we think you are just lying," [Goodman,] "We think you are just plain lying to us," and [Goodman] turned to Doc House and said, "Don't you think he is lying, Doc?" and House said, "Yes," and then he turned to Brandon and said, "Don't you think he is lying, Brandon?" and Brandon said, "Yes." So there I sat a great big liar in their estimation. That is all that they were doing is make me a big liar.

Q. Now, was there any discussion of a school, or what did this [Goodman] tell you about a school?

A. Well, he told me, he said, "You know about all these investigations that were going on?" and I said, "Yes, I read about them in the paper," and he said, "We are trying to help these fellows; we are not picking them up and accusing them of these criminal acts; we want to help them," and I says, "Fine," and he says, "We're setting up a rehabilitation, a psychiatric school or something, some kind of a training program here, that we are sending these fellows to school— I mean they are going to have psychiatric treatment," and he says, "We can do the same thing for you," and I said, "Well, I don't think I need any psychiatric treatment," and he says, "Well, your name won't be mentioned," he says. "You can go to this school; nobody's names will be mentioned, and nobody will know about it; you can go to these schools and be recuperated or rehabilitated, and so all we want you to do is to cooperate with us, and that's all we want you to do. You can go to this school, and no names will be mentioned."

Q. Now, did the occasion arise during this—how long do you think you were there with him before Doc House and Brandon left?

A. Oh, I must have been there a good hour or an hour and a half.

Q. Were they there all the time?

A. Yes, they were there all the time until [Goodman] said, "Well, maybe,"—he tried to get real friendly with me and he says, "Well, maybe, Gordon, you and I, you could talk better if you and I were just here alone."

Q. What did he call you then?

A. He called me "Gordie."

Q. Gordie. He wanted to talk to you alone, and then what happened?

A. So then he sent Doc House and Brandon and this cop out of the room and closed the door, and he says, "O.K., Gordie, let's talk man to man."

Q. Now, at that point I want to ask you, did the occasion ever arise during that afternoon when you were advised that there was a tape recording?

A. Yes. I didn't know it at first but, oh, I must have been there 45 minutes to an hour, and [Goodman] stood up and he said, "Will you excuse me a minute while I change the tape?" and that's the first time I knew that there was a tape recorder. So he took down some tapes off the filing cabinet up in back of him, and he says, "Of course, we aren't never going to use these; they are just for my record because I don't have a secretary," so I waited for him while he changed the tape.

Q. You personally know—at least the incident happened that there was a tape recording made?

A. Yes, right down here beside his chair.

Q. And that tape recording would show every answer and question?

A. As far as I know—

MR. EVANS: We are going to object to that, your Honor, as calling for a conclusion.

THE COURT: Objection is sustained.

If Larsen was telling the truth, then Goodman changed the tape before the others went out, so that Quinton and Brandon were lying. But perhaps Larsen misjudged the time.

Q. Now then, after the others left and he wanted to get buddy-buddy with you, proceed then with what happened.

A. Well, he tried to tell me, he started asking me, he says, "Come on now and tell us about this incident with Halverson, with this fellow that I just brought in," and I said, "There was no incident; I don't even recognize the man," and at that time I didn't recognize him, and so then he said, "Well, come on now, we know all about you and we know you did, so why don't you cooperate with us?" and he just kept dwelling on this cooperation deal, and so finally he says, "Well, you know we can make it tough on you if you don't cooperate," so then I began to wonder well now what should I do? I mean admit to something I didn't do, because the first thing that I could think of and the only thing I could think of at the time after all this publicity had been in the paper— . . . And all I could think of at the time was this publicity in the paper, and I was proposing marriage in January, the following month, and I had also just got this new job, which was actually a real position, and all I could think of was my name being spread all over the paper and everything going to pot, and that is all I could think of, and I mean when they started telling me that they would make it tough on me, then I began to wonder, well, if I cooperated in admitting something that I didn't do, would they let me go like they did with Halverson. I mean here Halverson stood right there and admitted a homosexual act, and they let him go because he was co-operative, so I thought to myself, well, I mean, if he can get away with it, I mean he actually admitted it right out and out and he's walking the streets free and his name hasn't been in the paper, I began to turn it over in my mind whether I should admit to something I didn't do in order to get the heck out of there.

Q. Now, did you even then admit it?

A. No, I did not.

Q. What happened then? What did he do?

A. Who?

Q. That is, Mr. [Goodman].

A. Well, he kept trying to get me to confess to this incident with Halverson, so I said that I think that that is the fellow who I met on the street corner, and I think it is the one who followed me up to my apartment, but there was no homosexual act committed, absolutely none, and he laughed and he says, "Well, we know you are lying now; you have come through with half of it and you won't come through with the rest," and so I told him the story about, if this was the guy, and I said in turning it over in my mind when they started talking about what date it was back in October and refreshing my memory, that there was a fellow who followed me home to my apartment and made a pass at me for a homosexual act, and I kicked him out.

Q. Now, in the course, while you were there alone, did something come up about you being misinformed?

A. Well, they told me that "You know we have interviewed lots of guys and let them go," or something to that effect, and that "You have been ill-advised, but you are not going to get off so easy," I mean threatening me with the fact that if I didn't cooperate that I would be doomed to all this publicity and everything.

Q. Now then, while you and Mr. [Goodman] were in there alone, did the occasion arise when Mr. [Goodman] made a telephone call?

A. Yes.

Q. Would you relate to the jury what was going on just before he made that call and what he said and then what happened on the call, as much as you know of?

A. Well, I don't know exactly who he called, but he said—

Q. Give me what led up to it.

A. Well, at the part when I told him that I admitted that this Halverson had followed me home to my apartment and everything, but I had not committed a homosexual act, he said, "Well, we'll show you," and then he picked up the 'phone and made a 'phone call, I don't know who to, and then he said, "O.K., if you don't want to cooperate with us, you are going to make it hard on yourself, that's all, you are just going to make it difficult for yourself." So he stood up and he paced the floor, and by that time it was practically dark in there and there was nothing but this desk lamp left, and he kept pounding out his ashes of his pipe on the ash tray, and he said, "Why don't you just admit to this insignificant incident and everything will be fine, just admit to this and I will make a 'phone call back and nothing will happen," so I kept turning it over in my mind, and I got up and paced the floor and wondered what should I do, I mean all I could see was my name being spread all over the morning paper, and then all I said was "O.K.," and he says, "O.K., buddy, you are a good boy; sit down." So then he made a 'phone call back to somebody and to whoever he talked to he says, "Well, Gordie is cooperating, he is going to be a good boy and he's going along with us," and so then they asked me a few more questions, and there at that time I believe that's when the rest of them came in and they took me down to the court-house.

Q. Now, did you ever admit to him up there that you had a homosexual act with this Halverson?

A. No, I never did.

Q. Did you ever admit to him that you took this Halverson's penis into your mouth?

A. I did not.

Q. Or vice versa?

A. No.

Q. As I understand, the most that you—you finally told him "Well, O.K."?

A. Yes, I told him, "Well, O.K."

Q. Now, what was your frame of mind at that time, if you didn't cooperate, what would happen to you?

A. Well, I was practically at the desperation point.

Q. What did you think would happen to you if you didn't cooperate with them?

A. If I didn't cooperate with them, I thought they would book me or pick me up, or whatever you want to call it, for suspicion, and my name would be in the paper anyhow.

Q. And if you did cooperate with them, what would happen?

A. I thought maybe I would get off like Halverson did. His name wasn't in the paper.

Q. Now then, so where did they take you then?

A. They took me down to Eugene Thomas' office.

Q. Had you ever been interrogated by police officers before?

A. Never.

Q. Have you ever been in trouble before?

A. No.

Q. Have you ever been charged with any crime?

A. No.

Q. Of any kind, misdeameanor or otherwise?

A. Nothing more than a parking ticket.

Q. This is your first experience with police officers?

A. Yes.

Q. Now, when they took you down to Eugene Thomas' office—that's where you left after you left that residence?

A. Yes.

Q. And Mr. Thomas was there?

A. Yes, he was.

Q. And incidentally, yes, now when you got down there what happened there? Who did the talking there?

A. Mr. Thomas did all the talking.

Q. And did—just relate what happened, as best you can recall, what happened there?

A. Well, it seems like we went in and this Quinton, the cop, stayed in the room, and Thomas started right in on this same old deal about this act that Halverson accused me of, and he kept telling—and then he mentioned again about this school, about this rehabilitation school and psychiatric treatment that they would give me, and they wanted to help me, and that's when he started to write on the yellow piece of paper there, and he tried to get me to confess to the homosexual act, of which I kept saying right up to the last minute that I did not take Halverson's penis in my mouth, and he was writing on this sheet of paper all the time he was talking to me, and then Quinton left the room, I believe.

Q. Now, this piece of paper—have you seen this Plaintiff's Exhibit 1 for identification before?

A. I just glanced at it.

Q. Who wrote that up?

A. Mr. Thomas.

Q. Is that in Mr. Thomas' own hand-writing?

A. Yes.

Q. And he was writing it up while you were sitting there in the room?

A. Yes.

Q. Now, did he hand it over to you and ask you to sign it?

A. Yes, he did.

Q. And what did you say to him about signing it?

A. I told him that "You left off of it that there was no attempted blow-job."

Q. Yes. Was there any further discussion about that aspect of it?

A. Well, he said, "Oh, yes," and took it back and added.

Q. Now, is that your signature?

A. Yes.

Q. What was your frame of mind at the time that you signed that paper?

A. Well, at the time I signed this paper I was almost at my wit's end as to what to do. I mean I thought—

Q. Go ahead.

A. I mean if you have got to admit to something you didn't do in order to save your job and your reputation, well, it would be easier than all this fighting.

Q. What was your state of mind, if you didn't sign it?

A. If I didn't sign it?

Q. Yes.

A. I thought they would take me in on suspicion, and my name would still be in the paper, when they had gone this far and made all these threats.

Q. Now then, were you present here yesterday when this officer Quinton testified?

A. Yes.

Q. Did you hear his testimony about the words "mutual masturbation"?

A. Yes.

Q. To your recollection was the word "masturbation" ever used during that day?

A. I don't—it was never used during that day.

Q. By anybody?

A. I have never heard the expression "mutual masturbation" by anybody.

Q. Is that the first time you have ever heard this expression?

A. That is the first time I have ever heard it.

Q. In connection with this case?

A. Yes.

Q. Now, did Mr. Thomas add to that statement about this not being a blow-job before you signed it?

A. Yes.

Q. And you wouldn't sign it until he would put that on. Was that language used throughout the day?

A. Yes, and lots worse.

Q. Who used it?

A. [Goodman] and Thomas.

Q. And it was—they talked in that parlance?

A. Yes.

Q. And did you all understand what the word "blow-job" meant?

A. Well, I picked up a lot of new expressions.

Q. What did the word, or how was the word used? What significance was given to that word?

A. Blow-job?

Q. Yes.

A. Taking the penis in one's mouth.

Q. And that was understood by everybody?

A. I suppose.

Q. Now, had you had anything to eat all this day?

A. No, I hadn't.

Q. Do you smoke?

A. Yes.

Q. Did you smoke then?

A. I didn't have any cigarettes.

Q. What is that?

A. I had run out of cigarettes.

Q. When?

A. Up there at that house.

Q. While you were there in Mr. Thomas' office, did everybody stay there?

A. No. Up there at the house Mr. [Goodman] kept saying, "Let's get this over with; I'm hungry; I want to go to dinner," so he didn't come down to the courthouse with us. So I understood he must have gone to dinner, and Brandon must have gone to dinner, and then when Brandon came back and relieved Quinton, Quinton went to dinner.

Q. Now, after you signed that statement did they let you go?

A. No.

Q. What did they do with you?

A. Well, they took me over to the police station and photographed me and took my fingerprints and made records, arrested me.

Q. And then where did they take you?

A. They took me back to the courthouse, and I waited around there until Thomas and Brandon took me up to Lampert's house.

Q. And what happened there at Judge Lampert's house?

A. Well, Mr. Lampert was sitting across, like a card table, in his home, and I was sitting across from him, and when they handed him

that document he said to me, "Is this true?" and I said, "No, sir," and
he said, "What part is not?" and he had the document facing him, and I
reached over the table and I pointed to the latter part of it about taking
the penis in my mouth, and I said, "That is not true," and he said, "Is
the rest of it?" and I said, "Well, yes, but that is the main point of it."

Q. Who was holding that complaint?

A. Lampert had it in front of him.

Q. You were looking at it upside down?

A. Yes.

Q. And you were complaining about the last part of it?

A. Yes.

Q. I am going to hand you what has been deemed marked as State's
Exhibit 2 for identification. I will ask you what part you were objecting to?

A. When I pointed to the last line, I mean my finger, I meant the
last part here about "taking the penis of one Eldon Halverson, a male
human being, and then and there sucking the same."

Q. Gordon, did you ever take the penis of this Halverson into your
mouth?

A. I did not.

Q. Did Halverson ever take his into yours [sic]?

A. He did not.

Q. Will you tell the jury what happened with that man Halverson
that sat on this stand yesterday? You tell your story now.

A. Well, I was taking orders for the restaurants, as I said. At that
time I was working as a salesman for Boise Fruit, and I had been to
the Boise Hotel, and I walked down the alley to Watson's Cafe, which
is adjacent to the Railways bus depot, and had taken my order from
Watson's Cafe, and I had my car parked up on the west side of
Hendren's Furniture Store, and as I was crossing the street this fellow
was standing on the street corner, and he spoke to me, and I didn't
know him, at least there was no recollection of an acquaintance there
at all, and he talked to me for a minute and asked me what I was
doing, and I told him, and he asked me where I was going, and I said
I was going home for lunch, and that was all that was about said there,
and I still could not recognize the guy; I mean I see men now and
then that I have gone to school with up at the university that I have
seen before but I don't know their names, and you just say "Hello," or
I mean you don't know them really. So I got in my car and started

home, and as I was coming up Eighth Street, at one of the stop lights, I can't remember which one it was, I looked in the rear view mirror, and he was following me; he was in his car behind me. I didn't know at the time that he was following me, and then I went on up home and drove in my usual parking lot and parked and got out of my car, and he also drove in and parked and got out of his car and followed me up to my apartment. Well, I thought right then that there is something funny, either I know the guy or I should know the guy, or it is one of those things that I have heard about, about some fruit trying to follow you home, so I went on up to my apartment, and he followed me up and he came right in the apartment, and he was still talking and fairly pleasant, and so I didn't, I didn't kick him out right at the time because I had heard about these things happening and I thought well finally, I mean, I am being made, and so he came into the apartment, and I fixed myself a sandwich and a glass of milk, and I walked in the bedroom for something, or in the bathroom, in the bedroom, I guess it was, for something, and he followed me in there and he started to, he grabbed ahold of my privates, and I says, "Well, man, you've got the wrong guy; you better hit the road," and so he didn't persist or resist; he left, and that was all that happened.

Q. Did you hear his story yesterday about you having driven up to his car and said, "Hi! Meet me at the Park"?

A. Yes.

Q. Did that occur?

A. Never.

Q. Did you hear his story about you then met him at the Park and drove up to the house?

A. I was never down to the Park.

Q. You were never down to the Park?

A. Well, I mean I have been to the Park over a period of years, but I was never at the Park that day.

MR. SMITH: That is all. You may cross-examine.

Larsen's testimony was fairly convincing. The fact that he had not had supper or cigarettes was also important, since it established duress. His insistence that he had never been at Julia Davis Park, and the fact that the prosecution had never corroborated that part of Halverson's testimony, was also in his favor. However, the fact that he let Halverson enter his apartment, that he was fas-

cinated by the guy, that he figured him to be "on the make," would suggest to the jury that Larsen certainly was a homosexual. It certainly did not help his case. Nevertheless, I'm quite sure that Larsen had swung the bout in his favor. If only he could come through the cross-examination! It was handled by Blaine Evans, not Thomas.

CROSS-EXAMINATION

By Mr. Evans:

Q. How old are you?
A. Thirty-two.
Q. And you say you were in the Army, were you?
A. Yes.
Q. When did you get out of the Army?
A. '46.
Q. And then you went to the University of Idaho?
A. Yes.
Q. How long were you up there?
A. Three years.

His records show two years.

Q. Did you graduate from the University?
A. No, I didn't.
Q. And when did you come to Boise?
A. In the fall of 1950.
Q. Where are you from originally?
A. Wallace, Idaho.
Q. Wallace; and you have lived in Boise continuously since 1950?
A. Up until last January.
Q. That was after your arrest?
A. Yes.
Q. Now, prior to October 3, 1955, have you ever known Eldon Halverson?
A. No.
Q. Have you ever seen him before?
A. I never have.
Q. Now, you say you saw him on the corner down there by Hendren's?
A. Yes.

Q. And did you have a conversation with him?

A. Yes, there was a conversation.

Q. And what was said?

A. Well, I can't remember exactly the nature of the conversation except that he asked me what I was doing, and I told him, and where I was going, and I told him.

Q. He asked you what you were doing and where you were going?

A. Yes.

Q. You have never seen him before?

Blaine had caught the weaknesses in Larsen's story and was hammering away.

A. No.

Q. Were you in your car there?

A. No. I was going to my car.

Q. You were going to your car. Was he in his car?

A. No.

Q. He passed you on the street?

A. Well, he was standing on the corner.

Q. He was standing on the corner?

A. Yes, and I came across the street.

Q. Was he just waiting for you to come across the street?

A. Well, it looked that way. He was just standing there.

Q. Well, then what did he say then as you came up to him on the corner?

A. Well, not exactly—he greeted me, "Hello," and there was some conversation, of which I don't remember the exact text of.

Q. Well, the substance would be enough on that. He asked you where you were going and you said you were going home for lunch?

A. Yes.

Q. Did you invite him to go home to have lunch with you?

A. No, I did not.

Q. And then what happened?

A. Then I went and got in my car.

Q. Where was your car parked?

A. It was parked on the side of Hendren's there. I believe it would be 9th Street.

Q. You were parked on the east side of the street?

A. Yes.

Q. Where had you been?

A. I had been to Watson's Cafe and the Boise Hotel.

Q. What were you doing in these two places?

A. I was taking orders.

Q. Taking orders for the Mode?

A. No. At the time this happened I was still working for Boise Fruit.

Q. Oh, I see. You were still working for the Boise Fruit?

A. On this October, whatever date it was.

Q. I see; and you were taking orders. Now, you were going in and getting orders?

A. Yes. I go into the kitchen door of most of the restaurants and talk to the buyer or the person in charge of the kitchen to take orders for produce.

Q. I see; and you had been into Watson's to get an order?

A. Yes.

Q. And you were coming out of Watson's?

A. Yes.

Q. And before that you had been to the Hotel Boise?

A. Yes.

Q. Where had you been before that?

A. Hotel Owyhee and the Royal Cafe.

Q. . . . Did you go into the Greyhound bus depot?

A. No.

Q. You didn't?

A. I didn't because it wasn't one of my accounts.

Q. I see. So you walked past him and you walked over and got into your car. What did Halverson do?

A. I don't know what he did then.

Q. You didn't see him?

A. I left him there at the corner.

Q. You don't know where he went?

A. No.

Q. Did you see him get into the car?

A. No, I didn't.

Q. And when you got in your car did you drive directly to your apartment house?

A. Yes.

Q. Yes; and how did you drive out to Hills Village?

A. To State Street and then over to 8th Street and then followed 8th Street out there.

Q. To Hills Village?

A. On Brumbach, yes.

Q. When did you first notice that anyone was following you?

A. I came here to one of the stop lights or a stop street or something or other, and I looked in my rear view mirror and I noticed that the same fellow was behind me in a car.

Q. What kind of car was he driving?

A. I can't remember the car.

Q. You recognized him in the car?

A. Yes.

Q. And did you wonder about why he was following you?

A. I didn't think too much about it at the time.

Q. Then you drove on out to Hills Village?

A. Yes.

Q. And where did you park?

A. In front of my unit.

Q. And where did Halverson park?

A. He parked—it was either a car or two up on the parking lot.

Q. Now, as I understand it, Mr. Larsen, you got out of your car and went to your apartment?

A. Yes.

Q. And he followed you?

A. Yes.

Q. When you went into your apartment you washed your hands first —is that correct?

A. No.

Q. You fixed your sandwich first?

A. If I remember correctly—it is sort of vague—I went up there and had a sandwich and a glass of milk.

Q. You ate the sandwich and a glass of milk?

A. Yes.

Q. And then you went into either the bedroom or the bathroom?

A. Yes.

Q. And when did he grab your privates?

A. While I was in the bedroom.

Q. While you were in the bedroom?

A. Yes.

Q. Did you have your pants undone?

A. No, I didn't.

Q. Did he try to unzip your trousers?

A. No, I didn't give him a chance.

Q. He just grabbed your privates?

A. Yes.

Q. And you told him to leave?

A. Yes.

Q. And did he leave?

A. Yes.

Q. Now, you said that when you were in front of Hills Village before you went to your apartment, you were on the lot, and you saw him get out of the car, at that point you realized that Halverson was probably—what did you call it, a "fruit"?

A. Yes.

Q. And you thought he was going to "make" you, to use your terminology?

A. Yes. Mainly, I heard the expression.

Q. So you went on up to your apartment and had a sandwich and glass of milk?

Blaine was really scoring now.

A. Yes.

Q. What was he doing while you were eating the sandwich and drinking the milk?

A. He was just standing there in the living room.

Q. Did you have a conversation with him?

A. No, there wasn't much conversation.

It was beginning to sound like a preposterously bad novel—even for Boise.

Q. Did you invite him into the apartment?

A. No, I did not.

Q. Did you offer to give him anything to eat?

A. No. I didn't offer him a sandwich.

Q. Now, this man was a complete and utter stranger to you?

A. Well, Blaine, as I said, I didn't know whether he was a complete stranger to me; I mean I could have gone to school with him or something but I could not recollect, but at the time I thought, "Well, I am being followed," and it sort of fascinated me.

Q. You didn't recognize him, though, on the corner there at Syms-York?

A. No, I didn't.

Q. He didn't know you by name either?

A. No. I don't think he called me by name.

Q. Well, let's go back for a few minutes here and discuss this matter of your interrogation in the prosecuting attorney's office on December 11, 1955. Mr. Quinton and Mr. Thomas were in the office with you, weren't they?

A. Here in the courthouse?

Q. Yes.

A. At the start of it, yes.

Q. And did you suggest to Mr. Thomas that you were hungry and you wanted to go and eat?

A. No, I didn't.

Q. Did you tell him you were out of cigarettes?

A. I can't remember.

Q. Didn't he offer you a cigarette?

A. I can't remember, Blaine, whether he did or not.

Q. As a matter of fact, wasn't Mr. Thomas very courteous to you?

A. Very courteous.

Q. Very polite?

A. Very sweet and soft spoken.

Q. Not harsh at all?

A. No.

Blaine was leading him into admitting that no duress had been involved.

Q. Very friendly, wasn't he?

A. Very friendly.

Q. And so was Officer Quinton, wasn't he?

A. He didn't have much to say.

Q. As a matter of fact, you weren't at all afraid of anybody or anything while you were down there in the prosecutor's office, were you?

A. Well, I was practically numb from fright, to tell you the truth.

Larsen didn't fall for the trick.

Q. Well, Mr. Thomas—

A. [Goodman] had broken me down before I had gotten there.

Q. Well, now, when you talked to Mr. Thomas, you knew that he was the deputy prosecuting attorney of Ada County, didn't you?

A. I didn't know that for sure, no.

Q. Well, let's put it to you this way: When you were standing in the outer office before you went into Mr. Thomas' office, do you remember standing there with Mr. Quinton?

A. I can't remember.

Q. Do you remember I came in the door?

A. I remember of seeing you out in the outer office.

Q. Don't you remember I came in and said, "Good evening, Gordon how are you tonight?" Do you remember that?

A. I remember seeing you in the outer office.

Q. Yes. Do you remember I talked to you for a minute? I don't remember the exact conversation now.

A. No; but I remember seeing you in the outer office, yes.

Q. You knew I was prosecuting attorney, didn't you?

A. Well, no; to tell the truth, I didn't.

Q. You didn't know that?

A. No.

Q. Well, what did you think I was doing there?

A. Well, I mean, then I knew; I mean I gathered as much.

Q. You knew that—

A. I mean I had never had any dealings with the prosecuting attorney before and had never followed it or realized it.

Q. Well, you had known both Mr. Thomas and myself previously, hadn't you?

A. I knew you previously, and I couldn't remember of meeting Mr. Thomas.

Q. Well, in any event when I came in you didn't make any complaint about this treatment you had received, did you?

A. No.

Q. You didn't say anything to Mr. Thomas about it either, did you?

A. No.

Q. One of the police officers was there, was there with Mr. Thomas, and had been out to [Goodman's], and you didn't say anything about it, did you?

A. No.

Q. And when you went to Judge Lampert's office—he is justice of the peace—you didn't say anything there about this treatment, did you?

A. No.

Q. Never mentioned it?

A. As I said, I was just humbly broken down completely.

This was a weak explanation of Larsen's failure to complain—and Blaine knew it.

Q. Well, you carried on a normal conversation with Mr. Thomas didn't you?

A. I don't know whether you could call it normal or not.

Q. Well, you carried on a conversation with him?

A. Well, if you want to call it a conversation.

Q. You went up to Judge Lampert's and carried on a conversation there, didn't you?

A. Not very much of one.

Q. Now, while you were sitting in Mr. Thomas' office, the prosecutor's office, when I came in, you recall I came in and talked to you there for a minute?

A. No, I don't remember that. I remember Mr. Quinton saying that when he was up here, but I don't remember of you coming in.

Q. Don't you remember when I came and we talked about the University of Idaho for a few minutes?

A. No, I can't remember, Blaine; really I can't remember that.

Q. And I asked you when you got started in this homosexual activities and you told me you got started in the Army?

MR. SMITH: Object to that question as being incompetent, irrelevant, and no foundation laid.

THE COURT: Overruled.

Q. Do you remember that?

A. No, I don't remember that.

Q. And don't you remember that I asked you how you got started in the Army and you said you were alone with men on the post a lot and you used to go in the shower room and that's where you got started?

A. No.

Q. You don't remember that?

A. No, I don't remember that at all.

Q. Do you remember discussing with Mr. Thomas other homosexual experiences you had?

A. No; because I haven't had any, Blaine.

Too late, Larsen realized that Evans was pulling the old have-you-stopped-beating-your-wife trick. When he finally began answering "No, because it isn't true" instead of "No, I don't remember," it only made it seem that he was lying more vehemently.

Q. You haven't had any other homosexual experiences?

A. No; no.

Q. Do you regard yourself as a homosexual?

A. I do not.

Q. Do you remember talking to Mr. Thomas about Bill Wilson? You know Bill Wilson, don't you?

A. No, I don't know Bill Wilson.

Q. I think he is known—

MR. SMITH: I object to this line of testimony as being beyond the scope of the direct examination.

THE COURT: Objection is overruled.

Q. I think he is known as Willard Wilson. Do you recall talking to Mr. Thomas about him?

Wilson was one of the convicted homosexuals.

A. No. Well, maybe he mentioned his name because I had seen his name in the paper.

Q. You had seen his name in the paper?

A. Yes.

Q. And do you remember Mr. Thomas asked you about Willard Wilson?

A. No, I can't remember.

Q. And don't you remember that you told him that you and Willard Wilson had had three homosexual experiences?

A. I certainly do not.

Q. You don't remember that?

A. I do not.

Q. Do you remember telling Mr. Thomas that you used to frequent bars and men would pick you up in the bar and you would have a homosexual affair with them?

A. I certainly do not.

Q. You don't remember that at all?

A. No.

Q. Do you remember talking about Mel Dir and * * * and * * *?

A. No.

Q. Never talked about any of them. How long were you in the office with Mr. Thomas?

A. Oh, it must have been a couple of hours.

Q. During this entire two hours all you ever talked about was this one affair with Eldon Halverson—is that right?

A. That's right.

Q. Don't you remember that you said that usually you had these affairs after you had had a few drinks of whiskey?

A. No, I don't remember that, because there was no affairs.

Q. Well, now, did you tell Mr. Thomas this story you have told us about Halverson following you out there and going to your apartment and your eating the sandwich and all that sort of thing?

A. Yes, I told him that story.

Q. You told him that story?

A. Yes.

Q. Who else was there when you told this story?

A. Quinton was there part of the time.

Q. Quinton was there, and Quinton heard this story?

A. I think so, either he or Brandon.

Q. One of the two were there?

A. And [Goodman] came in later.

Q. And [Goodman]. They all heard you tell this story?

A. Well, I don't know whether they were there when I told this story, but we went over and over and over this story.

Q. And you told them the same story that you have told on the stand today?

A. I told them Halverson was up to my apartment and there was no act committed.

Q. You told them that?

A. Yes.

Q. But did you tell them that you ordered him to leave your apartment, and that he had made a grab for your privates?

A. Yes.

Q. Now, did you read this States' exhibit before you signed it?

A. That yellow—

Q. That yellow sheet, you read that and then you signed it?

A. I read it, yes, very quickly.

Q. And you suggested, as I understand, to Mr. Thomas that he add a phrase to that?

A. Yes.

Q. And that phrase was that this wasn't a blow-job?

A. Yes.

Q. What is a blow-job?

A. Well, as I interpret it, it is taking the penis in one's mouth.

Q. Well, it means more than that, doesn't it? It means causing them to have an orgasm, doesn't it?

A. Well, I suppose.

Q. Well, the generally accepted term among homosexuals, that is what it means? Is that right?

A. I suppose; I don't know.

Q. Well, you used the term that night?

A. They had been using it all day.

Q. Well, irrespective of who had been using it, you used it that night? Isn't that right?

A. Yes.

Q. That's right; and by that you meant having an orgasm by mouth —isn't that right?

A. No, that's not right.

Q. What do you mean?

A. I just meant by a blow-job that they had been using all day long was taking the penis in one's mouth.

Q. Well, where is that exhibit? (Procuring St. Ex. 1) If that is what you meant, this statement says: "I recall taking his penis into my mouth and he took my penis into his," and then it goes on to say, "This was not a blow-job," why didn't you simply say, "Strike out that business about taking the penis into the mouth," if blow-job meant the same thing?

Now Evans was really striking home.

A. Because I thought by putting that amendment on that piece of paper that it would take care of the rest of it.

Q. What you actually meant was you admitted taking the penis in your mouth but you wanted to deny having an orgasm—isn't that right?

A. No, sir, Blaine.

Q. That is the reason you signed this?

MR. SMITH: Let him answer the question.

MR. EVANS: He answered it.

MR. SMITH: Finish your answer, if you have one.

A. What I mean is by not having a blow-job is by not even taking the penis into the mouth.

Q. Well, you say "involved playing around" here. What do you mean by "playing around"?

A. I said when he grabbed for my privates I supposed that is called "playing around."

Q. And so you took your pants down?

A. No.

Q. And he took his down?

A. He did not.

Q. Do you mean to tell me if you had such a horror of homosexual experiences that you would voluntarily admit to this type of action and sign your name to it?

A. At the state of mind I was in, I was ready to admit anything, Blaine.

Q. There was no pressure on you at the time you signed this?

A. No pressure?

Q. Everything was very pleasant in the prosecutor's office?

A. Very pleasant, yes, for you guys, but what about me?

Q. Did Mr. Thomas threaten you?

A. All but threatened me, yes. Not in so many words.

Q. You told me he had been very polite and very courteous?

A. Very polite and very courteous. That was a threat in itself.

Q. Now, when you went out to Bill [Goodman's], you went voluntarily out there with Officer Quinton, didn't you?

A. Yes, but when an officer comes and knocks at your door and shows you his badge, you don't really think it is voluntary.

Q. But you went out; you didn't refuse to go?

A. No, I didn't refuse to go.

Q. At that time you knew, of course, that you could refuse to go?

A. No, I did not.

After reading this section, I asked twelve men who were not lawyers—choosing them indiscriminately, eight at the bars of the

Royal Hotel and Boise Hotel and four at restaurants where I ate—
whether they would go with a policeman under such similar cir-
cumstances. All twelve answered yes. In New York or other big
cities, some at least would have answered, "Hell no." Goodman,
let us remember, insisted that women and homosexuals would go,
men would say, "Get a warrant." He was wrong—at least in Boise.

Q. You thought you had to go?

A. I thought I had to go. When an officer comes and knocks at your
door and asks you to go with him, I would say the average person
would go.

Q. Well, now, you were actually placed under arrest after you went
to Judge Lampert's, weren't you?

A. Well, I guess so. I don't know what—

Q. That is what you testified to this morning. So you weren't under
arrest at any time during this interrogation?

A. No.

Q. And you weren't under arrest when you were in the prosecutor's
office?

A. No.

Q. As a matter of fact, you could have left at any time if you so
desired?

A. Yes; but no one told me I could.

Q. As a matter of fact, both [Goodman] and Thomas told you you
could leave?

A. They did not; not once did they mention that.

Q. Now, when you were in the prosecutor's office you say, you have
told us that you signed this statement because you were afraid of the
publicity you were going to get?

A. Yes.

Q. Well, now, you recall when you signed this statement it says,
doesn't it, that it "might be used against me"?

A. I don't remember the exact text of it.

Q. Well, that is what it said.

A. And I can't remember the text that evening.

Q. So when you signed this you knew it might be used against you?

A. You guys had me so shook up I just didn't know which end was
up at the time.

Q. Well, I wasn't there conducting this hearing.

A. I mean your able assistant.

Q. So, in other words, being afraid of the publicity you were going to get, you nevertheless signed a document stating that it could be used against you, knowing full well when you signed it could be and probably would be used against you?

A. I had two alternatives.

Q. This was December 11th—

MR. SMITH: Just let him answer the question.

A. I had two alternatives, either confess to something I didn't do and go home, or resist and be charged.

Q. Did Mr. Thomas tell you you could go home if you signed this?

A. No; not in so many words.

Q. Well, this was on December 11th, wasn't it?

A. Yes.

Q. A number of these people had already been arrested, hadn't they?

A. Yes.

Q. And you knew that, didn't you?

A. Yes.

Q. And you were going to tell this jury that you thought if you signed this you would simply go home and forget about it?

A. That is my impression they led me to believe, yes.

Q. So you signed something that wasn't true, something that admitted on its face that you were a homosexual and had committed the infamous crime against nature?

A. I admitted everything up to the point of taking the penis in my mouth, and I resisted—I told Thomas time and time again that I didn't do it, but I thought I would be courteous and kind and go along with you guys as far as that point, if I could go home.

Q. Did you give them any information about—did you give them any information about * * *?

A. No, sir.

Q. Or * * *?

A. No.

Q. Or * * *?

A. No.

Q. Now, when you were talking to Mr. Thomas he told you, did he not, that whatever punishment would be meted out as a result of this crime you committed would be determined by the court—isn't that right?

A. No; I don't remember that at all.

Q. As a matter of fact, he told you several times that it was up to the court to impose punishment and he could not tell you what would happen as a result of your homosexual activity—isn't that right?

A. I can't remember that, Blaine. He kept talking about this school that they set up, that "If you cooperate with us we will send you to school and your name won't be mentioned," and led me to believe that, and I even admitted to going to this school if my name wouldn't be submitted.

Q. Now, when you first went to [Goodman's] and he started to talk to you, you could not remember anything about this fellow Halverson?

A. No; I didn't recognize him.

Q. And the interrogation went on apparently for several hours and you didn't remember anything about him?

A. Yes.

Q. And then Halverson came in and you saw him and you still didn't recollect him?

A. I didn't recollect him at first, no.

Q. And then after awhile, after you talked to [Goodman] a little bit longer, then suddenly you did remember that you had known Halverson? Is that correct?

A. Well, after all the threats and accusations—

Q. Never mind this stuff about threats. Just answer the question. Did you then remember that you had been with Halverson?

A. I recollected that could have been the person that they were referring to.

Q. And that was true, you had been with Halverson?

A. Yes.

Q. So that all this long interrogation resulted in your telling something that was the truth, that you had been with Halverson? Is that correct?

A. Well, I told you Halverson had followed me to my apartment.

Q. Now, you say that you were worried about having your name in the paper and [Goodman] said that Halverson wouldn't have his name in the paper—is that right?

A. No, he didn't say that, but he hadn't up until that time.

Q. As a matter of fact, since then his name has been in the paper several times, hasn't it?

A. Yes; linked with my name only.

Q. In connection with your case?

A. Yes.

Q. Now, you say that you told Mr. Thomas and Mr. Quinton everything except putting the penis in your mouth, is that correct, when you were down in their office?

A. I told him about the incident about him following me home and coming up to my apartment and everything except there was no homosexual act committed.

Q. Did you tell him about the, make the statement about masturbation?

A. There was no statement about masturbation; that word never came up.

Q. And what time was it that day when you got to your apartment on October 3rd?

A. Well, it must have been shortly after noon.

Q. After noon. As I understand it, when you got there you parked your car and he parked his car two cars away from you, and you got out of your car and went to your apartment. Was there any conversation at that time?

A. No.

Q. He simply followed you in?

A. Yes.

Q. Then when you got to the door of your apartment was there any conversation there?

A. No, not that I can remember.

Q. You just walked in and he followed you in?

A. Well, he said something about he didn't know that this Boise Hills Village was here and said something about the apartments or something like that.

Q. Now, at that time you thought he was a homosexual?

A. Yes. I began to get suspicious.

Q. And you were worried about being "made"?

A. Yes.

Q. But you walked into your apartment and he just docilely followed you along, and you said nothing whatsoever about it—is that your story?

A. Yes; because I was fascinated by—

Q. Well, then you had a sandwich and a glass of milk and still said nothing to him?

A. I was fascinated by the guy.

Q. Yes; and he stood by and watched you eat a sandwich and a glass of milk, and he said nothing?

A. Well—

Q. And then you got up and walked into your bedroom and he followed, and then he grabbed your private parts, and you said, "Get out," and he left—is that your story?

A. That's my story; that's the truth.

MR. EVANS: That's all.

MR. SMITH: That's all, Gordon. Thank you.

(Witness excused.)

It was a devastating cross-examination. Although everything could very well have happened as Larsen said, few were the jurors who would believe him. Evans had achieved his main goal: One could either believe Larsen or believe Quinton and Brandon and Thomas and Evans. Without putting Thomas or himself on the stand, Evans made sure that they too were directly linked with the prosecution's testimony in the minds of jurors. He also discredited Larsen's story that there had been no penetration. He did not insist that there had been any emission—this was not important. All Evans had to do was convince the jury that Larsen had taken Halverson's penis into his mouth, for the Idaho law does not define an "infamous crime against nature" by unnatural emission but by unnatural penetration.

* * *

Knowing as much as I did about Halverson (see appendices), I did not believe him. I believed Larsen. He was probably fascinated and flattered by a homosexual's advances, he probably let his fascination get the better of him, and he probably finally kicked Halverson out. Larsen may have had other homosexual affairs, but he was undoubtedly a much better human being than Halverson (which Blaine Evans himself admitted indirectly during his summation—see Appendix B-III). Larsen should never have been on trial. But there wasn't much that Smith could do after Evans' cross-examination. Only if he could produce the tape could he save the day for his client. Meanwhile, he put on the stand a few respected citizens as character witnesses for Larsen (including Gordon's seventy-year-old father, who testified that his son was a good boy, never lied, worked hard in mines in the summer while going to school in the fall). There were other incidental witnesses, including Quinton and Brandon again, but they did not fundamentally affect the trial.

Judge Koelsch then gave various instructions to the jury, including: that orgasm is not needed to convict, only proof of penetration (Instruction No. 4), that the jury must believe Halverson independently of the corroborating evidence and the corroborating evidence independently of Halverson's testimony (No. 6) and that the contended confession must have been obtained legitimately and voluntarily to be acceptable (No. 10). Shortly thereafter, Robert L. Erwin, the jury foreman, brought in the jury's verdict: Guilty.

Vernon K. Smith then had himself sworn in and testified that the prosecution had repeatedly offered him deals were his client to plead guilty. When this did not move the court, he then introduced into the record five other cases involving homosexuals where the court, and specifically Judge Koelsch himself, had handed out probation terms. Judge Koelsch replied that "every case that comes before me is dealt with individually on the basis of that particular case and that only, and the facts of that particular case and none other, so that while I am aware of these five particular cases, that is not going to influence me against you or in your behalf."

Attorney Smith was far from finished, however. He filed a series of affidavits as motions for a new trial (Appendix A) on the following grounds: that the prosecuting lawyer tried to imply the defendant's guilt by alluding to an interrogation he had had with the defendant (Appendix B-I); that the tone and manner used by the prosecution, both Evans and Thomas, implied that they had conclusive evidence that Larsen was a homosexual (Appendix B-II); that in his summation Evans admitted using Halverson as a tool to stop a "homosexual ring" that would "run the town" if Larsen was not convicted, all of which was never proven, and furthermore that Evans tried to accentuate the defendant's misdeed by referring to Halverson as "this boy under 21," which was false (Appendix B-III includes Evans's summation); that the court erred when it allowed Halverson to answer the question as to whether he knew Larsen, whom he had never met, to be a homosexual (Appendix B-IV); that new evidence is available (Appendix B-V) in the form of an affidavit by Dr. Butler (see below Appendix D); that defense's request for the tape was not sustained by the court (Appendix B-VI); that Goodman had been alone with the defendant, during which time duress, bribe, threat and inducement could all have been offered (Appendix B-VII); that the case was generally improperly handled (Appendix B-VIII); that Larsen was willing to take a lie-detector test and/or sodium amytal or sodium pentothal to prove he was not lying and that Dr. Butler, who had been away from Boise for four months preceding November 12, 1956, when told that Halverson had been the government witness, said that he knew him professionally to be a liar and psychopath (Appendix C).

Another ground for a new trial was Dr. Butler's affidavit (Appendix D). Dr. Butler had interviewed Halverson the year before, and his professional judgment was that Halverson "is a far developed sexual psychopath," and that such persons lie easily. Butler had interviewed Larsen after the trial and considered him not to be a psychopath. Dr. Butler's affidavit stated that he would be willing to testify to all this if a new trial was granted.

Smith also demanded a new trial (Appendix E) on the grounds that the extensive press coverage had prejudiced the jury, that there had been more than 150 stories on homosexuals in Boise in the *Statesman*, and that by bringing up the names of some of these past cases, the jury was led to link Larsen with them. And still another petition claimed that the court erred in refusing to let the defense see Larsen's confession before the trial (Appendix F).

Of all these grounds for a new trial, two seem to me irrefutable: The tape—a legal document in Idaho—was not produced (that is, Goodman was not forced to appear as a witness), and new evidence had been uncovered (Dr. Butler's affidavit). Goodman had acted with official status, even though he didn't have any, and he had been in charge of an investigation condoned, financed and aided by the police and the prosecution. As such, Goodman should not have been able to evade his responsibility, just as no police officer involved in the case could have. On this ground *alone,* a mistrial should have been declared—especially when all the prosecution witnesses confirmed the fact that Goodman and Larsen had been alone during part of the interrogation before Larsen's confession.

But Koelsch did not agree. He sentenced Gordon Larsen, who admittedly by all sides had never molested a child, to five years in the penitentiary. In my mind, this was an outrageous miscarriage of justice. It put the lie to all those sanctimonious officials I talked to—from Evans down—who claimed that they only wanted to stop child molesters.

19

CONCLUSION

VERNON K. SMITH KEPT FIGHTING. For years he filed appeal after appeal—but always lost. He even went to the U.S. Supreme Court, but since no policy issue was at stake, the Supreme Court refused to review the case. And so Larsen joined Moore, Wilson, Cooper, Shaffer, Gordon, Dir and the others in the pen.

A sprawling, antique institution, Idaho's State Penitentiary is run like any old-style prison—with coolers, holes, tough guards and not much of a rehabilitation program. There are shops, canning and license-plate factories and a couple of classrooms—for those who *want* to learn. (Inmates do the teaching, including a Dale Carnegie course in "How to Win Friends and Influence People.") The cell blocks, with thick gray stone walls, are bleak and dreary. Most of the cells, housing four inmates, are so small that desperate men easily become more desperate, and escapes or attempted escapes are frequent.

At first the homosexuals were segregated. Living in individual cells no bigger than a closet, with a bucket for water and a bucket for a toilet, they were kept away from other prisoners, who used to insult them whenever they saw them. "For a while," one of the ex-con homosexuals told me, "we worked making overalls. Then, finally, we got yard privileges. For me, it took four years. The guards were pretty nasty at the beginning, calling us girls and all that. But after one of the rich guys complained, the guards changed. The rich guys got out first, too, but I don't know if there was any pay-offs."

When I visited the pen, I had lunch with Warden Clapp and the guards. The food, including pork chops, various vegetables, an assortment of salads, and ice cream, was quite good. It was served by trustees. But I got to see the spaghetti that the cons ate that day, and it smelled like vomit. The recreation room, one huge gray hall, was more depressing than the courtyard. Scores of convicts were sitting on benches along the walls, chatting. The whistle for afternoon work jobs had not blown yet, but the single TV, which was on a platform high above head level, was not on.

"When they did put it on," another ex-con told me, "it was always ball games—even if the majority of the 500 or so guys in the pen didn't want to see it. There was one main radio, also on ball games. Once you got out of segregation, you could have your own radio, but without a speaker. You had to have earplugs, and then you could listen to anything you wanted. Otherwise, until last year, you weren't even allowed to play cards. When the weather was good, you played softball. In the winter, there was an old movie shown every two weeks. That was it. You got three packs of butts a week. If you smoked more you have to have money to buy them."

I got to inspect the maximum-security block: an all-gray fortress that we entered after getting the keys from armed guards standing on the wall nearby. But I could not get to see the hole—solitary confinement. The reason, said the guards, was that it was a dangerous place. But I gathered from those to whom I talked, and from Sam Day, the *Idaho Observer* editor who has long tried to get reforms initiated at the pen, that the conditions were simply too disgusting for a journalist to see.

Since neither Warden Clapp nor probation chief Maxwell has ever done much to install a meaningful rehabilitation program, the Idaho State Penitentiary has long been turning out hardened criminals instead of reformed ex-cons. On the record, both Clapp and Maxwell have often spoken in favor of a prison mental-health service. In practice, however, they have ignored it. In conversations with me, both gave me the impression that they didn't even believe in it. They scoffed at psychiatric reports and ridiculed the idea of preventive health, and Clapp even told me that he knew "a hell of a lot more than any head shrinker what to do with the cons."

The courts, however, have learned better. Or else, realizing the futility of their past harshness, they have completely altered their philosophy of punishment. On the facing page is a list of arrests on morals charges made in Boise during the year 1963, and their dispositions (the list does not include fourteen juveniles charged in Juvenile Court in 1963):

Of the twenty-four cases, only eight were brought before the District Court. There, not one of the convicted felons was sent to jail. Of the four found guilty of lewd and lascivious conduct in the District Court, one was sent to a state (mental) hospital, while three were freed on probation. The man guilty of an infamous crime against nature was also probated. In fact, of all the twenty-four cases, only two were convicted to jail terms: One got twenty days and another got one night. The toughest fine was $150.

I asked members of the Morals and Juvenile Squad whether this "softness" by the courts hampered their work. "Yes," replied Sergeant Don Jerome, who headed the squad in 1965, "but our job is not to prosecute but to prevent. This we accomplish by identifying the offender before he offends, as much as possible. Once we know him, we can watch him, and we can let him know that we're watching him, which is usually enough to scare him. If he persists in his habits, we try to catch him, arrest him. The arrest is pressure enough on him to mend his ways or to get help. And the courts often condition probation on getting such help anyway."

I asked how they identified the offenders. Sergeant Jerome and Dick Morse, one of his detectives, explained that they have a double-barreled program. On the one hand they try to enlist the help of the community by constantly educating it through lectures, posters, special films which are shown to YMCA officials, educators, the PTA, and so on. This trains those who work with youngsters to spot "people who don't belong around children, who have no excuse for being there, and brings them to our atten-

Charge	Disposition	Court
Lewd and lascivious conduct	Sent to State Hospital South	District
Disorderly conduct	Released on own Never appeared	City
Lewd and indecent	Plea guilty 30 days suspended	City
Disorderly conduct	Bond forfeited	City
Assault with intent to commit rape	Dismissed	District
Assault with intent to commit rape	Dismissed	District
Disorderly conduct	$100/30 days suspended	City
Disorderly conduct	5 days suspended	City
Disorderly conduct	$25 fine	City
Disorderly conduct	30 days probation	City
Disorderly conduct	30 days/10 suspended	City
Lewd and lascivious conduct	5 years probation	District
Lewd and lascivious conduct	5 years probation	District
Indecent exposure	Committed to Blackfoot	City
Infamous crime against nature	5 years probation	District
Lewdness and indecency	Posted bond Never appeared	City
Lewd and lascivious conduct	Found not guilty	District
Statutory rape	3 years probation	District
Lewdness and indecency	6 months probation to seek mental care	City
Lewdness and indecency	30 days suspended to seek mental care	City
Lewdness and indecency	Never prosecuted by complainant	City
Lewdness and indecency	Plea guilty/$150 fine	City
Disorderly conduct	Plea guilty/cont'd for mental report	City
Lewdness and indecency	Plea guilty/30 days suspended next day to return home to northern Idaho	City

tion." On the other hand, said Jerome, "we keep constant vigilance. This includes inspection of public places, spy holes in public toilets, stakeouts, patrols, et cetera." Morse added, "We also keep a very complete file, with photographs and characteristics, of known perverts. But it's a contant fight and we cannot let up, even if the courts are lenient."

Why such leniency? I asked .Jerome answered: "The 1955–1956 scandal boomeranged. Too many people were hurt. The city's reputation was too drastically damaged."

Indeed, the City Council finally decided to remain silent on such issues, and a new mayor was elected. The population at large was displeased either because the investigation did not go far enough or because it had gone too far. This fitted in with what Dr. Wardell Pomeroy told me: "It is quite common that following a witch hunt, a reaction sets in and the reverse happens—laxity becomes the practice. This is because a real crackdown often uncovers too many prominent men."

In Boise in 1955 and 1956, the crackdown never got that far. "The real big shots I knew as homosexuals were never arrested," one of the ex-cons told me. Others confirmed this. They were too big, too entrenched in Boise's power elite. "And they knew who that millionaire 'Queen' was," one of the ex-cons insisted. "They knew all about him before they picked me up, because they asked me about him. And, I'll tell you, I confirmed it."

More than 500 names had been on Goodman's list, but only sixteen were charged. The investigation was canceled, and the "crusading" *Statesman* did not complain.

Aimed at the city administration, the witch hunt had mushroomed beyond all its original intention. It had forced the prosecuting attorney to turn it into a *cause célèbre*, to push it with a vengeance. It did help him become famous—and win him election as state senator. But it was distasteful even to him. It also exposed Boiseans' intolerance, ignorance and blind stupidity. It made a mockery of Idahoan justice and revealed that such an investigation, once unchained, could turn up homosexuals in every sector of the community. That far, neither the courts nor the law-enforcement agencies were willing to go. Neither was the power elite, nor the *Statesman*.

But the *Statesman* has not always been impartial in other matters either. For example, the Park case. In the 1964 campaign for prosecuting attorney, the Republican incumbent was Martin Huff, his Democratic challenger was Tony Park. Park's campaign rested heavily on the fact that Huff had not prosecuted a man arraigned for a second-degree murder committed in February 1962. Although Park constantly repeated his charges before the election, the *Statesman* did not check them out until *after* the election, which Huff won. Then, and then only, did it assign a reporter to investigate Park's charges. The reporter found that they were justified and said so in a December 6, 1964, article headed by a five-column headline reading: "Ada County Lets Murder Case Sit for 34 Months." Two days later, a long *Statesman* editorial accused the prosecuting attorney of making "a mockery out of the State Constitution provision: 'In all criminal prosecutions, the party accused shall have the right to a fair and speedy trial.' " But of course Mr. Huff, a Republican, had already been elected, so the Republican *Statesman* did not mind criticizing him *now*. And fortunately there was no other daily newspaper around to accuse the *Statesman* of making a mockery of its responsibility to the public.

But, in fact, many public servants have not taken responsibility seriously in Boise. This was clear in 1955 when panic was created for political and economic purposes, when the court repeatedly contradicted itself, when juvenile prostitutes and stool pigeons were used to send sick men to the penitentiary, and when a professional investigator-interrogator was allowed to elicit confessions without having to defend or even explain his methods in court. Since then, that lack of responsibility has allowed Idaho to make a mockery of its progressive mental-health laws, its respectable civil rights legislation, its professed concern for education and its stated emphasis on the rehabilitation of those who "fall into error."

In 1965 that lack of responsibility made a mockery even of

the United States Constitution when the Ada County Board of Commissioners passed an ordinance forcing all ex-felons living in the county to appear at the sheriff's office to be registered, photographed and fingerprinted. When Prosecutor Martin Huff was told that the ordinance violated due process, he replied to Dwight Jensen, associate editor of the *Idaho Observer:* "I knew that was unconstitutional when I drew it [the ordinance] up." Huff added: "I didn't give a whoop, as long as we could scare some of these people around here." His remarks were printed in the March 4, 1965, *Observer.*

None of the Boise homosexuals sent to prison from 1955 to 1957 used force. Some were—and are—unchangeable, and violated the law only with other consenting adults, hurting no one. Others did molest children. They were sick and should have been treated. The kids too should have been treated. They were not—not one. Why?

APPENDIX A

Motion for Withholding Judgment on Gordon Larsen

COMES NOW, The defendant and moves this Honorable Court to withhold the pronouncement of judgment in the above entitled action, and for grounds and reasons therefor states as follows:

I

That at the time of the filing of this said motion for withholding judgment the defendant has filed a motion for new trial and moves this Honorable Court to act upon such motion before pronouncement of judgment; and in the event that such motion for new trial be denied, that pronouncement of judgment be further delayed in order that an appeal to the Supreme Court may be prosecuted from such order denying the motion for new trial; and in the event that such order denying a motion for new trial be sustained that the said defendant may then file an application for further withholding of pronouncement of judgment and parole.

Vernon K. Smith
_____
Vernon K. Smith
Attorney for Defendant
1900 Main Street
Boise, Idaho

Copy of the foregoing instrument
received, and service acknowledged
this 30 day of November, 1956.

BLAINE F. EVANS

PROSECUTING ATTORNEY

ADA COUNTY, IDAHO

By *Blaine F. Evans*
_____

(Filed: Nov. 30, 1956)

APPENDIX B

Motion for New Trial for Gordon Larsen

COMES NOW, The above named defendant and pursuant to Section 19–2406, I. C., and within 10 days after verdict of the jury, moves this Honorable Court to set aside and to vacate the verdict of guilty, heretofore returned in the above entitled action on the 20th day of November, 1956, and to grant a new trial, and for grounds and reasons therefor, this defendant alleges as follows:

I

The court erred in permitting the Prosecuting Attorney to interrogate the defendant on cross-examination concerning certain statements which were allegedly made by the defendant, Gordon Larsen, to the Prosecuting Attorney and his assistant, Eugene C. Thomas, at that certain interview in the office of the Prosecuting Attorney on the 11th day of December, 1955, and in particular erred in permitting the said Prosecuting Attorney to propound the following questions, to-wit: [Though Smith's version of the record is substantially the same as the official record, minor discrepancies do occur—due to the fact that Smith's version was transcribed by his secretary from a tape recording of the proceedings. Compare to the court version above, pp. 270–273 (when Smith filed a formal appeal to the Idaho Supreme Court, he used the official court record, which by then had been transcribed by the court reporter.)] Cross-Examination of the defendant Gordon Larsen by Blaine F. Evans, Prosecuting Attorney:

"Q. And I asked you when you got started in this homosexual activities and you told me you got started in the Army?

Mr. Smith: Object to that question as being incompetent, irrelevant and no foundation laid.

The Court: Overruled.

Q. You remember that?

A. No, I don't remember that.

Q. Don't you remember that I asked you how you got started in the Army and you said you were alone with men on the post a lot and you used to go in the shower and that's where you started?

A. No.

Q. You don't remember that?

A. No, I don't remember that at all.

Q. Do you remember discussing with Mr. Thomas other homosexual experiences you had?

A. No, because I haven't had any, Blaine.

Q. You haven't had any other homosexual experiences?

A. No, none.

Q. Do you regard yourself as a homosexual?

A. I do not.

Q. You remember talking to Mr. Thomas about Bill Wilson? You know Bill Wilson, don't you?

A. No, I don't know Bill Wilson.

Mr. Smith: I object to this line of testimony being beyond the scope of direct examination.

The Court: Objection overruled.

Q. I think he is known as Willard Wilson, you recall talking to Mr. Thomas about him?

A. No. Maybe he mentioned his name because I had seen his name in the papers.

Q. You had seen his name in the paper?

A. Yes.

Q. And you remember Mr. Thomas asked you about Willard Wilson?

A. No, I can't remember.

Q. Don't you remember that you told him you and Willard Wilson had had three homosexual experiences?

A. I certainly do not.

Q. You couldn't remember that?

A. I do not.

Q. You remember telling Mr. Thomas that you used to frequent bars and men would pick you up in the bar and you would have a homosexual relation? [The official record reads "homosexual affair with them." See p. 272.]

A. I certainly do not.

Q. You don't remember that?

A. No.

Q. Remember talking about Mel Dir and * * * and * * * ?

A. No.

Q. Never talked about any of them? How long were you in the office with Mr. Thomas?

A. Must have been a couple of hours.

Q. During the entire two hours all you ever talked about was this one affair with Eldon Halverson, is that right?

A. That's right.

Q. Don't you remember you said that you usually had these affairs after you had a few drinks of whiskey?

A. No, I couldn't remember that because there was no affairs."

II

That the said Prosecuting Attorney of Ada County, Idaho committed serious and high prejudicial error in the cross-examination of the defendant, Gordon Larsen, more in particular as follows, to-wit:

That in the cross-examination of the said defendant, Gordon Larsen, the Prosecuting Attorney was seated at counsel table in the personal company and attendance of his deputy, Eugene C. Thomas. That the said Prosecuting Attorney thereupon propounded the questions outlined and set forth in paragraph 1 hereof while both the said Blaine F. Evans and Eugene C. Thomas were personally present and seated at the counsel table; that the questions so propounded as set forth in paragraph 1 were so couched in language so as to infer that the said Prosecuting Attorney and his deputy, being quasi judicial officers of this court had personal knowledge that the said Gordon Larsen had admitted to them that he got started in homosexual activities while in the Army; that the said Gordon Larsen got started in homosexual activities as a result of being alone on Army posts and would go into the shower rooms and have such homosexual activities; that the said Gordon Larsen admitted to the Deputy Prosecuting Attorney, as a quasi judicial officer of this court, that he had had three homosexual relationships with Willard Wilson; that the said Gordon Larsen had admitted to Eugene C. Thomas that he did frequent bars and there be picked up for homosexual relationships; that the said defendant had admitted that he was acquainted with * * *, * * *, and Mel Dir; that the said defendant had admitted to Eugene C. Thomas that he, the said defendant, usually had these affairs after having had a few drinks. That the foregoing questions outlined in paragraph 1 hereof by a quasi judicial officer of this court couched in such language as to imply that they, the Prosecuting Attorney and the Deputy Prosecuting Attorney, had personal knowledge of such admissions were made and propounded under such circumstances wherein the said Prosecuting Attorney made no pretense or showed no good faith in intending to rebut the denials of the defendant by rebuttal testimony, and in fact did not offer any affirmative proof or evidence that the accused did make such statements and admissions, but by and through such prejudicial misconduct on the part of the Prosecuting Attorney during cross-examination sought to imply the existence of immaterial facts with the purpose of im*pun*ing, prejudicing and degrading the defendant unfairly by insinuation and innuendo, rather than by evidence.

III

That the Prosecuting Attorney, Blaine F. Evans, in his summation and argument to the jury committed further serious and high prejudicial error by comments and arguments as follows:

" * * * *an issue which has nothing to do with this case,* gentlemen, but an issue which I think you want answered. Why hasn't he been prosecuted? Well I am going to tell you why he hasn't been prosecuted. *You have this situation where you have all these homosexuals knowing each other and being together— * * *, * * *, * * *, this defendant and Brocaw* [usually spelled Brokaw]. In each case Halverson, as Mr. Smith brought out, is the complaining witness. Let's be frank about it. *I don't like Halverson. I had to subpoena him to get him to come here and testify. He didn't want to do it, but he did—I forced him to do it.* All right, *what can you do when you have a ring operating in your community?* You have to have somebody get up on that stand and testify that the act was committed. Now there are only two people present when this act is committed, one has to testify to prove the case, and it is the only way—the only way under the law that we can *prosecute these men* and they must be prosecuted. It is the only way it can be done. One must testify. So, what do you do? *You look this group over,* you take the youngest, *this boy under 21, the least culpable and use him as your complaining witness in order to prosecute the others.* * * *, * * *, * * * *and Brocaw, all prosecuted—convicted, the last one in the group with Halverson involved this defendant and his trial is here* and when this case is finished we can deal with Halverson. We couldn't do it before. We simply couldn't do it before unless we wanted to dismiss every one of these cases because Halverson called Smith Sunday night. You know what he called about? He didn't want to testify. If we had prosecuted him *he'd had a lawyer, claimed his privilege against self-incrimination, all these cases go by the board, the investigation is at an end and the homosexuals run the town—we are through.* The only way we can proceed is the way we have done. Maybe it isn't nice. I don't like it, but believe me, it is the only way—*the only way you can do it if you are going to take care of this situation.* Now you have the evidence before you. You know in your own minds, *as I know,* that the defendant did the thing he is accused of. He put that penis in his mouth as is accused. Gentlemen, I am asking you, please go out in that jury room, convict [sic] he did it. You have sworn on your oath that if you find he did that act you will convict. We are asking you to do your duty, stand by your community and bring in a conviction." (Emphasis supplied)

That there was no evidence to substantiate there was a ring of homosexuals in which Gordon Larsen was involved; that there was no evidence from which it could be logically argued that * * *, * * *, * * *, this defendant and Brocaw knew each other, and had been together; that there was no evidence from which it could have been argued that there was a ring of homosexuals operating in your community; that there was no evidence from which it could be logically argued that Halverson was a boy under 21, and that he was the least culpable as a complaining witness to prosecute the others; that there was no evidence that the homosexuals would run the town.

That the remarks and argument of the Prosecuting Attorney were highly prejudicial and were invoked for the obvious and sole purpose of creating prejudice against this defendant when the Prosecuting Attorney argued unfairly and outside the facts that Gordon Larsen was a member of a homosexual gang and a member of a homosexual ring, which was operating in the community. That the comments and argument of the Prosecuting Attorney were for the obvious purpose of creating passion and prejudice by implying that * * *, * * *, * * * and Brocaw had all *be* [been] convicted and upon such hypothesis that this defendant should also be convicted as he was the last one in this group in which Halverson was involved, and further appealed to the prejudices and passions of the jury by repeating and arguing that there was a gang of homosexuals in the community, of which Gordon Larsen was a member, and that if these men were not prosecuted the homosexuals would run the town, and we'd be through. That the said Prosecuting Attorney further perpetuated the prejudicial error of his cross-examination of Gordon Larsen by arguing in his argument to the jury based upon the unfair inferences developed on cross-examination of Gordon Larsen, as set forth in paragraph 1 hereof, that Gordon Larsen was a homosexual and that he, Blaine F. Evans, knew it.

IV

The court erred in a ruling concerning the admissibility of certain evidence during the re-direct examination of Eldon Halverson, more in particular as follows: [Here, too, Smith's version varies slightly from the official court record. See pp. 211–212 for the official version.] Re-direct examination of Eldon Halverson, the State's witness, by Blaine F. Evans, Prosecuting Attorney:

"Q. Now you say you told this fellow Bill [Goodman], or whatever his name is, about * * *, * * * and * * *, is that right?

A. Yes.

Q. And they were homosexuals?

A. Yes.

Q. And you also told [Goodman] about the defendant, Gordon Larsen?

A. Yes.

Q. And he was known to you to be a homosexual?

Mr. Smith: Now just a moment, I object to that calling for hearsay.

Mr. Evans: Well I am trying to find out what he told [Goodman]. You opened it up.

The Court: Objection overruled.

Mr. Evans: Now, go ahead and answer.

A. Yes.

Q. That's right. Now of the four people you told Mr. [Goodman] about, * * *, * * *, * * * and the defendant Larsen, three of them have been convicted of committing the infamous crime against nature.

[The official court record has an answer—"yes"—here.]

Mr. Smith: Object to that as being incompetent, irrelevant, immaterial.

The Court: Objection sustained. Strike the answer. Gentlemen of the jury when I say that anything is to be stricken from the record that means you are to disregard it, put it out of your mind.

Q. So when you saw the defendant Gordon Larsen on the streets of Boise on October 3rd and he approached you, you knew at that time he was a homosexual?

A. Yes.

Mr. Smith: I object to that question as being highly leading and highly suggestive. Calls for opinions and conclusion of the witness.

The Court: Objection overruled. The answer may stand.

Q. You did.

A. Yes."

v

That subsequent to the trial and in particular on the 22nd day of November, 1956, there was discovered new material and probative evidence which could not have been discovered through due diligence prior to the time of trial and could not have been produced at the trial. That the newly discovered evidence and the facts surrounding its unavailability prior to the time of trial are set forth in the affidavit of Dr. John Butler, Director of the Division of Mental Health, Idaho State Board of Health, and the affidavit of Vernon K. Smith, attached hereto and made a part hereof.

vi

That the court erred in sustaining defendant's questions to the witness Quinton upon cross-examination, which were propounded fcr the purposes of ascertaining whether there was a tape recording taken of the inquisition and interrogation of Gordon Larsen at the home of Bill [Goodman] on the 11th day of December, 1955, and further erred in denying defendant's offer to prove that such a tape recording was in fact taken and would show each and every statement, question, admonition, answer and comments, threats, promises and inducements by all parties concerned as the same might relate to whether or not any inducements or promises were held out, or threats made to the said Gordon Larsen, which such rulings of the court were made upon the misrepresentations of the Prosecuting Attorney that he was not laying a foundation for a confession but was merely showing to the jury the occurrences of the day.

VII

That there was an insufficiency of the evidence to sustain a verdict of guilty upon the charge of infamous crime against nature, such insufficiency being more particularly specified as follows:

That the evidence produced at the trial against the defendant consisted of direct statements by Eldon Halverson, the State's witness, together with corroboration thereof by certain alleged admissions which were made by the defendant while in the Prosecuting Attorney's office in the presence of Eugene C. Thomas and James Brandon following the hour of 8:00 o'clock p.m. on the night of December 11, 1955; that the evidence of the trial conclusively shows that for a period of approximately 1½ hours to 2 hours the defendant was alone in the house of one William [Goodman] at which time he was being interrogated and interviewed by the said [Goodman]; that the evidence further shows conclusively that during said interview between the said Gordon Larsen and the said William [Goodman] that the said William [Goodman] held out an inducement to the defendant, Gordon Larsen, to cooperate by telling the said Gordon Larsen that they did not want to hurt him, but to help him, and if he would cooperate they would send him to a school; that the evidence further undeniably shows that the said William [Goodman] demonstrated that such an inducement was highly probable in that he called in before Gordon Larsen the witness Eldon Halverson who in the presence of the defendant and the said [Goodman] claimed that he had had an homosexual relationship with the defendant Gordon Larsen by his (the said Halverson) and the said defendant having taken each other's penis into their mouths and that after making such a claim the said Bill [Goodman] gave the witness Halverson money to buy gas to go back to Payette and to leave; that the evidence further conclusively shows that when the defendant Gordon Larsen refused to cooperate or to admit any involvement with the said Halverson the said William [Goodman] admonished him that he (the said Larsen) had been misadvised and that he would not get off so easily by not co-operating and thereupon made a telephone call wherein the unwillingness of Gordon Larsen to cooperate was discussed and the statement was made to the effect that they would have to take tougher measures; that the evidence undeniably shows that at the conclusion of the interviews between the said William [Goodman] and Gordon Larsen the said Gordon Larsen was numb with fright for the effect that his refusal to cooperate would have upon him in the light of his impending marriage and acquisition of a new substantial employment; that the evidence further conclusively shows that the defendant believed that if he did not cooperate by admitting to a lie he would be charged publicly and disgraced, whereas, if he would cooperate he would probably be dealt with in the same manner as the witness Halverson. The evidence further conclusively shows that the above facts were testified to by the defendant Gordon Larsen; that the said Gordon Larsen was a credible witness and that his testimony concerning the interview and the inducements and threats held out and made by the said Bill [Goodman] were inherently probably [sic] and not improbable. That such testimony concerning the interview between the said Bill [Goodman] and Gordon Larsen was wholly and completely uncontradicted. The evidence further shows that following such interview with Bill [Goodman] the defendant was taken to the Prosecuting Attorney's office where an alleged oral admission of a homosexual act was claimed to have been made by the defendant in the testimony of James

Brandon; that such oral admission and confession was under such circumstances being made immediately following the softening up process and interview with Bill [Goodman], was as a matter of law inadmissible as a confession as not having been voluntarily made and free of inducement; that the State's Exhibit "1" for identification, being an equivocal and not an unequivocal admission on the part of the defendant, as a matter of law does not amount to corroboration of the testimony of the accomplice Eldon Halverson, and as a matter of law was inadmissible as a confession as not having been voluntarily made and free from inducements; that State's Exhibit "2" for identification, together with the testimony of James Brandon, did not constitute an unequivocal admission of the act, but was equivocal testimony and not sufficient in law to amount to a corroboration of the testimony of the accomplice Eldon Halverson; that all such pretended corroboration was insufficient in that the alleged oral admission and confession as related by the witness James Brandon, and the written admission or confession failed to corroborate the particular alleged act in point of time as charged in the information.

VIII

The court erred in giving each and every charge to the jury.

This motion for new trial is made and based upon the records and files, together with the notes and transcript of all evidence and exhibits taken and produced at the trial, together with the affidavit of John Butler and Vernon K. Smith relative to the motion for new trial, and the further affidavit of the said Vernon K. Smith pertaining to the cross-examination of the defendant Gordon Larsen and the remarks and comments of the Prosecuting Attorney in his final argument to the jury, and the further affidavits of Vernon K. Smith and Violet Sykes wherein the exact

arguments of Blaine F. Evans in his closing argument to the jury
are set forth in exact words.

Vernon K. Smith
_____
Vernon K. Smith
Attorney for Defendant
1900 Main Street
Boise, Idaho

Copy of the foregoing instrument received,
and service acknowledged, including affidavit
of John R. Butler, Vernon K. Smith, Violet Sykes and
Vernon K. Smith, this 30 day
of November, 1956.

BLAINE F. EVANS
PROSECUTING ATTORNEY
ADA COUNTY, IDAHO
By *Blaine F. Evans*
_____

(Filed: 3:40 P.M. Nov. 30, 1956)

APPENDIX C

*Affidavit in Support of Motion for New Trial for
Gordon Larsen re. Newly Discovered Evidence*

STATE OF IDAHO)
) ss.
County of Ada)

Vernon K. Smith, being first duly sworn upon oath, deposes and says:

I am the attorney for Gordon Larsen, the above named defendant, and I make this affidavit in support of a motion for a new trial for the above named defendant on the grounds of newly discovered evidence, and do set forth herein the facts and reasons why it is contended that this newly discovered evidence could not with reasonable diligence have been discovered and produced at the time of trial.

I say that the trial of the above entitled action was set for 10:00 o'clock a.m. commencing on the 19th day of November, 1956; that as late as 10:00 o'clock p.m. on the 15th day of November, 1956, I had a conversation with Blaine F. Evans concerning an inquiry as to whether or not said action would be tried on the 19th day of November, 1956, and while no decision or determination was made at such time, an appointment was made between myself and Blaine F. Evans to discuss the matter as to whether or not the said case would be tried, said appointment to have been on the 16th day of November, 1956 at the hour of 9:00 o'clock a.m.; that such contemplated discussions had nothing to do with the said Gordon Larsen ever entering a plea of guilty. That such appointment at the said hour of 9:00 o'clock a.m. on the 16th day of November, 1956 was not kept by the said Blaine F. Evans and towards the end of the day the said Blaine F. Evans informed me that the case would be tried on the 19th day of November, 1956.

Following the trial of the case and the verdict of guilty having been returned by the jury, I further discussed with the defendant the fact as to whether or not the defendant had had a homosexual relationship with Eldon Halverson as charged in the complaint, and upon the defendant's continued denials I inquired of the defendant as to whether or not he would be willing to submit to a lie detector test or be interviewed by a psychiatrist while under the influence of sodium amytal or sodium pentothal; that upon the defendant's assurance that he would, I undertook to find a psychiatrist or doctor who would give such a test. I further say that I contacted Dr. Dale Cornell and Dr. Burkholder, of Boise, Idaho, and Shadel's of Idaho in Wendell, Idaho, and received generally the advice from such sources that an interview under the influence of sodium amytal or sodium pentothal would not necessarily reflect an absolute statement of the truth by the person so under the influence. That is to say, a denial of homosexual activity by the person so under the influence of sodium amytal or sodium pentothal might not be the truth and a general reluctance was expressed by Dr. Cornell, Dr. Burkholder and Shadel's of Idaho to extend such service.

That having heard a rumor that Dr. John Butler, the Director of the Mental Health Division of the State of Idaho Board of Health, used hypnosis in connection with the interviews of the suspects in the recent arson cases at the University of Idaho, I called Dr. John Butler in an effort to seek his services in this connection and was able to obtain an interview for 3:00 o'clock p.m. on the 22nd day of November, 1956, the purpose of which such interview was to inquire into the possibility of subjecting Gordon Larsen to a hypnotic trance and to generally evaluate him as a homosexual or psychopath.

I further say that in the course of the interview it became known to me for the first time that Dr. John Butler had seen, interviewed and evaluated Eldon Halverson, the State's witness against this defendant, and I further say that my discovery of the fact that this specialist in the field of psychiatry and mental health had seen, interviewed and evaluated Eldon Halverson was a result of almost pure accident.

I therefore say that my discovery of this new evidence concerning the fact that Eldon Halverson has been evaluated by a specialist as a far developed sexual psychopath, together with the discovery that the said Eldon Halverson has a high potential for low credibility as regards his truth and veracity and that the said Eldon Halverson was a psychopath and mentally ill could not have been discovered by reasonable diligence. I further say that I am informed by the said Dr. Butler, and upon such information I believe the facts to be, that the said Dr. Butler was away from Boise City almost continuously for the 4 months next preceding the 12th day of November, 1956 and that the possibilities of an interview with him during the period from November 12, 1956 to November 19, 1956, at which time I might have discovered this evidence was highly remote for the reason that he did inform me that during the first week that he was back in Boise he was virtually unavailable for interviews or discussions due to the press of business which had piled up in his absence from his Boise office.

I further say that I am a practicing attorney and have been a member of the Bar of the State of Idaho for the past 15 years during which time I have actively participated in numerous criminal proceedings as attorney for defendants. I further say that in my opinion that there was a sharp and direct conflict between the testimony of Eldon Halverson, the State's prosecuting witness, and the defendant, Gordon Larsen. I further say that the corroboration and claimed admissions that were made by Gordon Larsen in the course of his interviews by the police officers on the 11th day of December, 1955 were made under such circumstances of fright, fear and pressure; that it is reasonable to believe that the admissions claimed to have been made by the said Gordon Larsen to the corroborating witnesses were made in the hope of avoiding being prosecuted if he would cooperate, and it is therefore reasonable to believe that such admissions so made by the said Gordon Larsen were untrue as he so testified at the trial. I further say that according to the evaluation of the said Gordon Larsen by Dr. John Butler, the said Gordon Larsen has no tendencies of being a psychopath, and at the time of the trial his general reputation for truth and veracity was supported and testified to by four witnesses, whereas, the reputation for truth and veracity on the part of Eldon Halverson was not corroborated. I therefore say as a practicing attorney that the newly discovered evidence which would be available at a new trial through the testimony of Dr. John Butler goes to the very capacity of the witness Eldon Halverson as a witness and would reveal a general personality defect, mental illness, and psychological inherent high potentiality for lack of credibility insofar as truth and veracity are concerned. I therefore say that I believe that the newly discovered testimony and evidence of Dr. John Butler is not only highly material to the defense of this defendant in the charge against him, but that such testimony, if the same had been, or could be made available to a jury hearing said cause, might well result in a verdict of not guilty.

Vernon K. Smith
_____
Vernon K. Smith

Subscribed and sworn to before me this 29th day of November, 1956.

(NOTARIAL SEAL)

Violet Sykes
_____
Notary Public for Idaho
Residing at Boise, Idaho

(Filed: Nov. 30, 1956)

APPENDIX D

Affidavit of Witness re. *Motion for New Trial for Gordon Larsen*

STATE OF IDAHO)
) ss.
County of Ada)

John L. Butler, being first duly sworn on oath, deposes and says:

I am the Director of the Mental Health Division of the Idaho State Board of Health.

I further say that I am a duly licensed and practicing physician in the State of Idaho. I was graduated from Johns Hopkin [sic] University School of Medicine; that thereafter I served a rotating internship and studied psychiatry at Saint Elizabeth's Hospital in Washington, D. C., the said Saint Elizabeth's Hospital being primarily a mental hospital; that thereafter I served a psychiatric residency at the Bethesda Naval Hospital. That thereafter for the ensuing twenty (20) months I served as psychiatrist at the Naval Prison System at Norfolk, Virginia during which time I was actively engaged in security investigations dealing with homosexual[s] and psychopaths in connection with the security investigations, which were conducted and carried on by the government of the United States. I further say that I attended Cornell University for two (2) years majoring in social psychiatry; that subsequently I was actively engaged as an industrial psychiatrist with the Mutual Security Agency of the United States and was assigned to foreign duty in Europe, having returned to the United States of America in the early fall of 1955.

That during the month of Decemver [sic] of 1955 I became actively interested and engaged in the so-called homosexual investigations which were carried on in Boise City, Ada County, State of Idaho, commencing during the last of December, 1955, and was subsequently assigned and employed as Director of the Mental Health Division of the Idaho State Board of Health, in which capacity I am now serving.

I further say that during my professional practice in the field of psychiatry that I have studied, interviewed and evaluated a large number of homosexuals and psychopaths and estimate that I have evaluated in excess of two thousand (2,000) such homosexuals and psychopaths.

I further say that after having been appointed as Director of the Mental Health Division of the State Board of Health in the State of Idaho I was almost continuously out of the City of Boise for the period of approximately four (4) months next preceding the 12th day of November, 1956, and was virtualy unavailable for consultation, interviews or discussions during the first week that I returned to my office on the 12th day of November, 1956.

I further say that on about the 22nd day of November, 1956 I received a call from Vernon K. Smith requesting the possibility of an interview with the above named defendant, it having been the request and suggestion of the said Vernon K. Smith that I subject the said defendant to hypnosis or the administration of sodium pentothal or sodium amytal in an effort to better evaluate his own client, the above named defendant, as to whether or not he was telling the truth concerning an alleged homosexual relationship for which the said defendant had been charged and also for the purpose of ascertaining and determining from the medical and psychiatric point of view whether the said defendant was a homosexual person. I further say that the first available appointment in the light of the press of my duties was set for 3:00 o'clock p.m. on the afternoon of November 27, 1956.

I further say that in the course of my interview with the said Vernon K. Smith and Gordon Larsen, I learned that the prosecuting witness in the above entitled action was one Eldon Halverson, and as to the said Eldon Halverson I make the following statement, and in the event that a new trial be granted I would be willing to appear as a witness and to testify substantially to the following facts:

That during the month of December, 1955 Eldon Halverson was referred to me by the Prosecuting Attorney of Ada County, State of Idaho for interview and evaluation concerning certain

alleged homosexual activities on the part of the said Eldon Halverson. I further say, and would so testify, that I had two interviews with the said Eldon Halverson on two separate occasions,
each of which lasted approximately 1½ hours. I further say that
in the course of my interviews with the said Eldon Halverson
I found him, the said Eldon Halverson, to have been confused,
and in his statements to me I found them to be frequently contradictory and inconsistent. I observed that he was a person pos-
sessed of practically no sense of guilt or any desire to change his
ways. I further found that he was a self-centered person and
quickly and readily inclined to blame others for his own difficulties. I further concluded from my interviews with the said Eldon
Halverson, did evaluate him, and would be willing to testify that
in my professional opinion as a psychiatrist, that the said Eldon
Halverson is a far developed sexual psychopath.

I further say that it is my professional opinion as a psychiatrist,
and it is a well established and recognized belief in the field of
psychiatry that the credibility for truth and veracity by psychopaths, including sexual psychopaths, is very low. I further say
that it is my opinion, based upon my experiences in evaluating
psychopaths and sexual psychopaths, and that it is a generally
accepted belief in the field of psychiatry that a sexual psychopath is prone to lie without compunction, reticence or feeling of
guilt in order to justify his own actions or shortcomings, and are
particularly prone to lie to obtain favor or to avoid personal
punishment for their own offenses or misdeeds. I further say that
it is my experience as a practicing psychiatrist based upon my
numerous experiences and evaluations of psychopaths and that
it is the accepted belief in the field of psychiatry that sexual
psychopaths are prone to even wrongfully accuse others without
compunction, guilt or reticence under circumstances when such
wrongful accusation might possibly obtain favor for the psychopath or avert difficulties which he might otherwise encounter
on account of his known conduct. I further say that it is my professional opinion based upon my numerous experiences in evaluating psychopaths and sexual psychopaths, and it is my profes-

sional opinion based upon my interviews with Eldon Halverson that the said Eldon Halverson has a high potentiality as a far developed sexual psychopath to make false statements and even false accusations under circumstances where it might be to his personal advantage to make such false statements.

I further say that I have interviewed Gordon Larsen on the 22nd day of November, 1956 and as a result of a one (1) hour interview it is my professional opinion that he is not a psychopath.

I further say that following my interview with the said Eldon Halverson as hereinabove outlined and my evaluation of him that I communicated such evaluation to the Prosecuting Attorney of Ada County, Idaho, and did in such evaluations advise the said Prosecuting Attorney of Ada County, Idaho that the credibility of Eldon Halverson was subject to serious scrutiny and that any statement made by the said Eldon Halverson wherein he attempted to accuse or involve any other person should by reason of his, the said Eldon Halverson, being a sexual psychopath, be evaluated with the most cautious scrutiny. I further say that in the event that a new trial be granted I would be willing to appear and testify concerning my interviews with the said Eldon Halverson and my evaluation of him insofar as his psychopathic tendencies are concerned and would be further willing to testify concerning my professional opinions of Eldon Halverson and Gordon Larsen, as the same have been set forth in this affidavit.

John L. Butler
_____
John L. Butler

Subscribed and sworn to before me this 28th day of November, 1956.

Vernon K. Smith
_____
Notary Public for Idaho
Residing at Boise, Idaho

(NOTARIAL SEAL)
(Filed: Nov. 30, 1956)

APPENDIX E

Affidavit re. *Cross-Examination of the Defendant Gordon Larsen & re. Comments of the Prosecuting Attorney in His Final Argument to the Jury*

STATE OF IDAHO)
) ss.
County of Ada)

Vernon K. Smith, being first duly sworn on oath, deposes and says:

I am a duly licensed and practicing attorney in Boise City, Idaho, a member of the Idaho State Bar and an attorney for the defendant in the above entitled action. I further say that I personally resided in Boise City, Ada County, Idaho during the months of September, 1955 to the date hereof and that I read numerous reports, news stories and articles in the Idaho Daily Statesman concerning certain alleged homosexual activities and investigations which were being conducted in Boise City during the fall of 1955, together with the news stories and releases which had to do with the disposition of the numerous cases. I further say that the name Willard Wilson was prominently publicized by extended news stories when he was arrested as a homosexual and that when he plead[ed] guilty and was sentenced to 5 years in the penitentiary such news story received prominent display in the Idaho Daily Statesman. I further say that when * * *, * * * and * * * were each arrested that the fact of their arrests was prominently publicized in the Idaho Daily Statesman and as their cases were disposed of on pleas of guilty and terms of probation were granted, such facts were further prominently publicized. I further say that when one Charles Brocaw was arrested in Boise City on a charge of an alleged act of homosexuality his arrest was prominently publicized in the Idaho Daily Statesman as was the fact that he plead[ed] guilty and was sentenced to a commuted jail sentence in the Ada County Jail. I therefore say that the names of Wilson, * * *, * * *, Brocaw and * * * were so prominently publicized that the names were almost of common knowledge in Ada County, Idaho during the investigations that were carried on during the fall of 1955 and as their individual cases were disposed of into the year 1956. I further say that I believe that such news stories concerning the arrests, appearances and court dispositions of the 16 persons arrested in Ada County exceeded easily 150 news stories. I further say that during said period I circulated about the City of Boise, Idaho and talked to numerous people and that the subject of homosexual investigations, the prosecution, the pleas and dispositions of such cases were almost common talk and gossip to such an extent that the names of * * *, * * *, * * *, Brocaw, Mel Dir, and the name of Gordon Larsen carried almost a secondary meaning of homosexuality by reason of the extensive publicity and that by reason of such secondary meaning to such names the mention of such names on cross-examination and in the comments of the Prosecuting Attorney in his final remarks needed no further explanation as to whom these men were, but that the mention of the name itself was sufficient to quickly refresh a recollection for a secondary meaning which had come to be attached to such names.

Vernon K. Smith
_____
Vernon K. Smith

Subscribed and sworn to before me this 29th day of November, 1956.

Violet Sykes
_____
Notary Public for Idaho
Residing at Boise, Idaho

(NOTARIAL SEAL)
(Filed: Nov. 30, 1956)

APPENDIX F

Amendment to Motion for New Trial for Gordon Larsen

COMES NOW, The above named defendant, by and through his attorney, Vernon K. Smith, and files this amendment to the motion for new trial heretofore filed in the above entitled action on the 30th day of November, 1956, and by such amendment assigns and sets forth a further ground for new trial to be numbered as IX, said further ground to be as follows:

IX

The court erred in denying defendant's motion to inspect documents before trial.

Dated this 5th day of December, 1956.

Vernon K. Smith
_____

Vernon K. Smith
Attorney for Defendant
1900 Main Street
Boise, Idaho

Copy of the foregoing instrument
received, and service acknowledged
this 7th day of Decemver [sic], 1956.

BLAINE F. EFANS [EVANS]

PROSECUTING ATTORNEY

ADA COUNTY, IDAHO

By *E. C. Thomas*
_____

(Lodged: Dec. 7, 1956)

INDEX

INDEX

Lightning Source UK Ltd.
Milton Keynes UK
UKHW011956150622
404478UK00001B/32